IMAGES
*of America*

# YUBA FEATHER HILLS

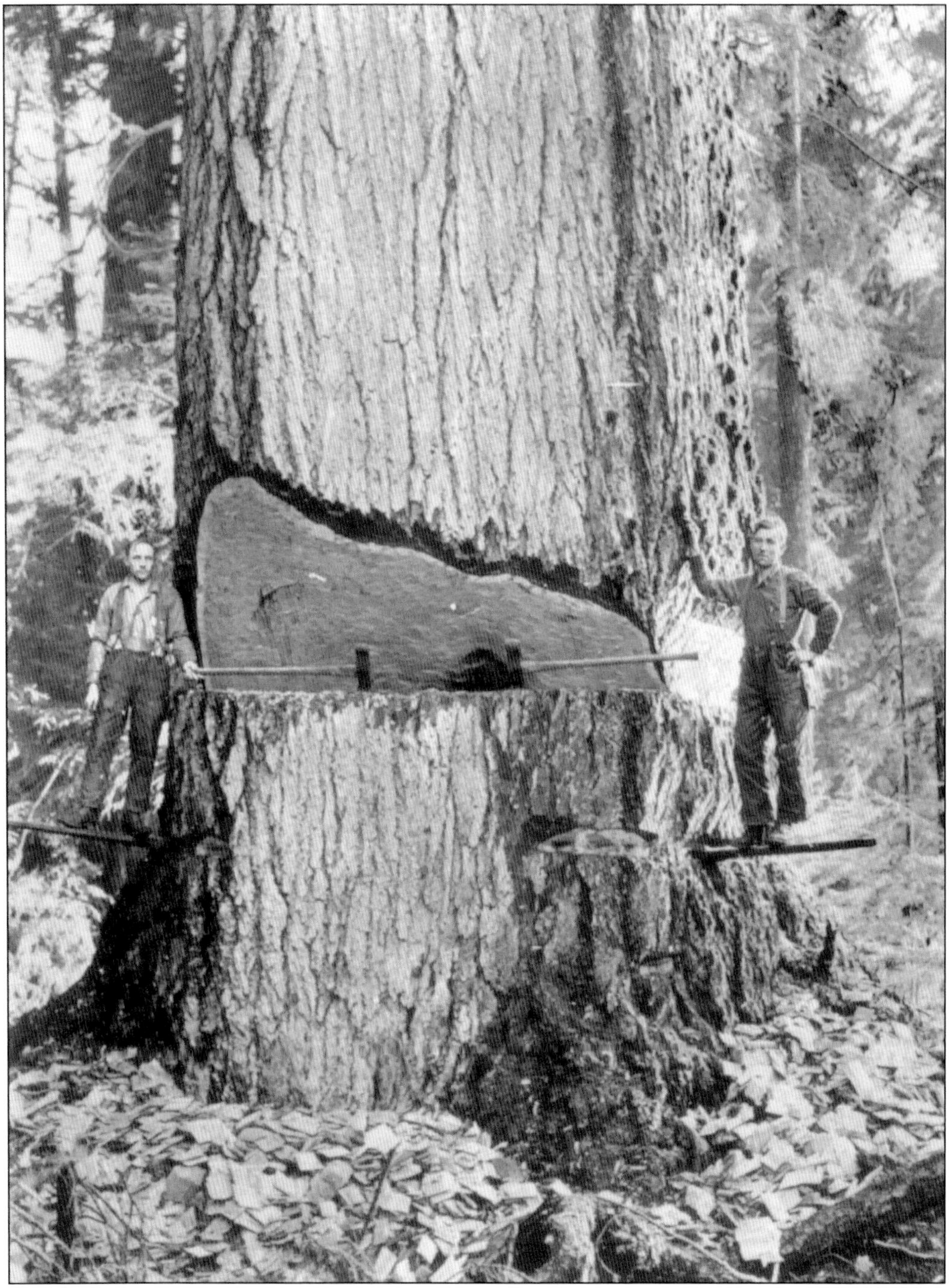

Will Foss stands on the springboard at right, while he and an unidentified coworker fell an enormous Douglas fir on his family's property near Brownsville.

**ON THE COVER:** This steam-traction engine provides power to run reciprocating saws at a logging site in the Yuba Feather Hills in 1890. The engine used wood fuel, but sparks from the chimney threatened to set the woods on fire, so the crews switched to oil.

IMAGES
*of America*

# YUBA FEATHER HILLS

Rosemarie Mossinger and the
Yuba Feather Museum

ARCADIA
PUBLISHING

ISBN 978-0-7385-3102-1

Published by Arcadia Publishing
Charleston, South Carolina

Printed in the United States of America

Library of Congress Catalog Card Number: 2005936292

For all general information contact Arcadia Publishing at:
Telephone 843-853-2070
Fax 843-853-0044
E-mail sales@arcadiapublishing.com
For customer service and orders:
Toll-Free 1-888-313-2665

Visit us on the Internet at www.arcadiapublishing.com

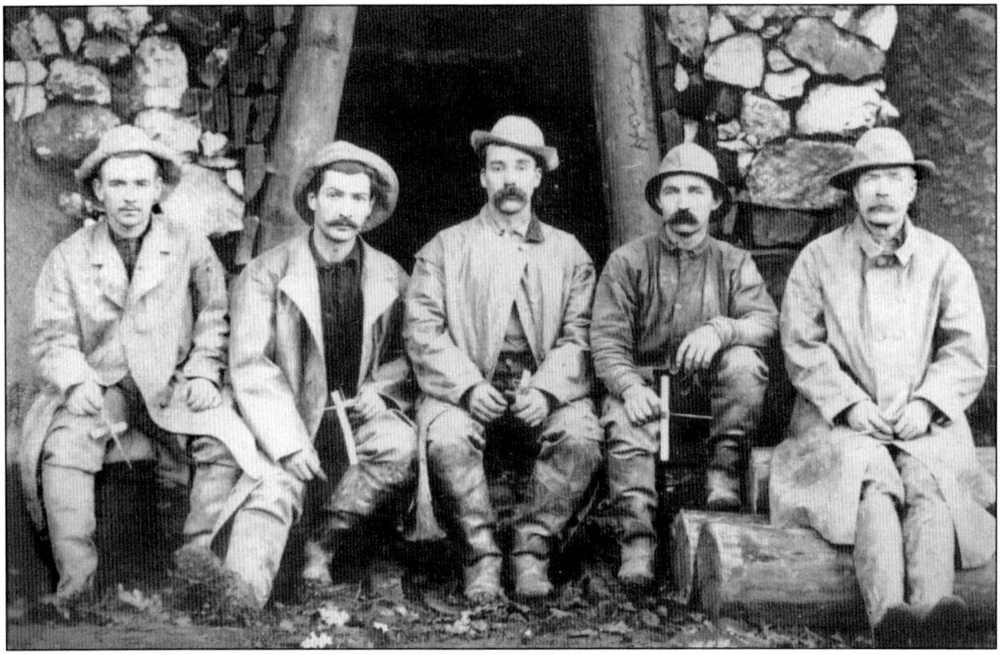

In front of the Locust Point tunnel near Forbestown, these miners are, left to right, Dave Eddy, ? DeFontrill, Frank Philbrick, Horace Hawkins, and Superintendent Patterson. They each carry a candle and candleholder, which is made with a sharp point at one end to jab into mine timber. Locust Point was part of the Goldbank Mine.

# Contents

# ACKNOWLEDGMENTS

We offer sincere thanks to those who contributed photographs and documents from their collections, advice, and information from their research to help provide an interesting perspective of the 10 towns in this book: Janet Baur, Janet Bond, Ben Falck, the Foothill Volunteer Fire Department, Jann Garvis, Janice Hammontre, A. Dale Johnson, Aleta Joseph, Lona Lahore, Frances Martin Family, Carl Mautz, Phil McDonald, Heather Moldenauer, Mike Muths, Florence Prater, Kathy Sedler, Brad Sharpe, Cassie Simmons, Leonard Travis, the Yuba County Library, and the Yuba County Water Agency. Jim Morgan and Shirley Crompton generously shared photographs and research as they prepared their forthcoming book, *Golden Memories of the Oregon House and Dobbins Areas.*

The Yuba Feather Museum is greatly indebted to Jim Lague, who collected more than 3,000 negatives during the past 25 years. Since his death in 2004, volunteers have worked tirelessly to identify, document, and catalogue the collection. A recent anonymous gift of more than 100 photographs, documents, ledgers, and ephemera have added to our archives of vintage photographs and glass plates, providing a priceless record from which we could choose. The illustrations used in this book without credit lines are from the museum's archives.

We of the Yuba Feather Museum thank Arcadia Publishing for the opportunity to publish the stories of our towns, sharing the treasures of the Yuba Feather Hills.

—Rosemarie Mossinger
Yuba Feather Museum

# INTRODUCTION

The towns in the Yuba Feather Hills were born in the gold rush, as thousands of treasure seekers swarmed up the slopes of the rugged Sierra Nevada. Within a few years, more than 60 hotels were strung along the trails and toll roads, some only a few miles apart. They provided lodging and meals for travelers and fresh teams of horses and mules for freight wagons and stagecoaches. Families settled around these centers, building homes, churches, shops, and schools. As horses and carriages faded into the past and motor vehicles took their place, travelers could go longer distances in shorter times. One by one, the enormous old hotels disappeared, along with neighboring schools and stores. Of all the camps, inns, houses, and way stations of the early days, only 10 developed into towns that thrive today, 150 years later. Three of the grand hotels have survived, in Woodleaf, Strawberry Valley, and La Porte, and these are treasured links with the past.

The mining boom was long gone by World War I, a bleak time when many left for military service, and others moved to cities where better paying and less dangerous jobs were available. Without manpower, most of the gold mines closed. Later, people flocked to the hills, nostalgic for a more peaceful past. Locals picked up trade from tourists driving automobiles with money to spend. Bootleggers provided liquor, and the old hotels were revived. Developers bought up property and put in golf courses, tennis courts, cabins, swimming pools, and sold lots for summer homes. When the Great Depression hit, entrepreneurs shut down or abandoned their property, and the hotels were desolate once again.

Then a rather surprising thing happened. People began to move back to old, familiar places where rent and land prices were at rock bottom, with land often selling for the price of back taxes. Families tended gardens and livestock, mining for gold on the side for cash. Fruit orchards and grain fields on the old ranches still produced, and slowly some mines reopened.

The onset of World War II dealt a deathblow to gold mining, but boosted lumbering because of military needs and the influx of people to the West Coast. Small mills already dotted the hills when the post-war market simply exploded, and larger mills were built to fill the demand for construction materials. Lumber remains an important industry today. Oroville Dam, along with its complex waterways and hydroelectric systems, came in the 1960s.

At the beginning of the 21st century, residents of each town continue to show great diversity where the descendants of pioneers live side by side with former city folk and retired people are neighbors to young families. New industry and commerce continue, but a few independent residents still mine for gold. Although each town changed in different ways and at varying paces, they share a deep commitment to care for each other, especially for those with special needs. Numerous service and volunteer organizations attest to that commitment. And each of the 10 towns has fascinating stories and truly unique character and charm, told through priceless photographs and documents. This is a sampler of the rich history of the Yuba Feather Hills.

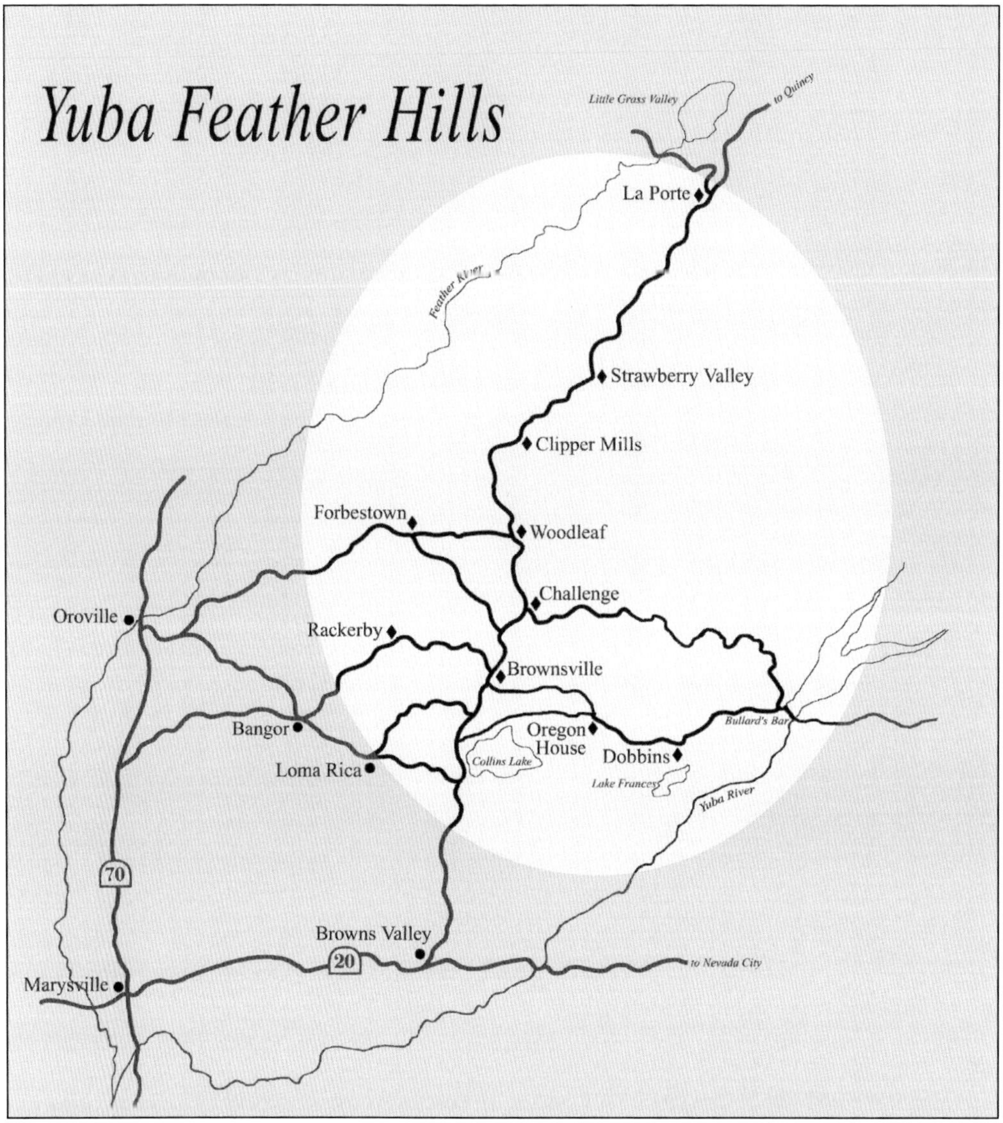


The highlighted area on this map shows the location of the 10 towns featured in this book, generally north-northeast of Oroville and Marysville, California. The Yuba Feather Hills region is so named because the Feather River is the boundary to the north and the Yuba River to the south. One of the main roads through the hills travels up the ridge between the two watersheds.

# *One*

# Oregon House

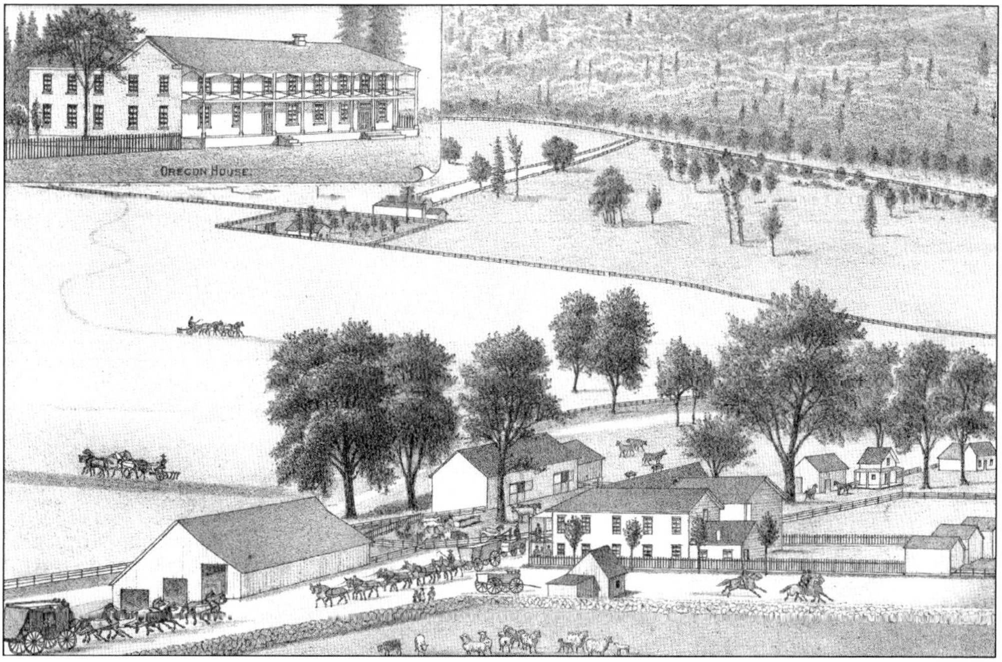


Larry Young's log cabin was far from any town when he built it in 1850, but the gold-seekers beat a trail right past his door. Two years later, the Oregon House was built, possibly named for the many pioneers who came by way of the Oregon Trail. It quickly became a popular stage stop and freight station. James H. Haun, a miner who struck it rich, frequently traveled the route. He wrote in his journal on December 6, 1854, "Paid $10 to ride up to the Columbus House [Strawberry Valley] in the stage; Dinner $1 at the Oregon House; got to Columbus at 8." When the owners of Oregon House hosted a party in 1853 to celebrate the anniversary of the Battle of New Orleans, 250 tickets were sold, and among all those guests there were only 18 ladies. (Illustration from *History of Yuba County*, Wells and Chamberlain, 1879.)

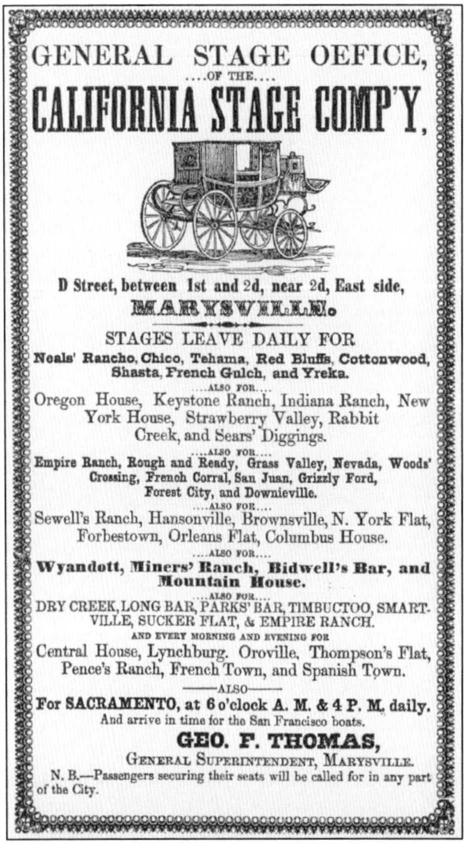


The Oregon House was on the schedule for daily California Stage Company stops, along with the neighboring Keystone and Indiana Ranches. The post office was first established in Oregon House in 1854 and Peter Rice was the first postmaster.

Theseus Vernet "Ford" Clark was a teamster who hauled freight from Marysville northward to both valley and mountain towns and mines. According to historian Jim Morgan, he often took loads up Stanfield Hill by "double hauling." He and other freight men hooked their combined teams to one set of wagons, hauled them to the top of the hill, unhitched them, and then took the teams back down for the other wagons.

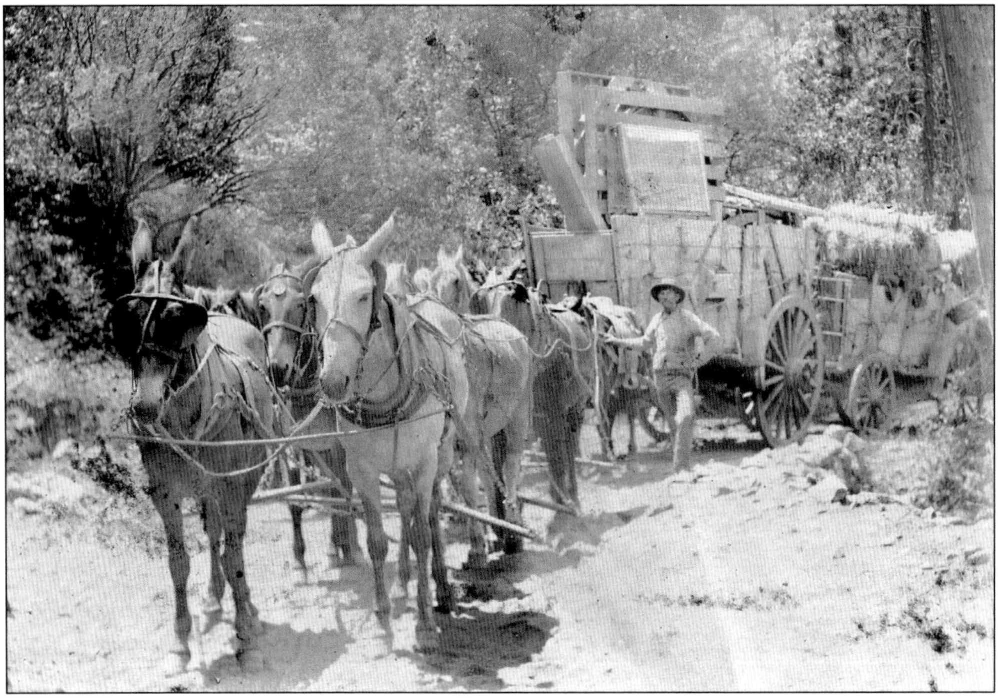

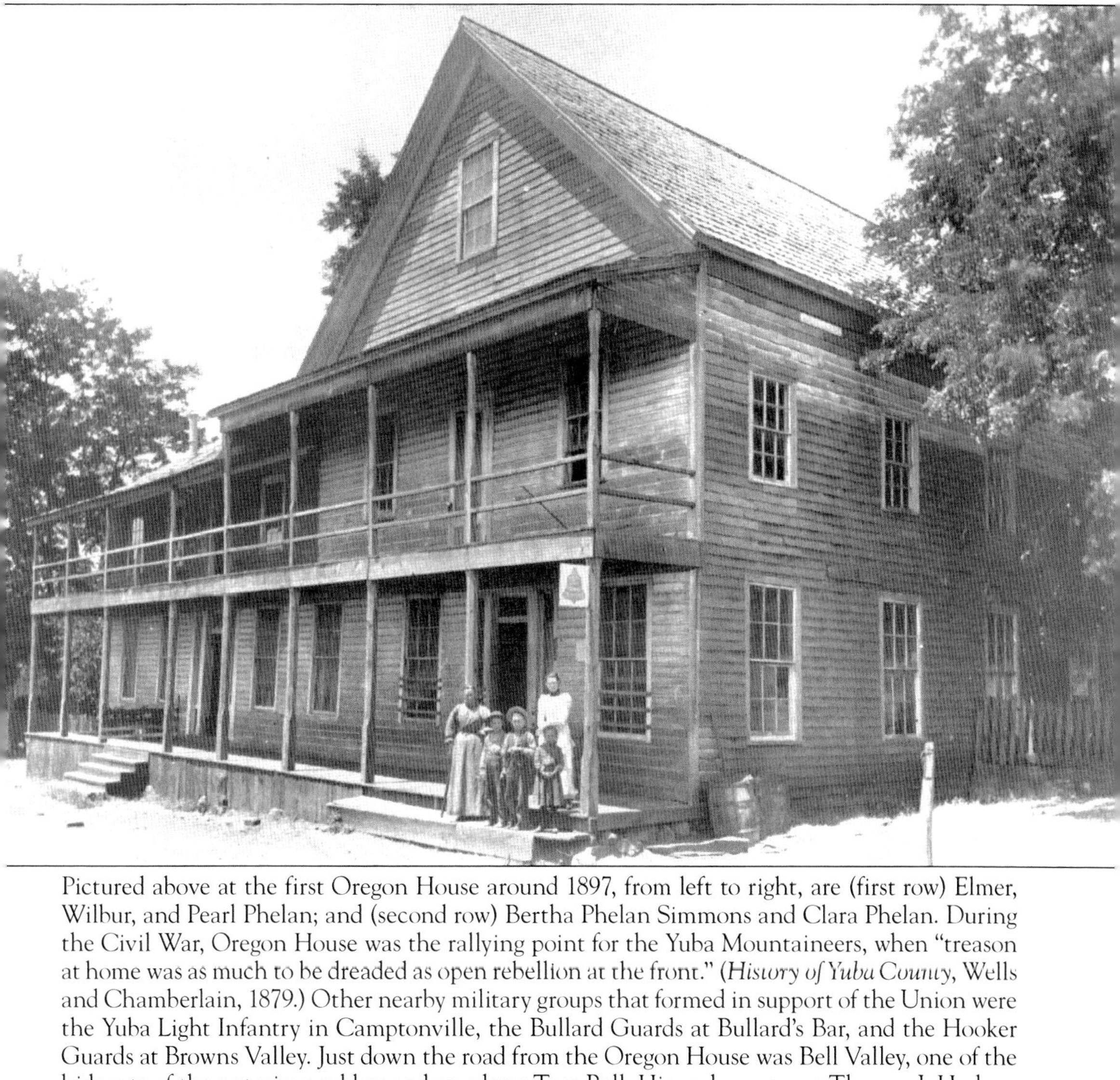

Pictured above at the first Oregon House around 1897, from left to right, are (first row) Elmer, Wilbur, and Pearl Phelan; and (second row) Bertha Phelan Simmons and Clara Phelan. During the Civil War, Oregon House was the rallying point for the Yuba Mountaineers, when "treason at home was as much to be dreaded as open rebellion at the front." (*History of Yuba County*, Wells and Chamberlain, 1879.) Other nearby military groups that formed in support of the Union were the Yuba Light Infantry in Camptonville, the Bullard Guards at Bullard's Bar, and the Hooker Guards at Browns Valley. Just down the road from the Oregon House was Bell Valley, one of the hideouts of the notorious robber and murderer Tom Bell. His real name was Thomas J. Hodges, and he was a brilliant surgeon in the army before turning to crime. He was captured near the San Joaquin River in 1856 and four hours later was hung by vigilantes. The Oregon House was destroyed by fire in 1909, and a new hotel was built within a year. It burned to the ground in 1936, and only a grove of trees and charred wood mark the spot today. (Courtesy Jim Morgan and Cassie Simmons.)

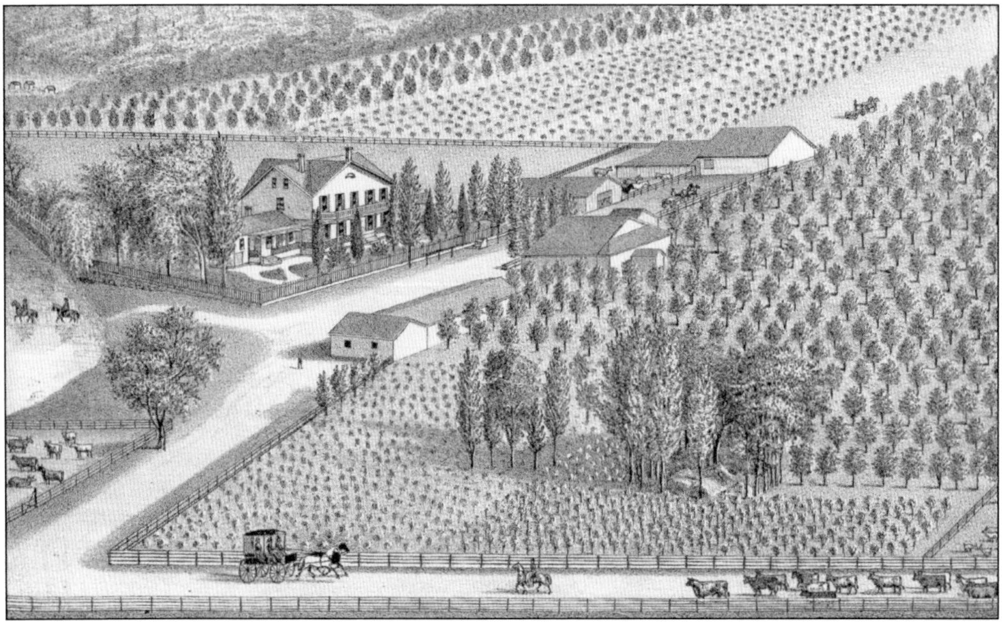

The Virginia Ranch had a choice location in a fertile valley planted with orchards and field crops where large herds of livestock were raised. Most of the area is now covered by Collins Lake. (Illustration from *History of Yuba County*, Wells and Chamberlain, 1879.)

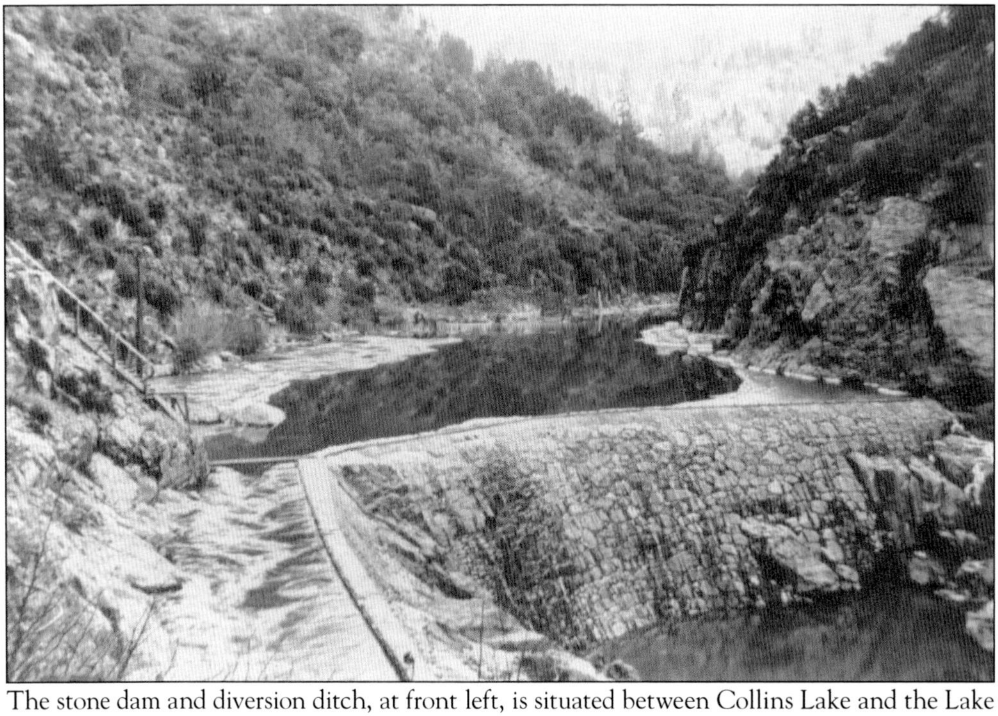

The stone dam and diversion ditch, at front left, is situated between Collins Lake and the Lake Mildred dam. The quality of the workmanship is evident in this structure and it has lasted for many decades. (Courtesy Yuba County Water Agency.)

The first Oregon House School was built in 1854, and by 1879, 28 boys and 23 girls were enrolled. Bill and Roma Johnson, at right, donated property on Rice's Crossing Road across from their home to build the new Oregon House School, pictured below. (Courtesy Jim Morgan.)

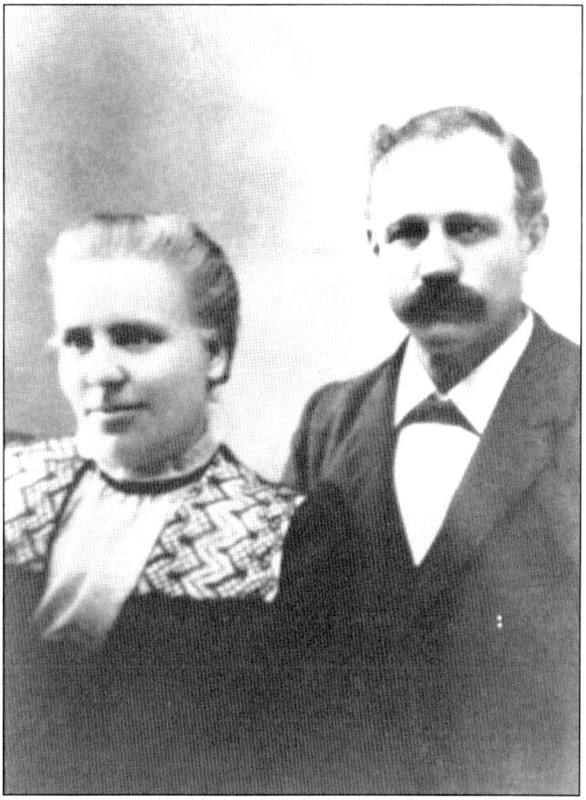

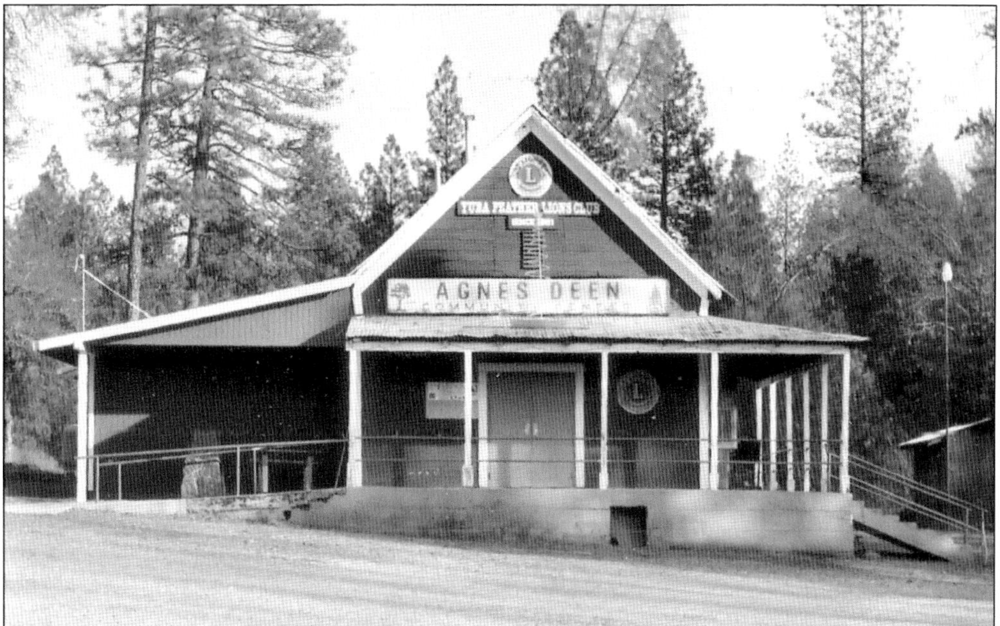


After the Oregon House School District merged with Dobbins, a town a few miles west, the building was named the Agnes Deen Community Center, as shown in this contemporary view. (Courtesy Jim Morgan.)

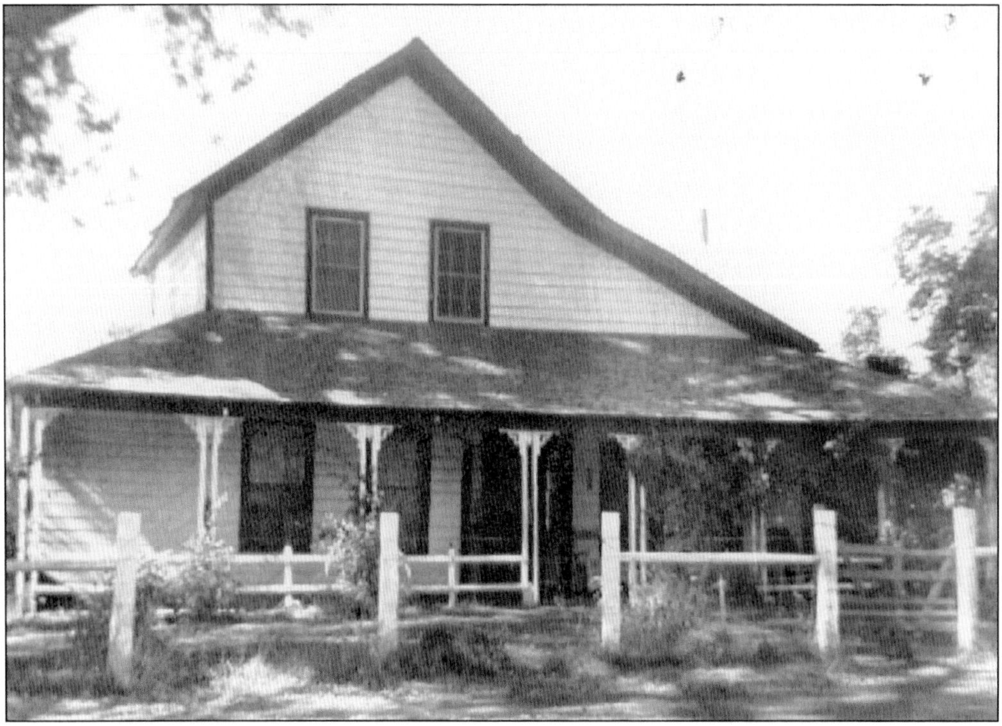

In 1849, John Scott built this home, which may be the oldest structure in Yuba Feather Hills. John came to California alone before his wife, Katherine Maria (Marquardt), and two daughters arrived in 1854. When the new road, built by Atchison and Rice in 1860, bypassed their hotel, New York Star House, the Scotts put the house on skids and moved it with a team of oxen. A towing chain broke before the building reached the desired side of the road, but after a bottle was passed around, they left it where it was. It remains in the same place on Marysville Road today, and after being remodeled in the 1950s, it is a private home. (Courtesy Jim Morgan.)

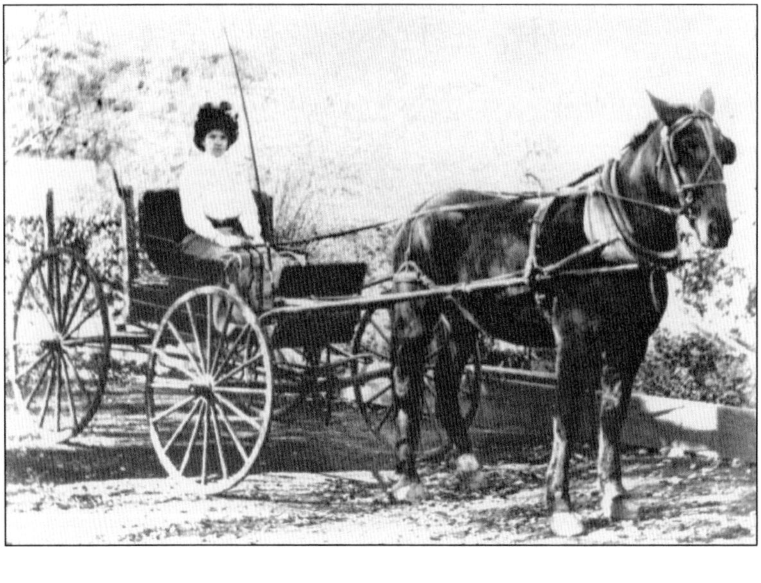

Ada Emma Scott, daughter of John and Katherine, drove her buggy to the Frenchtown School, where she taught for three years. Her wage started at $75 per month, and by 1915 it had increased by $10. (Courtesy Jim Morgan.)

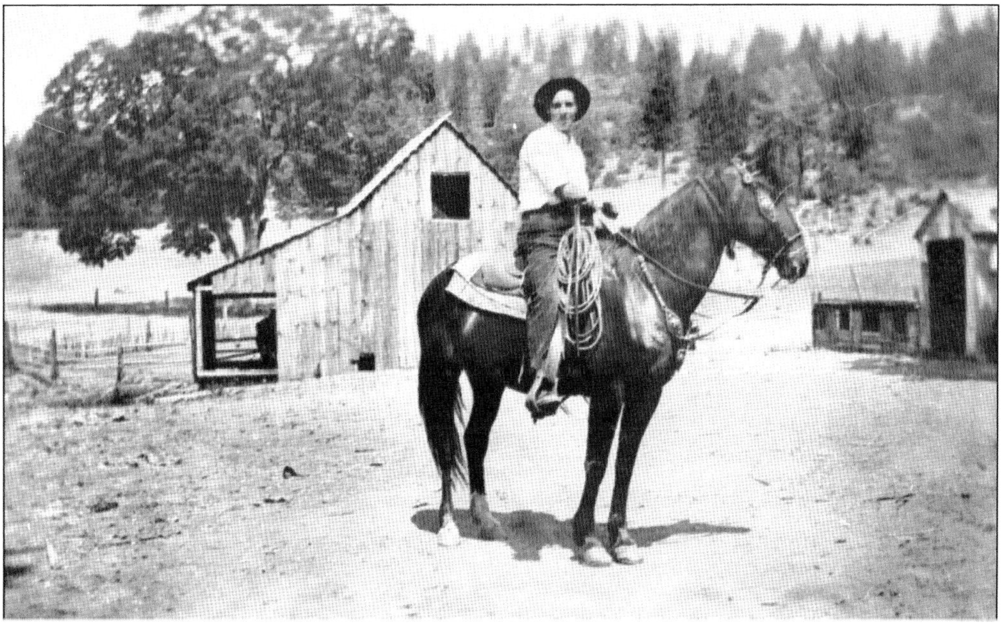

Warren Chittenden rides one of the horses on his family's ranch at Frenchtown, where he was born in 1899. The ranch had large herds of cattle and grew grain crops.

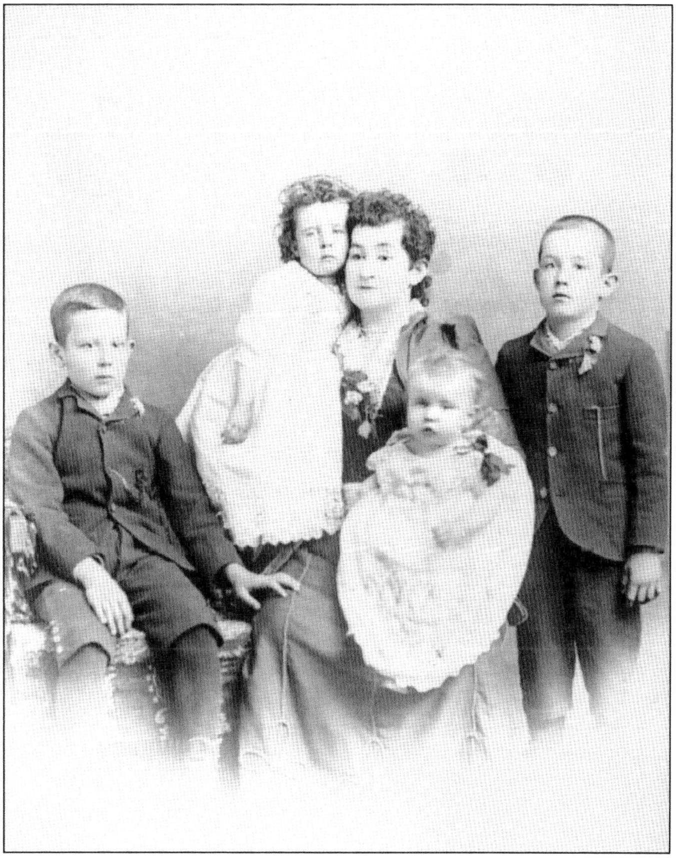

Henry Chittenden's wife, Catherine, was photographed with four of their children, all born in a mining town beyond La Porte called Howland Flat. Catherine taught school at La Porte at one time, and the family later settled on a ranch at Frenchtown.

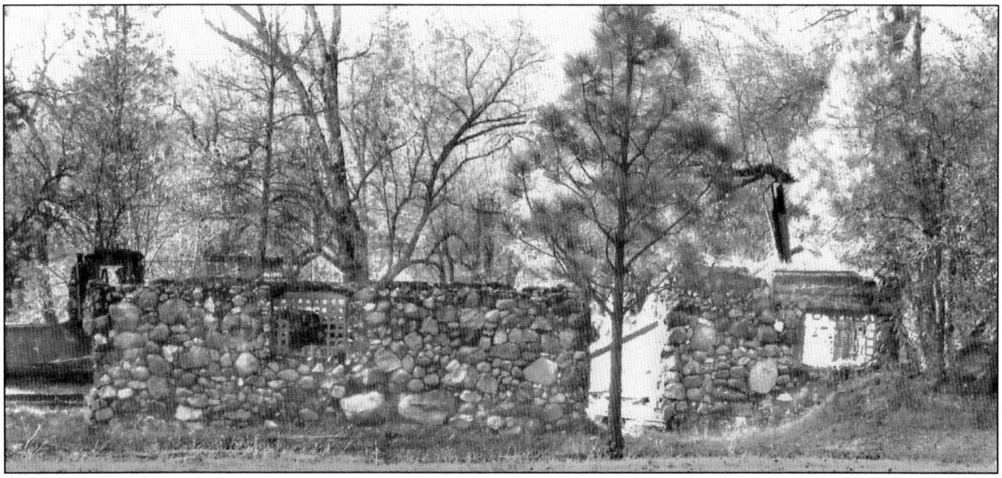

Paul Vavaseur built a hotel, bar, and store, and planted a vineyard here in 1854, bottling his own wine. Five hundred men, most of them French, were mining in the surrounding hills and streams. Within a few years, Frenchtown had four stores, three saloons, three hotels, two blacksmiths, a bakery, and a barbershop. When it was a thriving community, each family had one day a week to bring their bread to bake in the community ovens. Most of the town was destroyed by fire in the 1880s and only these crumbling walls mark the site.

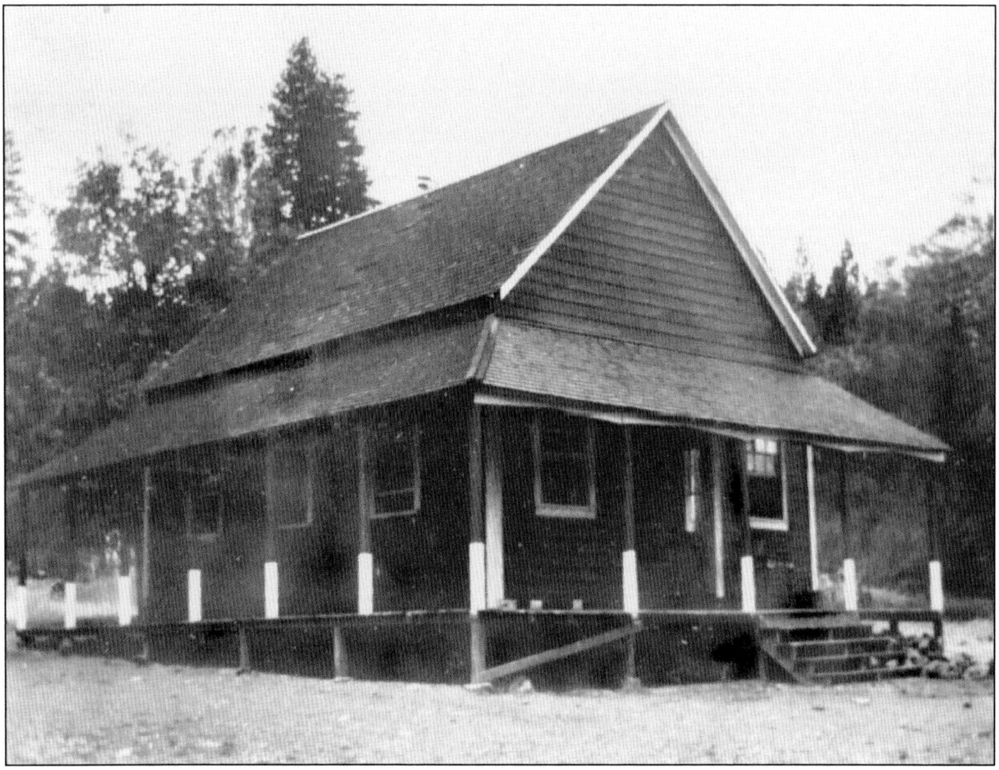

Frenchtown School was open until 1925, at times suspending classes when the number of students dwindled and at others requiring two teachers for the eight grades. The annual wage was $300 in 1884, and by the time the school closed, it had risen to $1,260.

Edwin A. Forbes was the son of Alexander R. and Catherine M. (Kracher) Forbes. Alexander was a pioneer who came to Canada via Scotland before settling in California and raising livestock on his ranch in Oregon House. Edwin married Elizabeth Jane Yore in 1885. He was a major in the California U.S. Volunteers, a teacher, an attorney, an owner of the *Marysville Appeal* newspaper, and an adjutant general in the California National Guard.

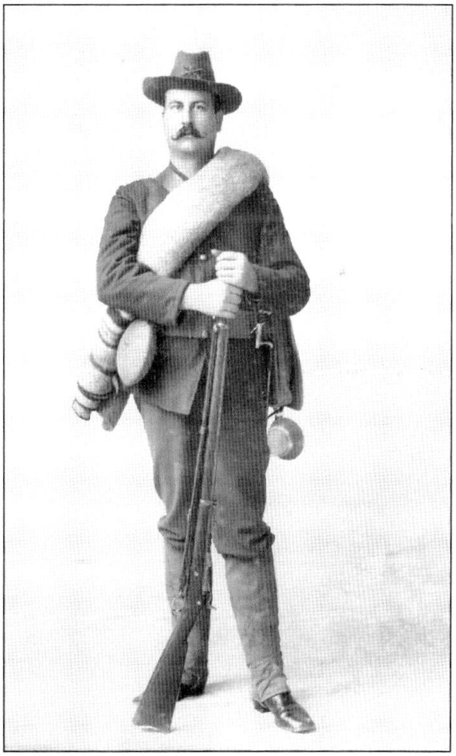

The crew of the Bercut-Richards Mill gathered in the saw-filing room for a photograph. The huge band saws were routinely sharpened and changed when the old saws became dull. The mill ran during the late 1940s and early 1950s. (Courtesy Jim Morgan.)

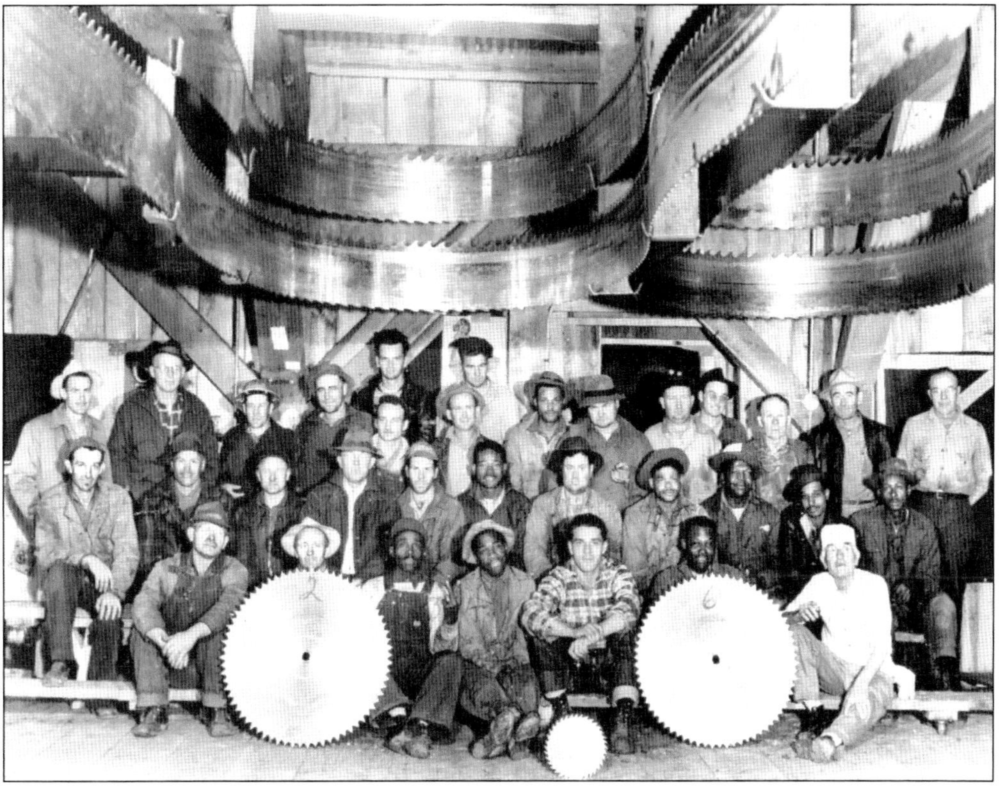

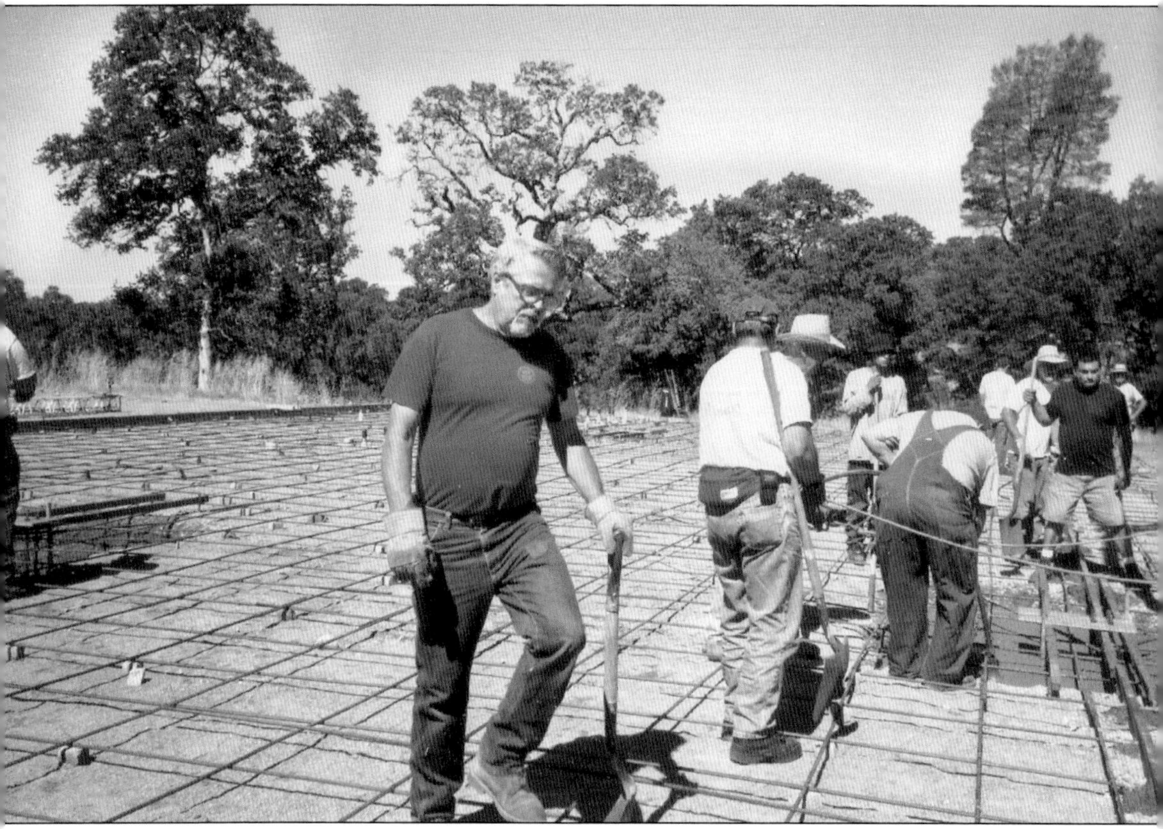

In a fine example of neighboring towns cooperating for shared benefits, Oregon House and Dobbins have jointly raised funds and furnished the labor to build a community center on Marysville Road, north of the Dobbins-Oregon House Fire Station. The building will also be equipped to provide shelter during emergencies such as fire and flood. The group plans to eventually construct a playground and picnic area on the property. The exterior of the 10,000-square-foot building is complete and currents efforts are focused on the interior work. (Courtesy Mike Muths.)

# *Two*

# DOBBINS

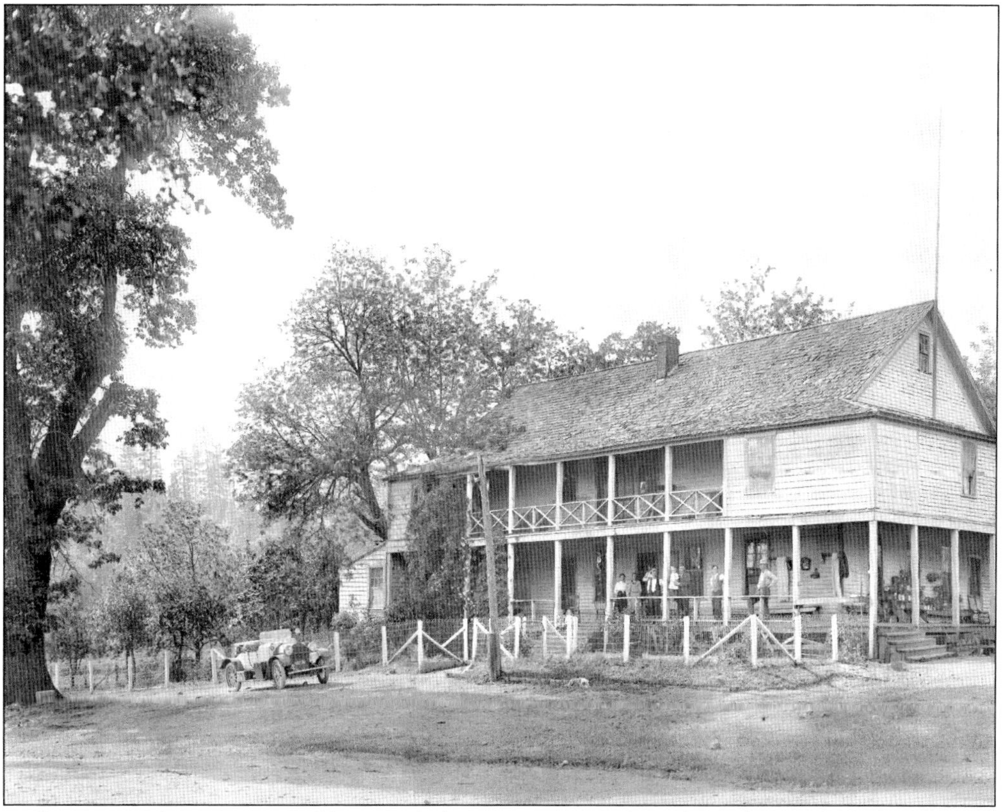

William M. and Marcus D. Dobbins settled on 160 acres in a broad meadow in the lower foothills in 1849, and within a year their ranch and store had become a terminus for Langton's Pioneer Express. The post office, designated Dobbins Ranch, opened in 1851, the earliest in the Yuba Feather Hills region. By 1854, it was discontinued, and the postmarks are very rare. The Dobbins brothers sold out in 1855, and when Joseph and Marinda (Rugg) Merriam came from Massachusetts in 1863, they purchased the hotel, ranch, and store. A new post office was granted in 1887, this time named Dobbins.

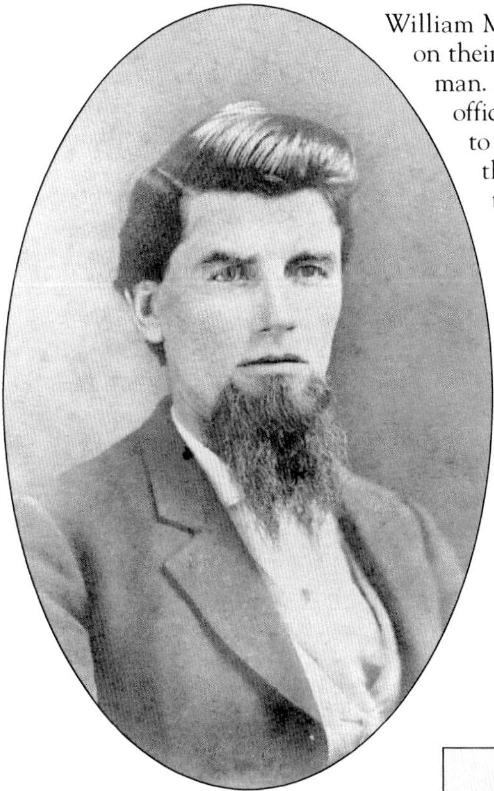

William M. Dobbins, his wife, and three children lived on their ranch only a few years, but Dobbins was a busy man. Besides running the large ranch, store, and post office, he served as a Yuba County justice from 1849 to 1854, then became county clerk. After selling the ranch in 1855, he went east as a delegate to the national presidential convention, nominating James Buchanan. Dobbins and his family spent the remainder of their lives in the eastern states. (Courtesy Carl Mautz.)

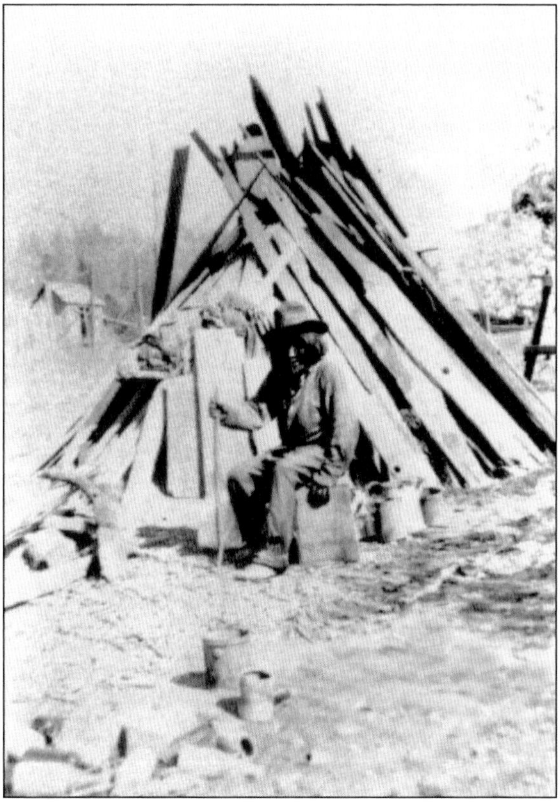

The native Maidu had lived in the region thousands of years, sustained by wild game, acorns from the abundant oak trees, and many springs of water. This Maidu sits outside his bark home, or *hubo*, at Dobbins. Descendents of the tribe still make their homes in the Yuba Feather Hills. (Courtesy Jim Morgan.)

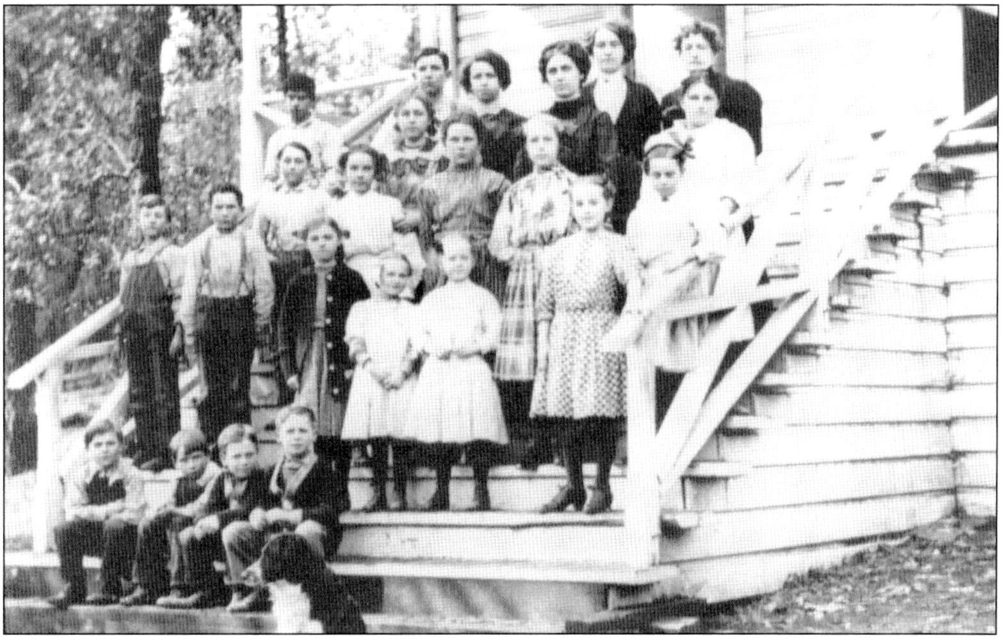

The teacher and students stand on the steps for the photographer at the Dobbins School, while a friendly dog takes the front row. The building is now the Lake Francis Grange Hall. (Courtesy Jim Morgan.)

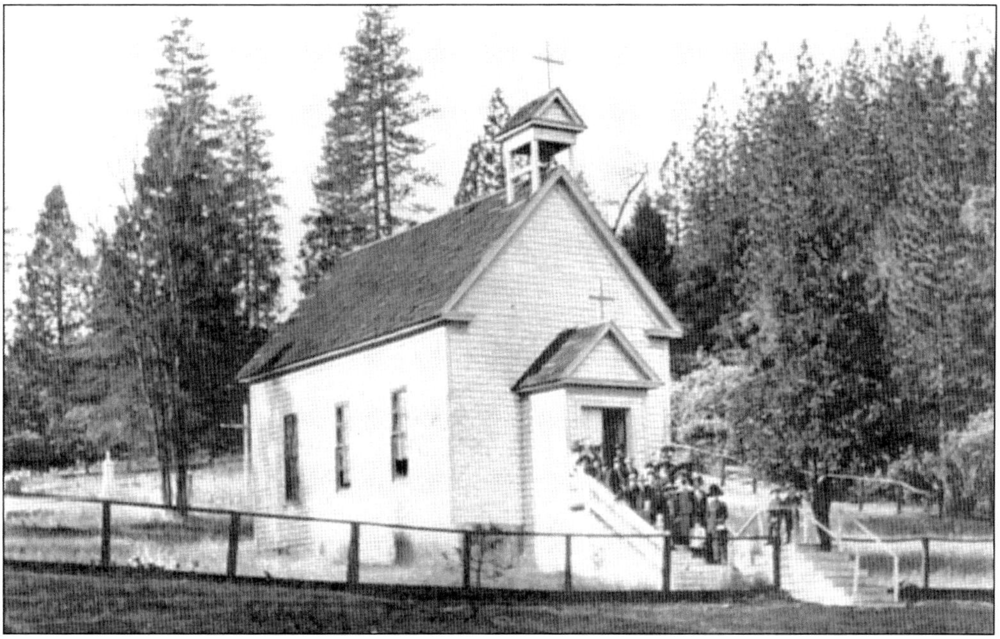

Before the Catholic church was built, services were held in the home of Mary Slingsby's uncle, James McMenamin. The Sacred Heart Catholic Church was built 1897 on land donated by Joseph and Merinda Merriam. At the dedication, the Brownsville band played on the porch of the hotel. The church closed in 1982 and quickly deteriorated. When local residents learned it was to be razed, they rallied support and restored the building from foundation to belfry. Now the bell rings at 3:00 p.m. Sunday for worship services.

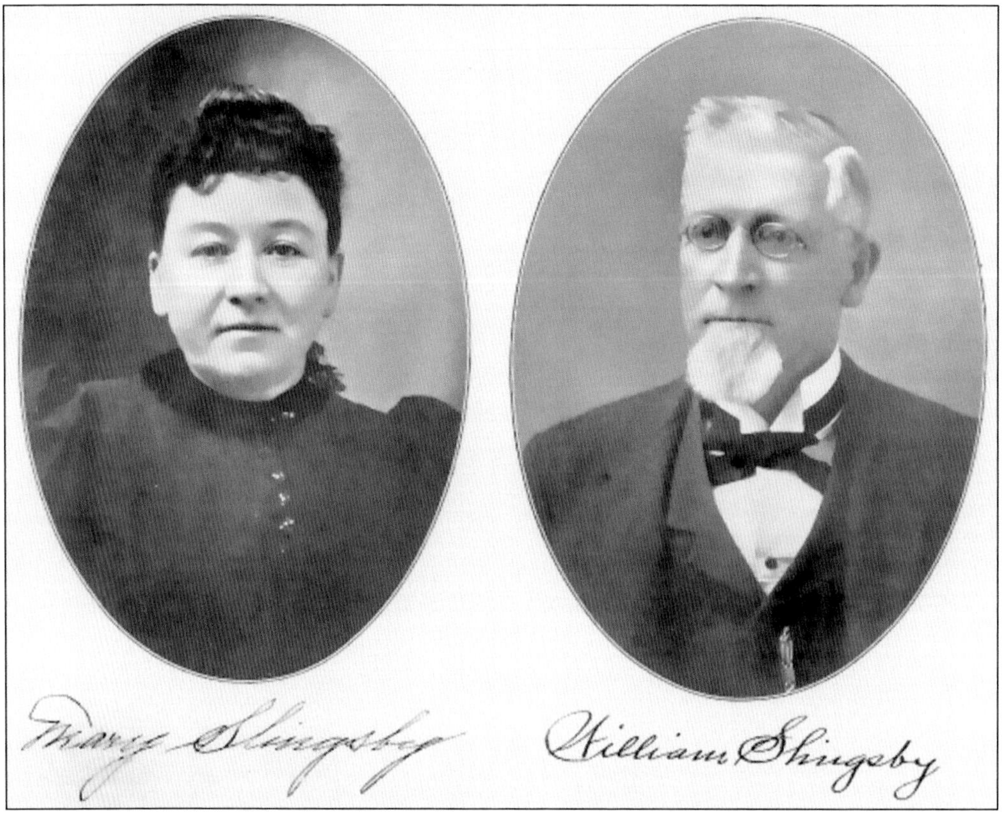


William Slingsby and Daniel Gettens opened a store in 1867 and maintained a pack train on the Downieville Trail for a number of years. When William died, Joseph Merriam took over the store, and later his son Chester ran it.

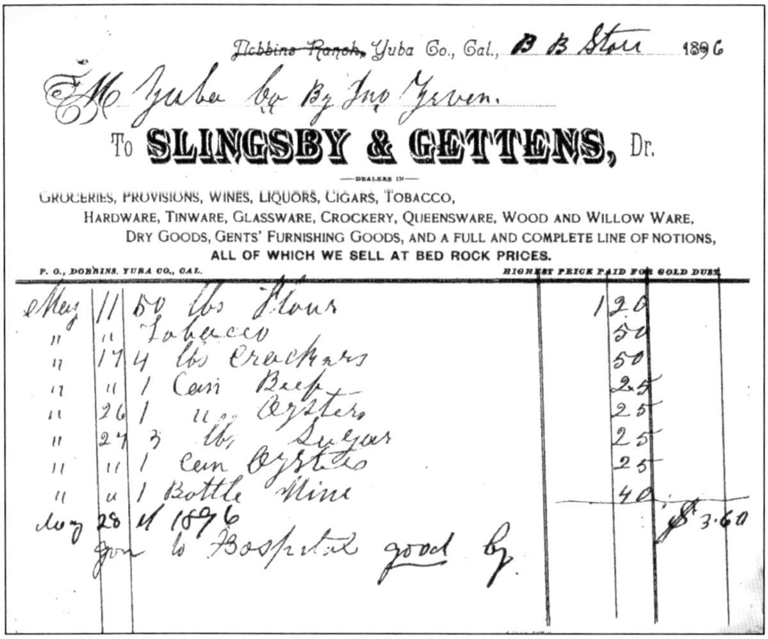

~~Dobbins Ranch,~~ Yuba Co., Cal., B B Store 1896

M Yuba Co By Jno Greven.

To **SLINGSBY & GETTENS,** Dr.

—DEALERS IN—

GROCERIES, PROVISIONS, WINES, LIQUORS, CIGARS, TOBACCO,
HARDWARE, TINWARE, GLASSWARE, CROCKERY, QUEENSWARE, WOOD AND WILLOW WARE,
DRY GOODS, GENTS' FURNISHING GOODS, AND A FULL AND COMPLETE LINE OF NOTIONS,
ALL OF WHICH WE SELL AT BED ROCK PRICES.

P. O., DOBBINS, YUBA CO., CAL. HIGHEST PRICE PAID FOR GOLD DUST.

| | | | |
|---|---|---|---|
| May | 11 | 50 lbs Flour | 1.20 |
| " | " | Tobacco | 50 |
| " | 17 | 4 lbs Crackers | 50 |
| " | " | 1 Can Beef | 25 |
| " | 26 | 1 " " Oysters | 25 |
| " | 27 | 3 lbs Sugar | 25 |
| " | " | 1 Can Oysters | 25 |
| " | " | 1 Bottle Wine | 40 |
| Aug | 28 | " 1896 | $3.60 |
| | | gone to Hospital good by. | |

At the store, customers could buy almost everything they needed, including furniture, clothing, and dishes. The receipt bears the name Dobbins Ranch in 1896, when a client purchased oysters, flour, and wine, paid the bill, and the clerk ended with a cryptic note that some read as "gone to hospital. good by."

Lake Frances was an idyllic scene in 1915. John Martin named the lake, which dams Dobbins Creek, for his daughter Frances. He was an entrepreneur who founded the Yuba Electric Power Company in partnership with Eugene de Sabla Jr. With funds from Romulus Riggs Colgate (grandson of Colgate Soap Company founder), the men built the Colgate Powerhouse on the Yuba River. The lake, first filled in 1899, was an emergency water supply for the powerhouse if the eight miles of the wood flume failed. (Courtesy Yuba County Library.)

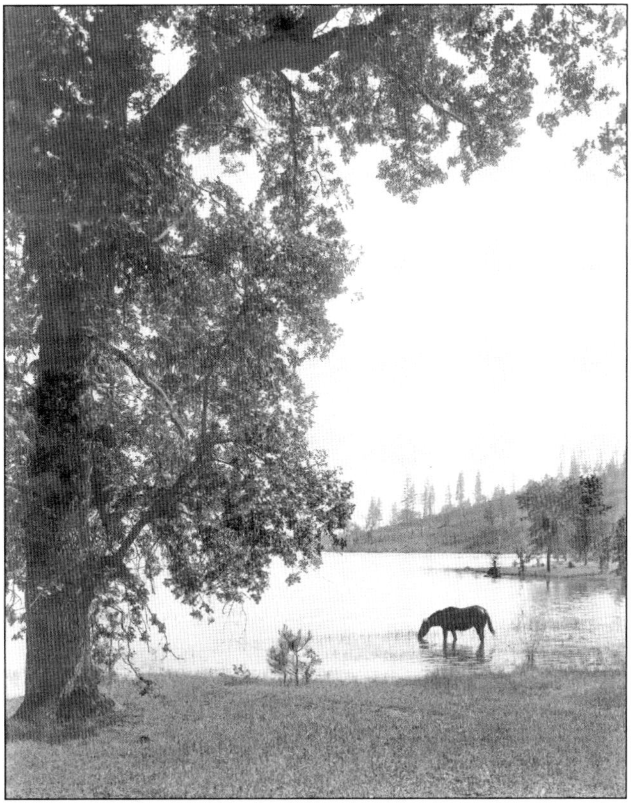

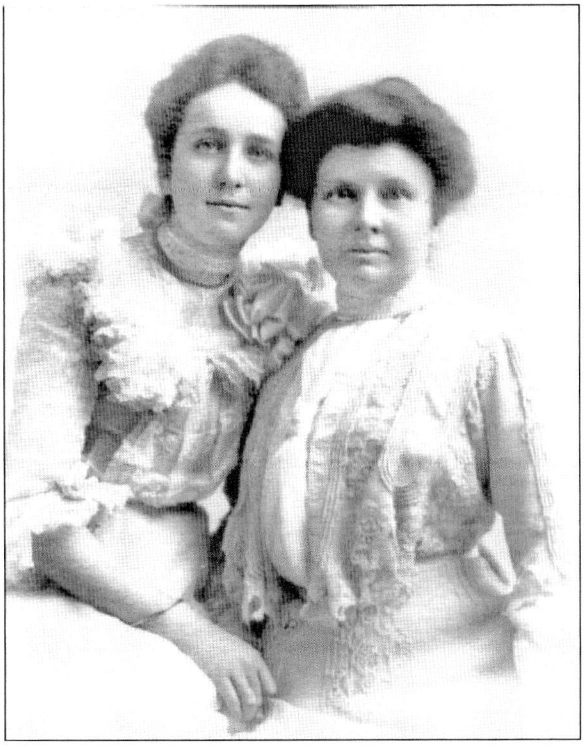

Frances Marianna Martin was the eldest of John and Abigail Martin's five children, born December 18, 1888. Frances and Abigail were photographed around 1910. (Courtesy Frances Martin Family and A. Dale Johnson.)

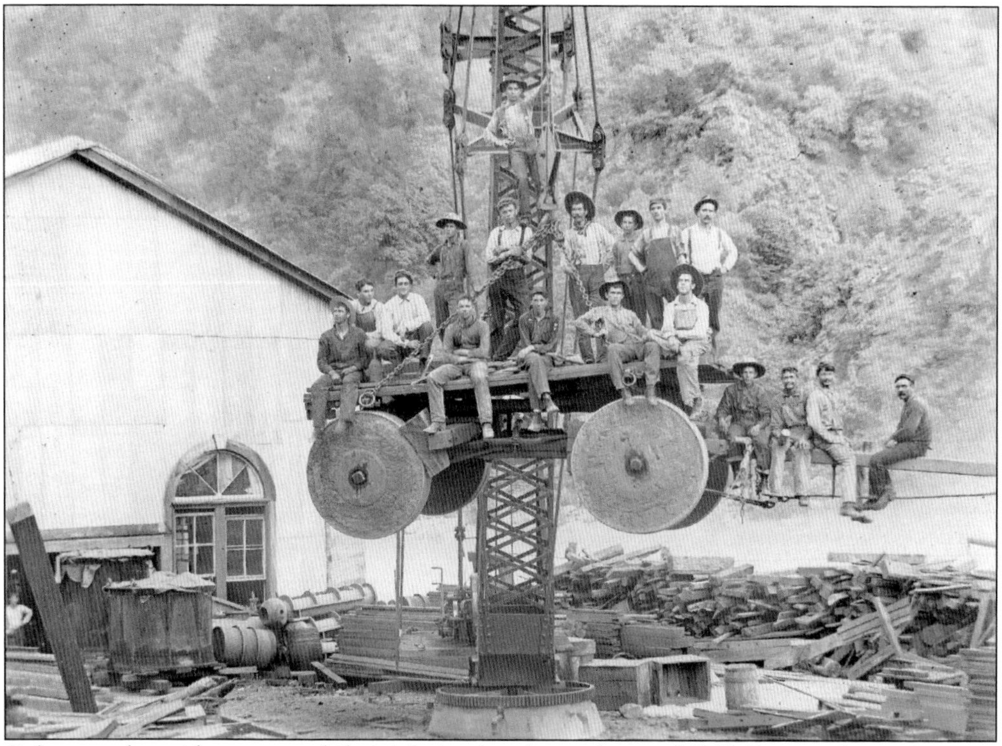

Colgate workers ride a wagon while it is hoisted to the road around 1899. Seventy-five mule teams and more than 200 men were employed to build the flumes and powerhouse.

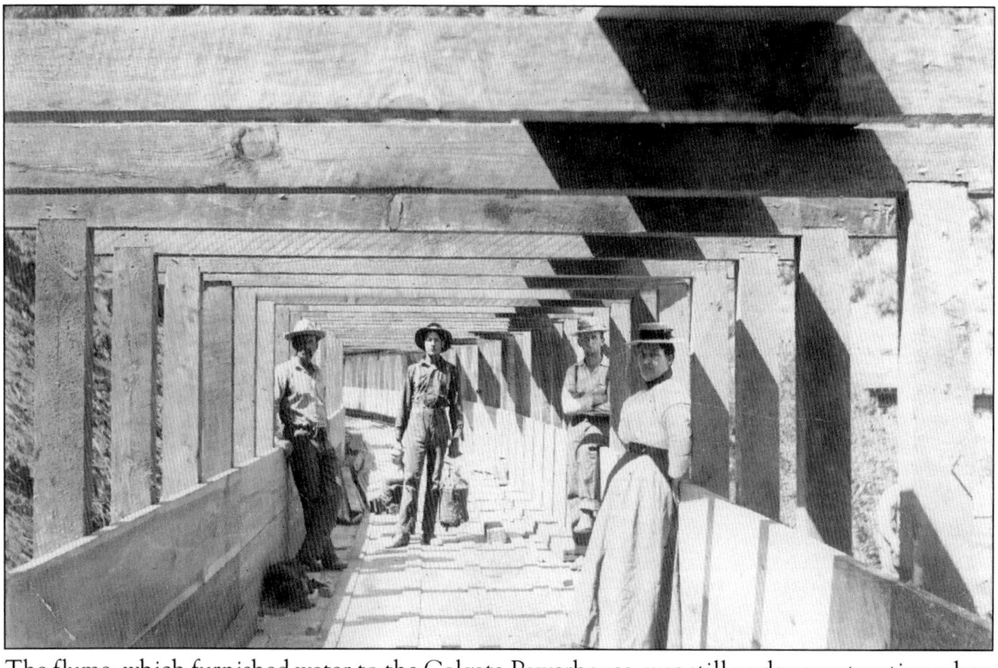

The flume, which furnished water to the Colgate Powerhouse, was still under construction when visited by an unidentified lady around 1890. The plank overhead was used to patrol the flume and watch for places that needed repair.

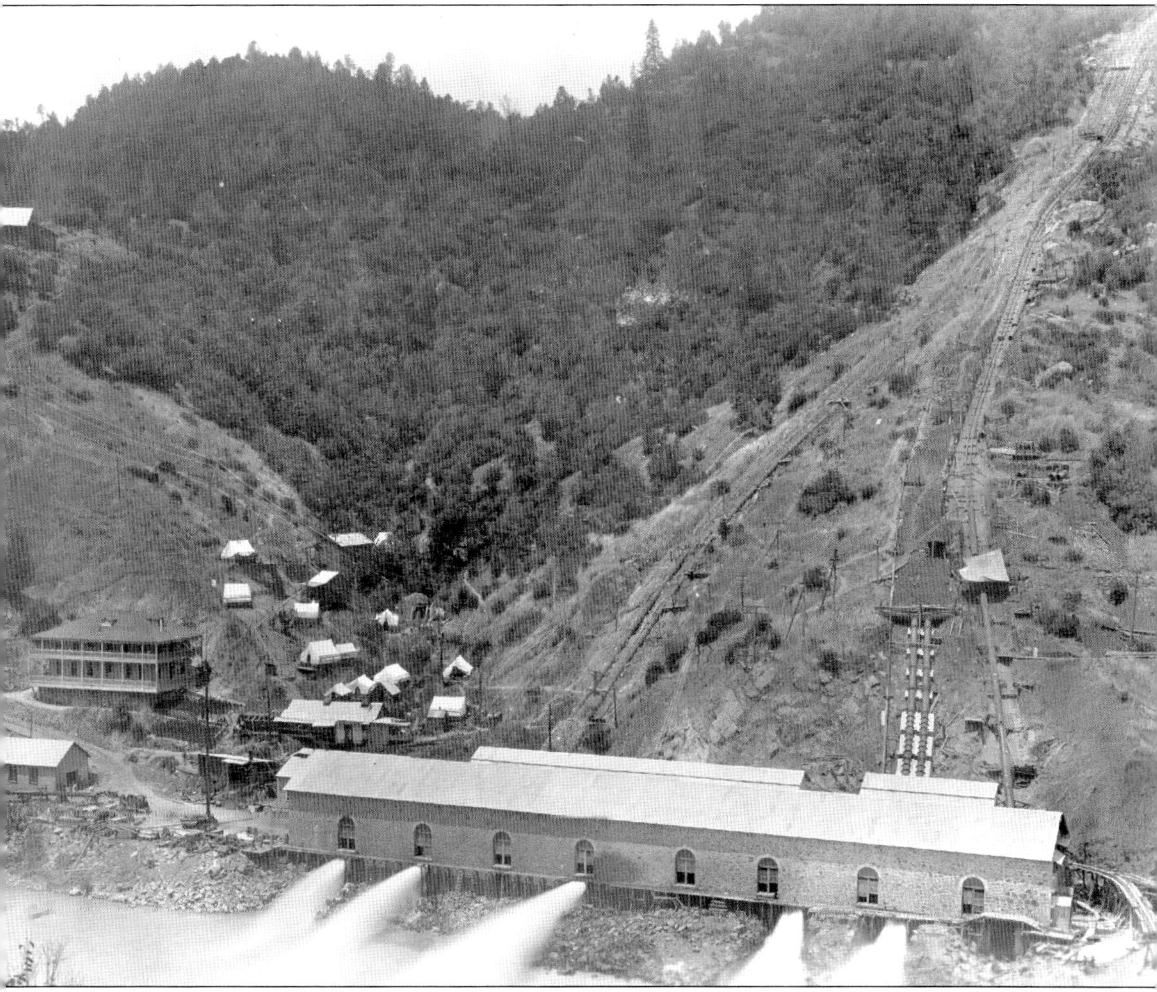

Workers' tents dot the ravine above the Colgate Powerhouse, and pipelines are being installed below Lake Frances and the flumes, which are still under construction. The Yuba River is in the foreground. On September 5, 1899, the first power was transmitted to Sacramento, and by December lines extended to Oroville. Colgate Powerhouse is still operating, and furnishes electricity for most of the Yuba Feather Hills region.

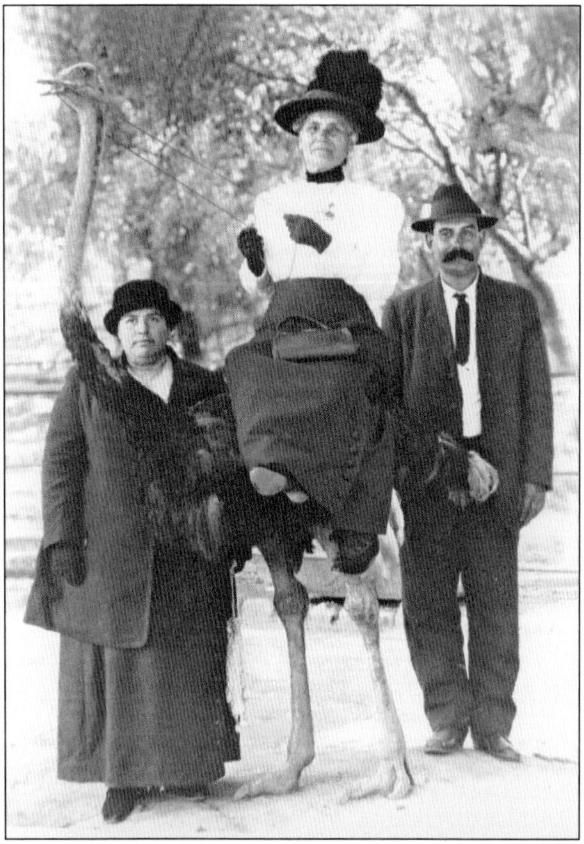

The occasion during which Nellie Royat rode the ostrich has been lost to memory, but the photograph is charming. Her friends Mary and Charlie Lucero stand alongside. (Courtesy Dan Lucero family.)

At the Dobbins Saloon, *c.* 1925, the patrons stood at the bar rather than sit on stools, as was the custom of the time.

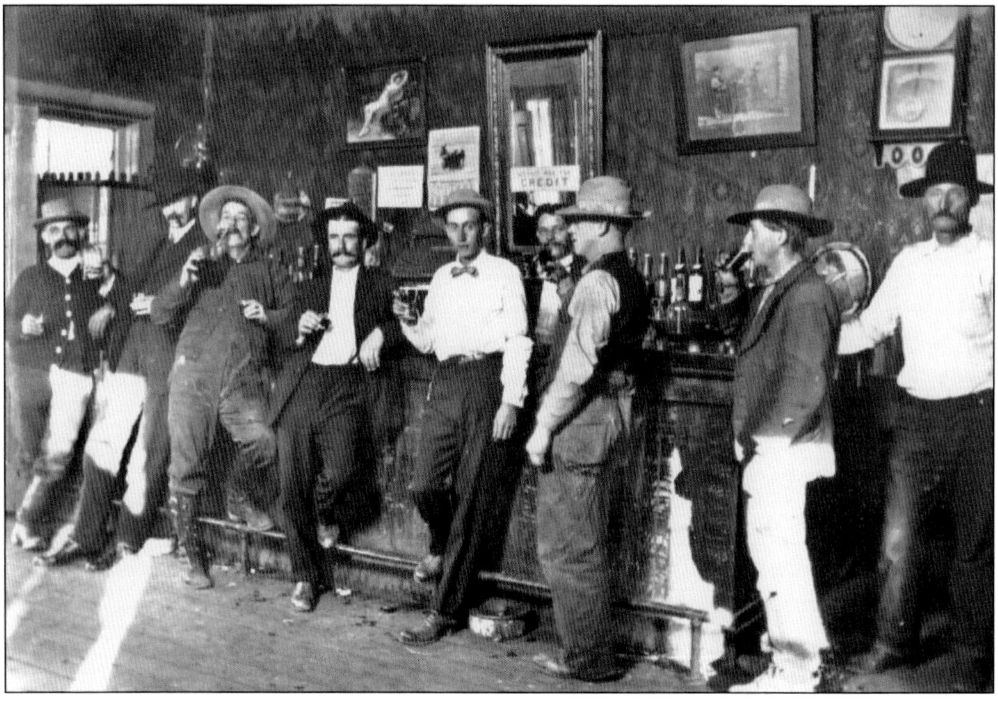

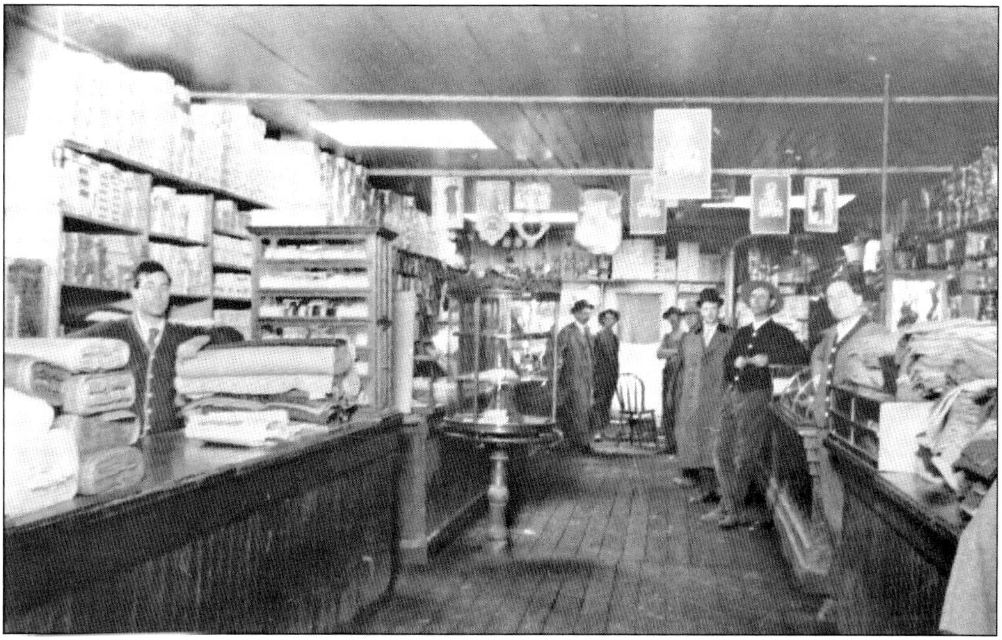

A group of men stop to pose at Dobbins Store in 1925. Chester Merriam and Bill Simmons were the clerks at the time. A great variety of goods were displayed throughout the store, and Merriam also had a large scale for weighing gold brought in by miners. (Courtesy Jim Morgan.)

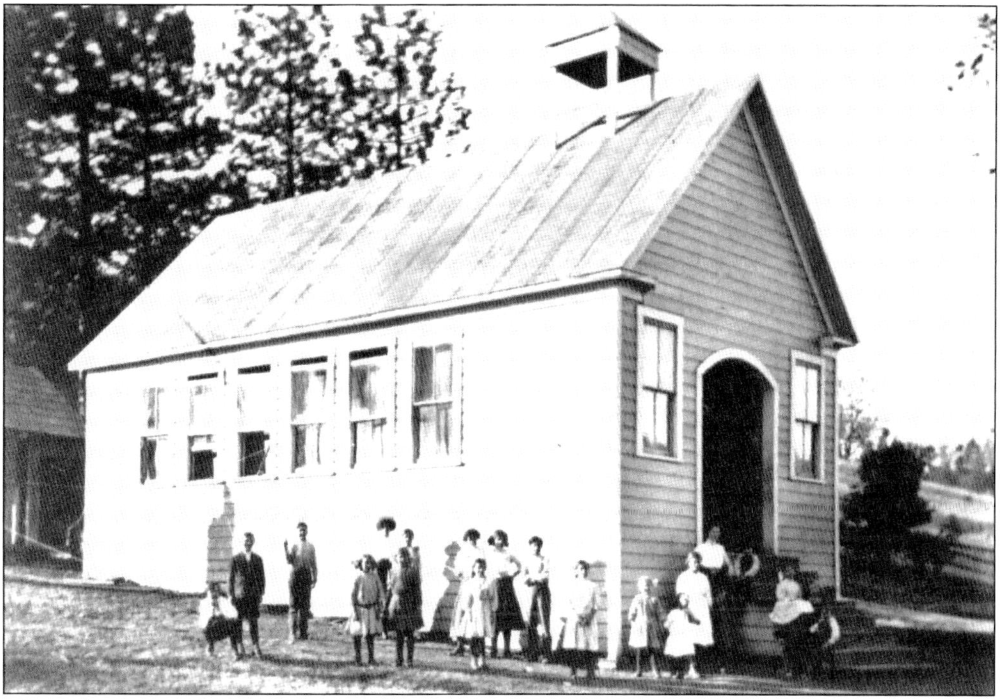

The Indiana Ranch School was built in 1856. Methodist Episcopalian services were first held in private homes by circuit-riding preachers, beginning around 1855. Later, they took place in the school and were conducted by Mr. Satterfield, who also worked in the mines on weekdays. This building is now a private home. (Courtesy Jim Morgan.)

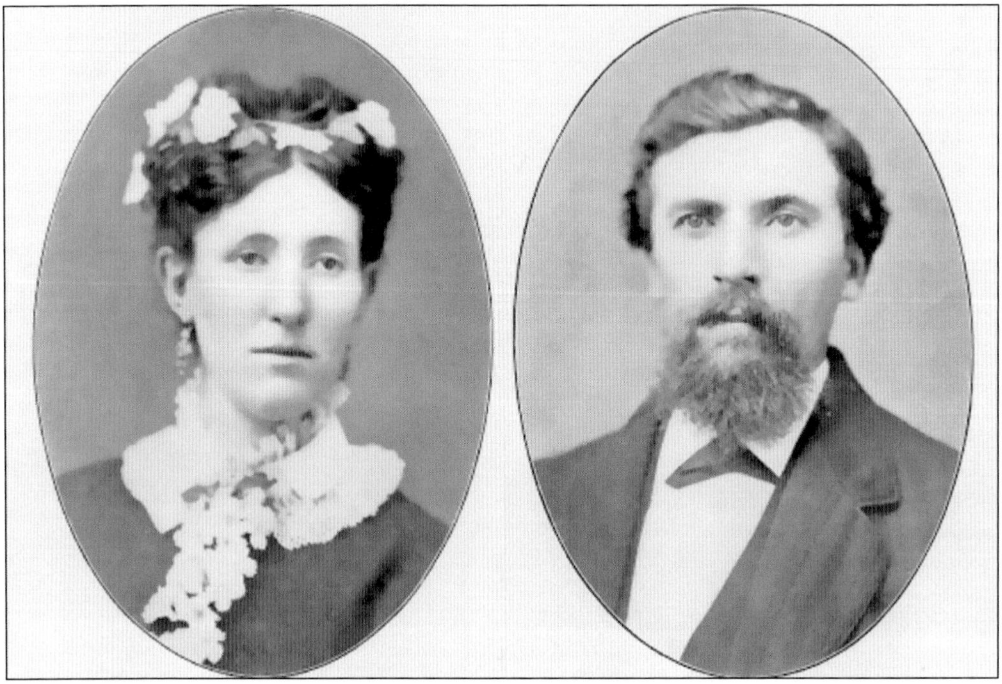

Henry A. Klenzendorf came from Germany with his parents when he was 15 and they joined his uncle, who was mining at Bullard's Bar. This place on the Yuba River was named for Dr. Bullard of New York, one of the 1849 miners. A military group, the Bullard Guards, was organized in 1852, and a post office opened in 1866. By 1879, there were two stores, a hotel, and about 30 Caucasian and Chinese residents. Henry was the manager of the Pacific Gas and Electric's (PG&E) lumberyard at the tramway above the dam. The site was inundated by the waters of Bullard's Bar Dam.

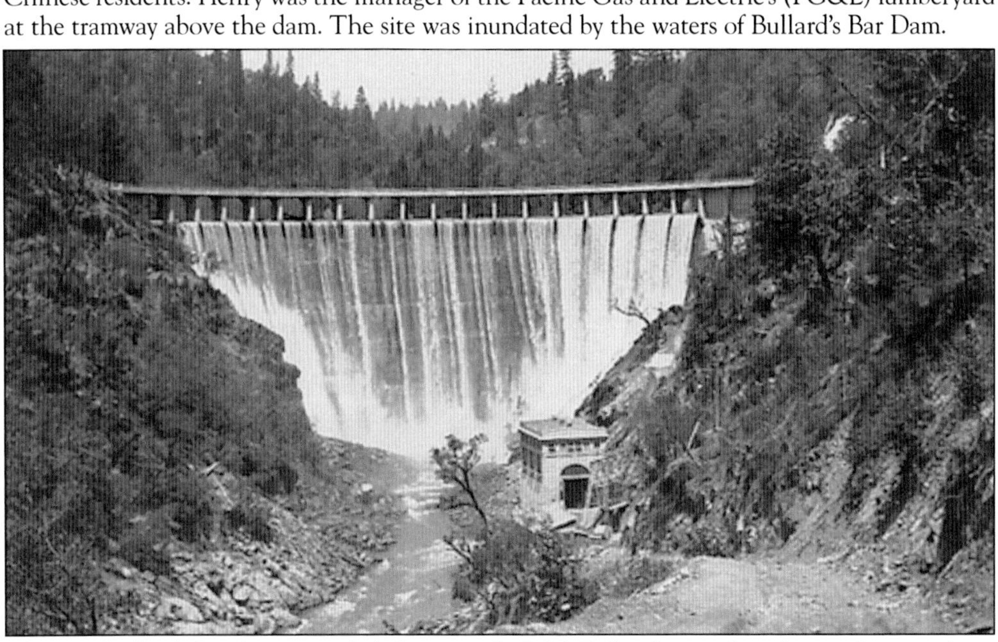

The 1942 Bullard's Bar Dam provided electricity for PG&E, flood control, and water for agriculture and recreation. It was replaced by a new structure in the 1960s, built by the Yuba County Water Agency, which had purchased all the PG&E facilities in the Dobbins area.

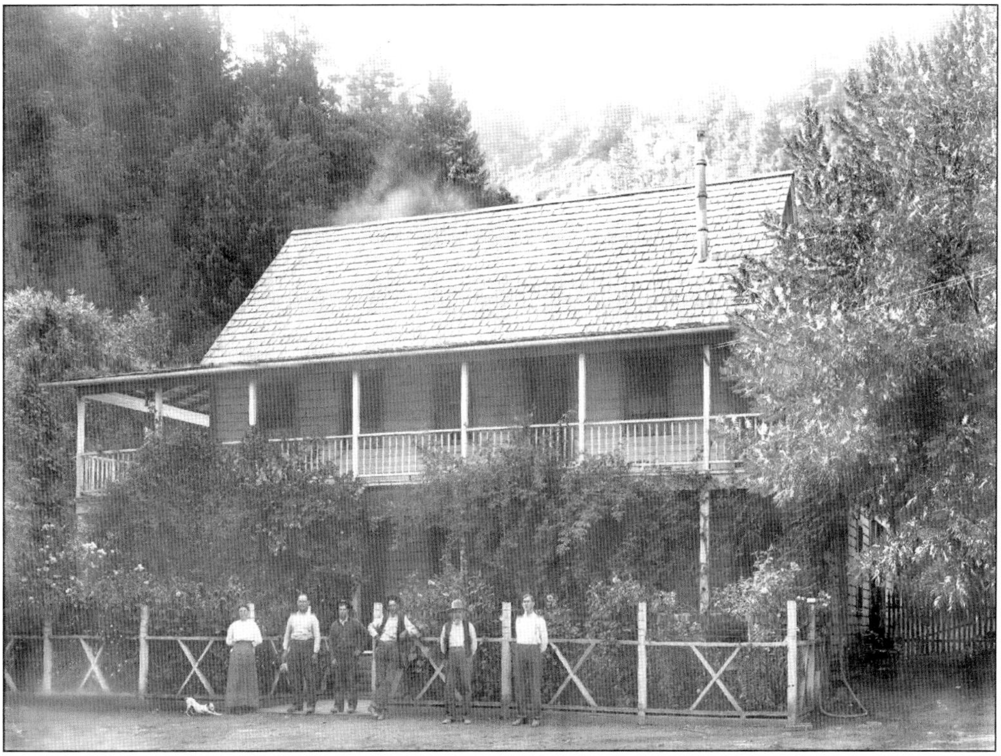

Pictured here in 1890, the Greenville Hotel on Oregon Hill Road was operated for years by the Skinner family. The community also had stores and a blacksmith at one time.

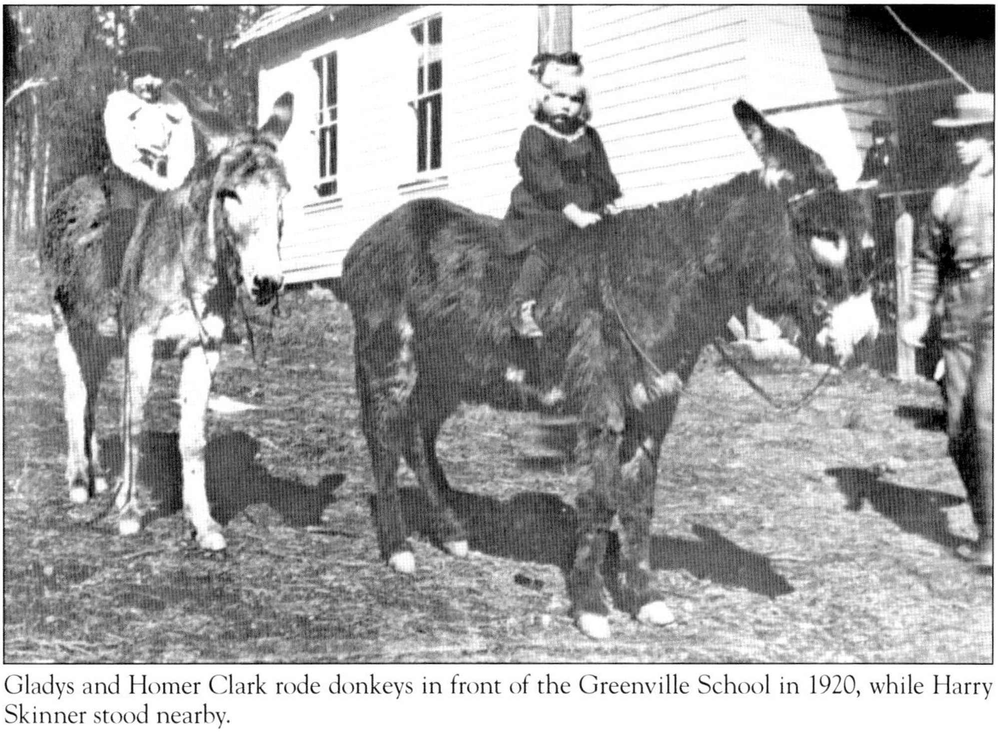

Gladys and Homer Clark rode donkeys in front of the Greenville School in 1920, while Harry Skinner stood nearby.

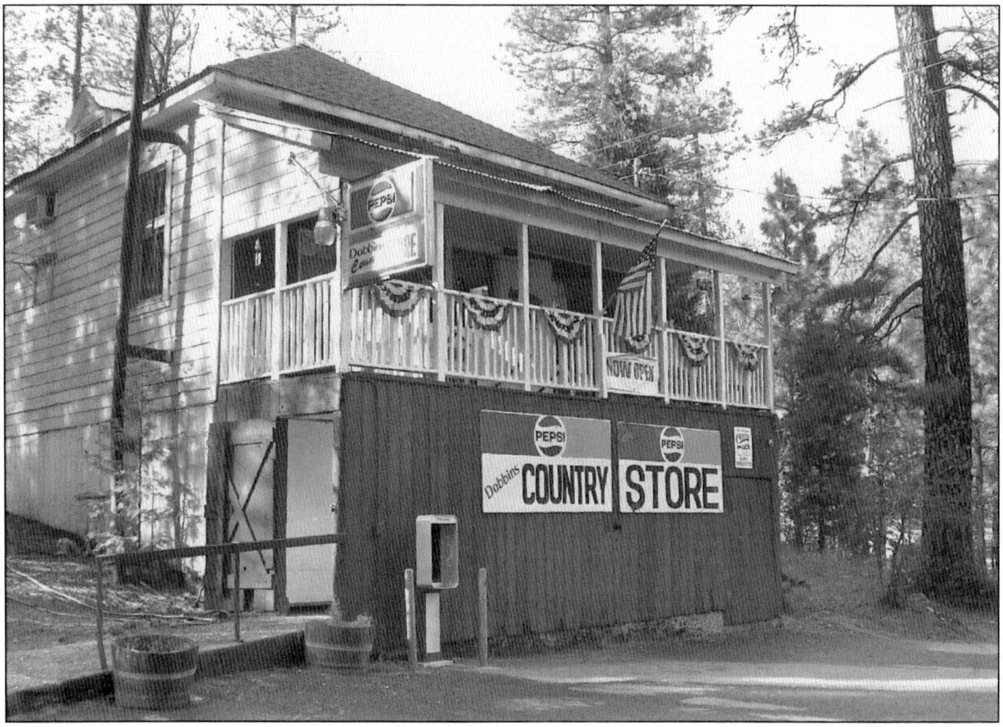


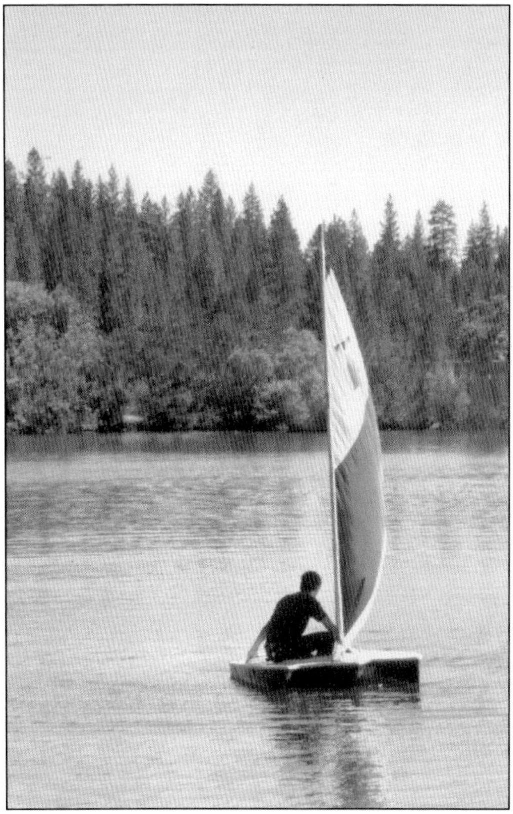

The present Dobbins Country Store was a high school in 1923, but in recent years it has been a general store, serving the needs of residents in the community. Wilma Steiner, honorary mayor of Dobbins, recalls that it was used for large gatherings, such as graduation ceremonies in the 1930s. The honorary mayor position is won in an annual election where voters pay $1 for each vote, and they are encouraged to "vote early and often." The proceeds go toward the community hall project.

The new Lake Frances Dam was recently rebuilt to modern, earthquake-proof standards, and the lake offers a pleasant place for sailing, swimming, and picnicking. Several annual events, such as Vintage Tractor Days and boat races, draw crowds from miles around.

# *Three*

# BROWNSVILLE

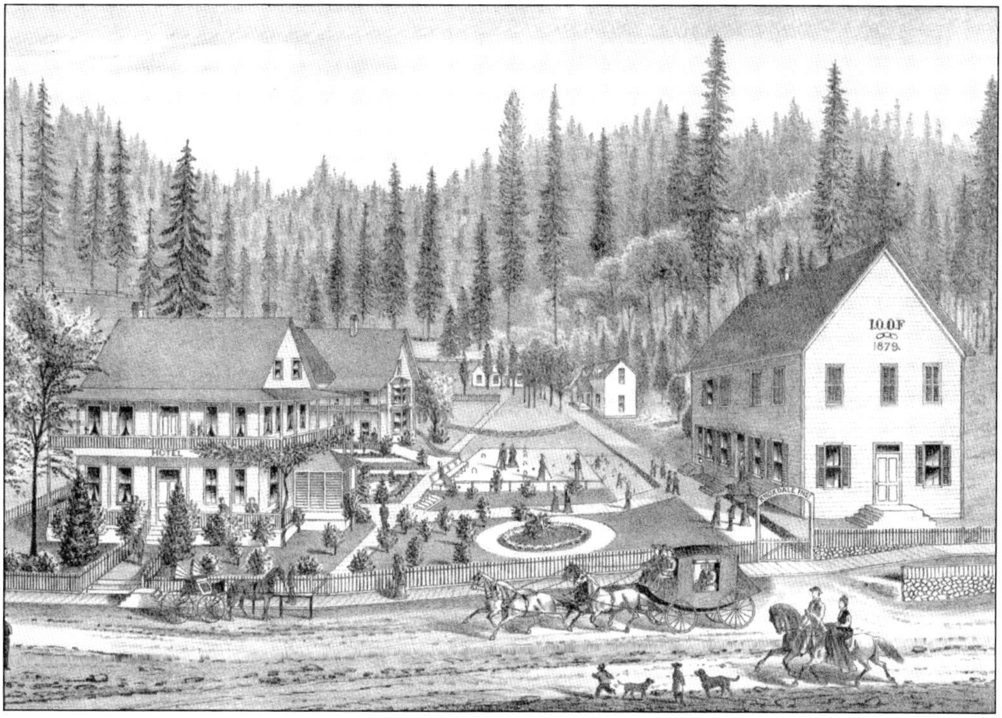


Isaac E. Brown ran a small sawmill here in 1850, and it was known as Brown's Place until 1862, when a post office was established. Martin and Sena Knox came from Springfield, Illinois, around 1855. They built the Knox Hotel and the Institute, at left, which provided advanced education for young people. They also kept saddle and driving horses and a fine croquet lawn for their guests. The lower floor of the International Order of Odd Fellows Hall, at right, was used for classrooms. Wells Fargo Express Company opened an office here in 1879, and A. T. Hankins was one of the first agents. His wife, Mary, taught music at the institute, and their five children were students there. (*History of Yuba County*, Wells and Chamberlain, 1879.)

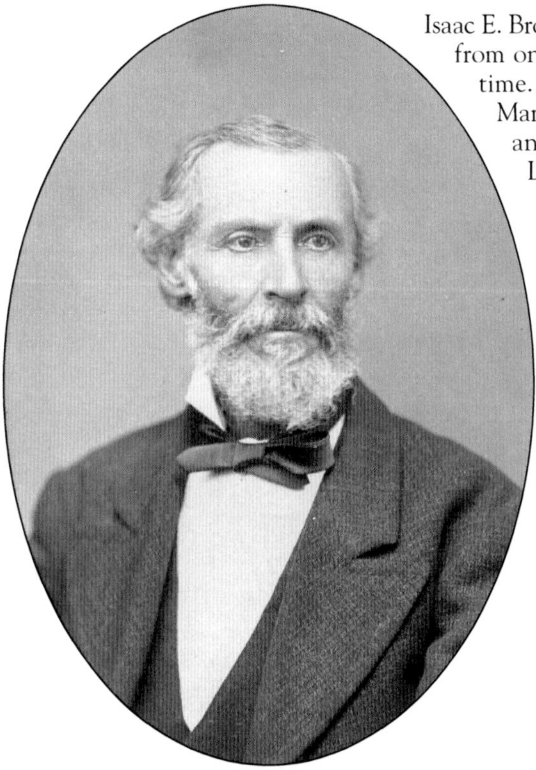

Isaac E. Brown arrived from Maine in 1849 and jumped from one scheme to another, making money each time. He opened a blacksmith shop in a tent in Marysville, cut hay to sell to wagon trains, bought and sold numerous properties, joined the Gold Lake rush to the hills, bought Barker House (Woodleaf) and took up 160 acres there (along with more land in Rackerby), built a road to Barker House, took a trip to Maine and back to California, served as justice of the peace, bought interests in mines in the high country around La Porte, and was state assemblyman in 1870 and 1871. By 1879, he described himself as a "retired farmer and miner" on 200 acres in Brownsville.

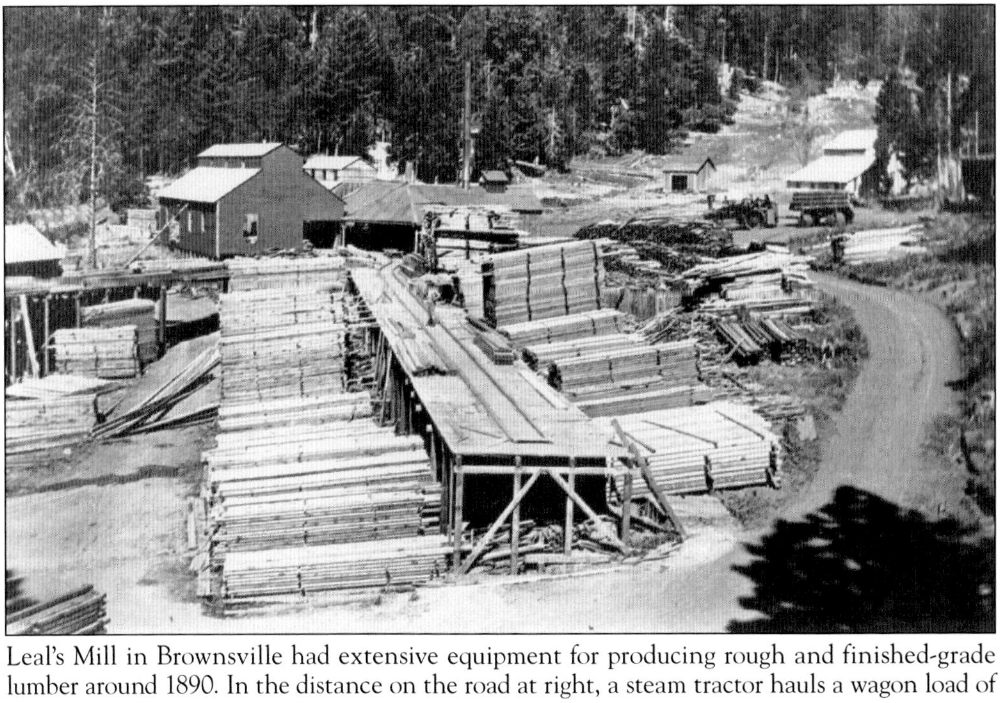

Leal's Mill in Brownsville had extensive equipment for producing rough and finished-grade lumber around 1890. In the distance on the road at right, a steam tractor hauls a wagon load of logs to the mill.

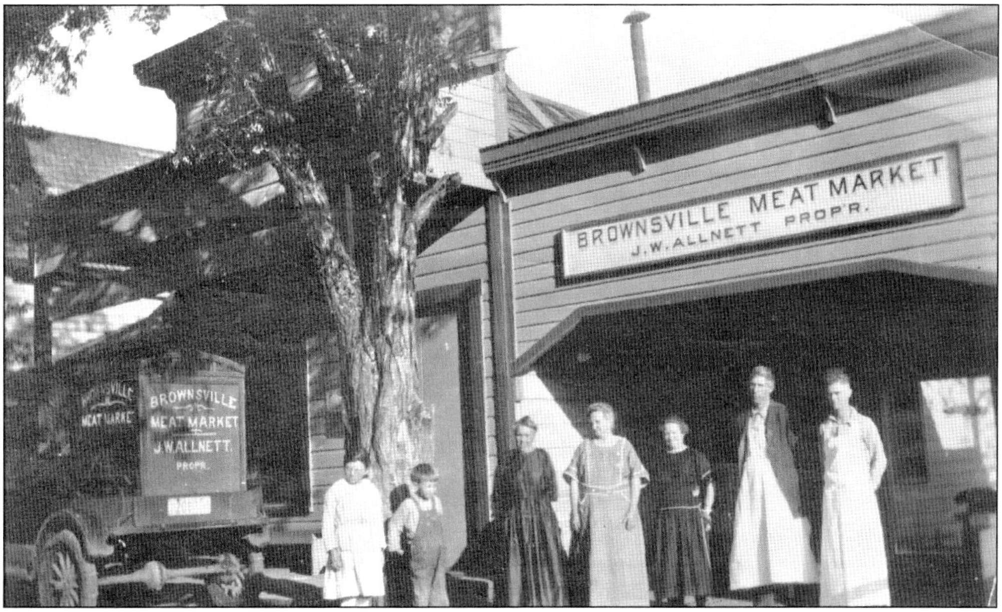

J. W. Allnett's meat market delivered meat throughout the region and served as traveling butcher to ranches. He also kept an ice house and rented space for cold storage.

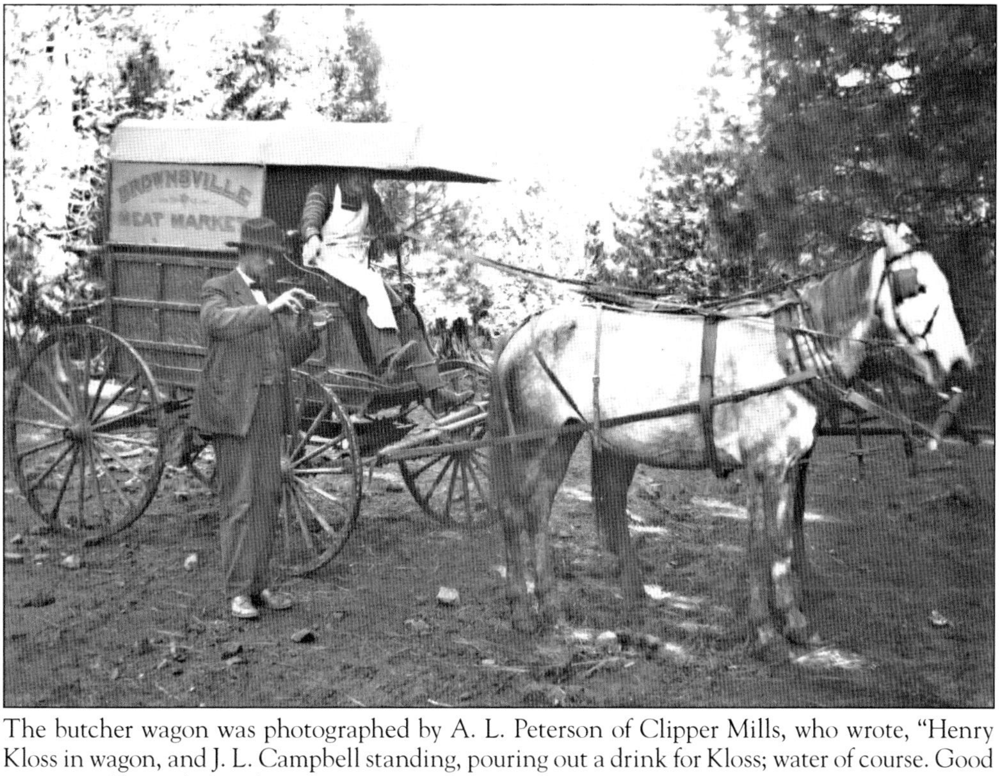

The butcher wagon was photographed by A. L. Peterson of Clipper Mills, who wrote, "Henry Kloss in wagon, and J. L. Campbell standing, pouring out a drink for Kloss; water of course. Good many would say that's a lie."

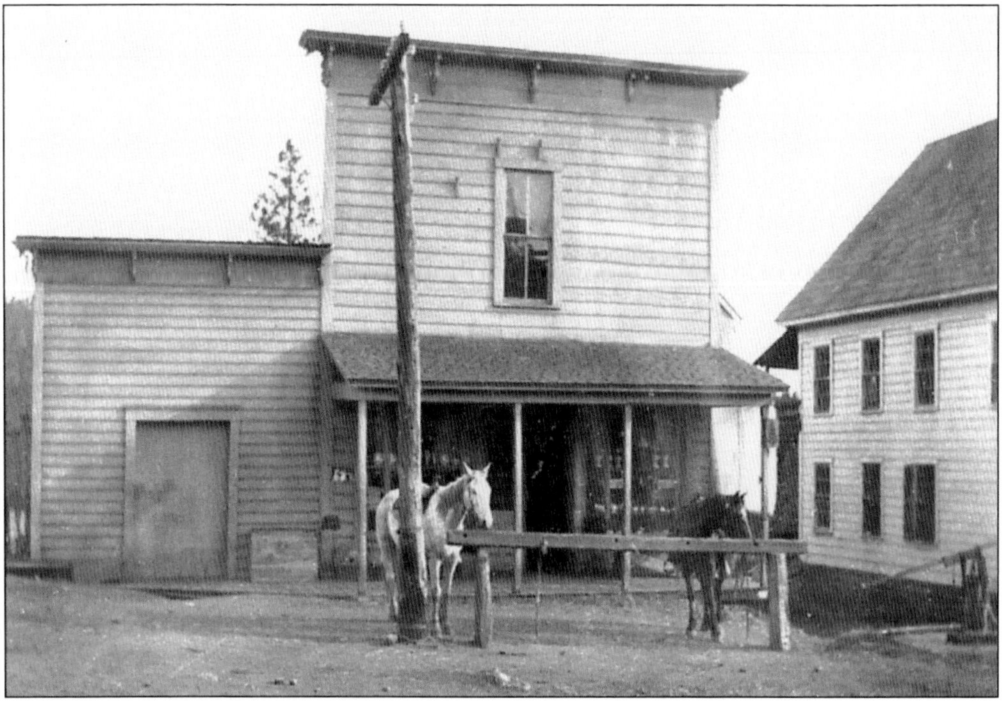

The Henry A. Conwell Hardware store, located on the south side of La Porte Road, carried a vast array of household goods. They were especially known for their selection of ornate kerosene lamps and fancy glass shades. Conwell was born in Delaware in 1832 and came to California in 1853.

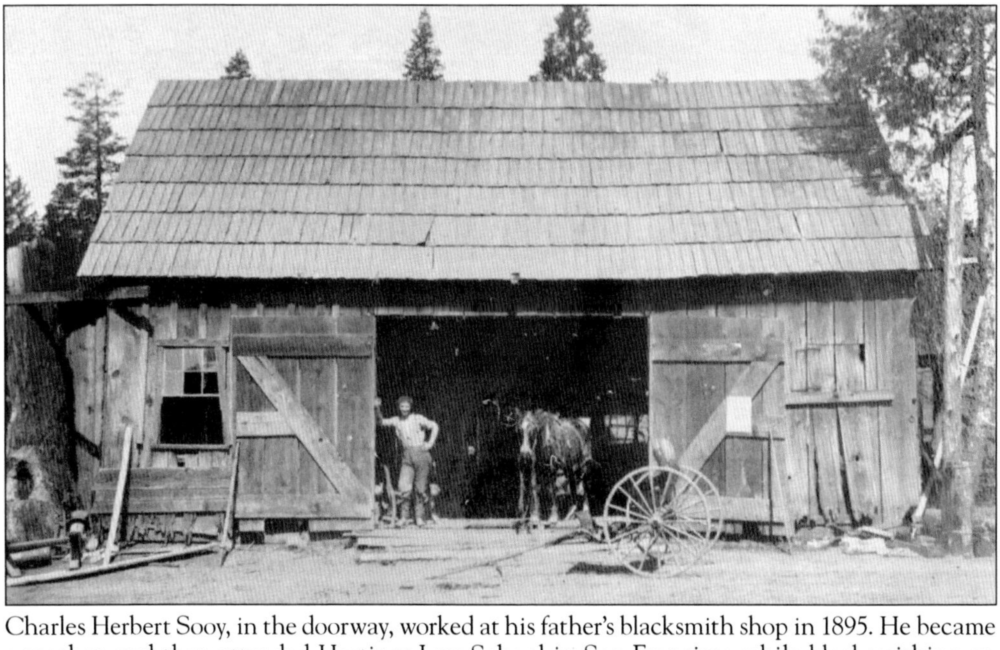

Charles Herbert Sooy, in the doorway, worked at his father's blacksmith shop in 1895. He became a teacher, and then attended Hastings Law School in San Francisco while blacksmithing on Saturdays to help support himself and his brothers and sisters. He spent much of his time raising funds for a livestock showplace in the Bay Area, and realized his dream when the Cow Palace opened for the first Grand National Stock show in 1941.

This school was originally built in 1860 near Crane's Mill in Sharon Valley. Seven years later, it was put on log rollers and moved to Brownsville, but retained the name Sharon Valley School. It also served as the church on Sundays. The local district joined Yuba Feather School District in 1949 and the old school became a private home that is still in use.

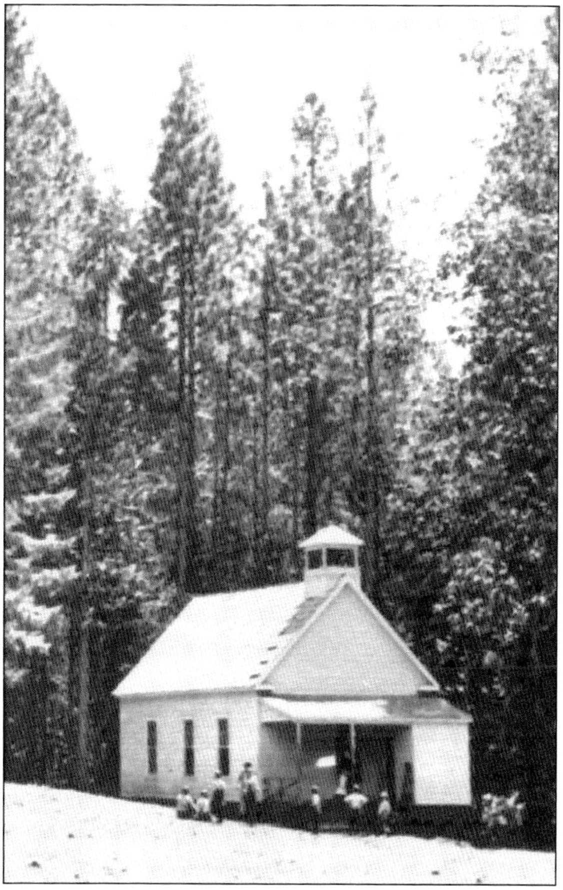

G. S. W. TWOGOOD. E. G. TWOGOOD.

BROWNSVILLE, CAL., ______ 189__

M ______

Bought of **G. S. W. TWOGOOD & SON,**

....DEALERS IN....

**General Merchandise, Dry Goods and Groceries,**

TOILET ARTICLES, DRUGS, FANCY GOODS, ETC.

G. S. W. Twogood, the proprietor of the general merchandise store in Brownville, was also a surveyor and assessor. He spent summers at the Woodleaf Tollhouse while his wife and son ran the Brownsville store. His wife was also the postal clerk.

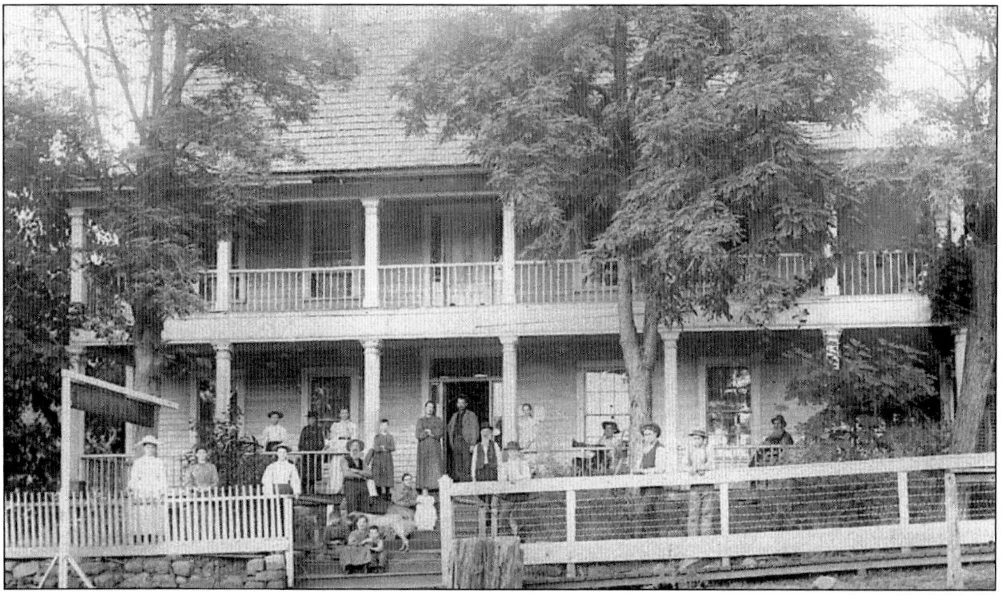

The grand, two-story Knox Hotel was the center of much of the social life in Brownville and provided accommodations for those visiting their children at the Knoxdale Institute. Boardwalks lined the side of the street from one end of town to the other. The hotel was torn down in the 1930s.

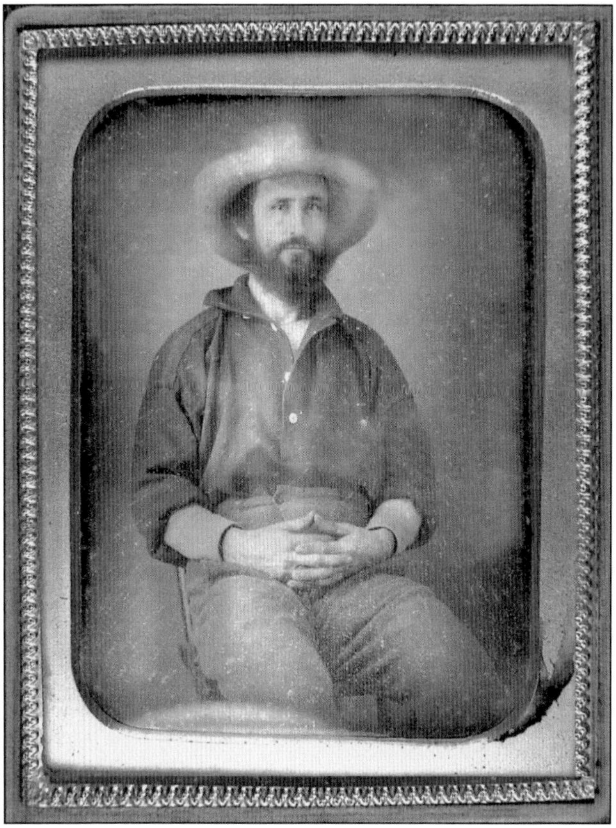

Lemuel Foss, his wife, Susan, and their six sons came from Biddleford Maine and settled at New York Flat. The Fosses had Sunday school classes and services in their living room until money was raised to build a church. Alice and Welcome Snow, originally from Maine, lived near the Foss family. Unfortunately, there is no record of how Welcome got his name. Another neighbor was Alfred Scott, born a slave in Tennessee around 1820. He escaped and enlisted in the Union Army during the Civil War before coming to California and becoming a farmer and gold miner.

Alice May Foss of Portland, Maine, was affectionately known as Lady May. In 1888, she stayed with her cousins at the Foss Ranch for a year, enjoying horseback riding and evenings of games. When back at home, she wrote, "Thursday evening I heard some ladies and gentlemen singing in the street and it made me think of the sings we had on New York Flat. I thought how long it would be before we sung together again, and perhaps never."

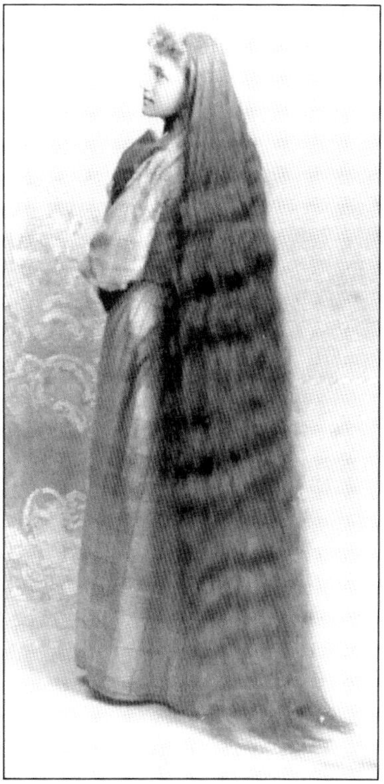

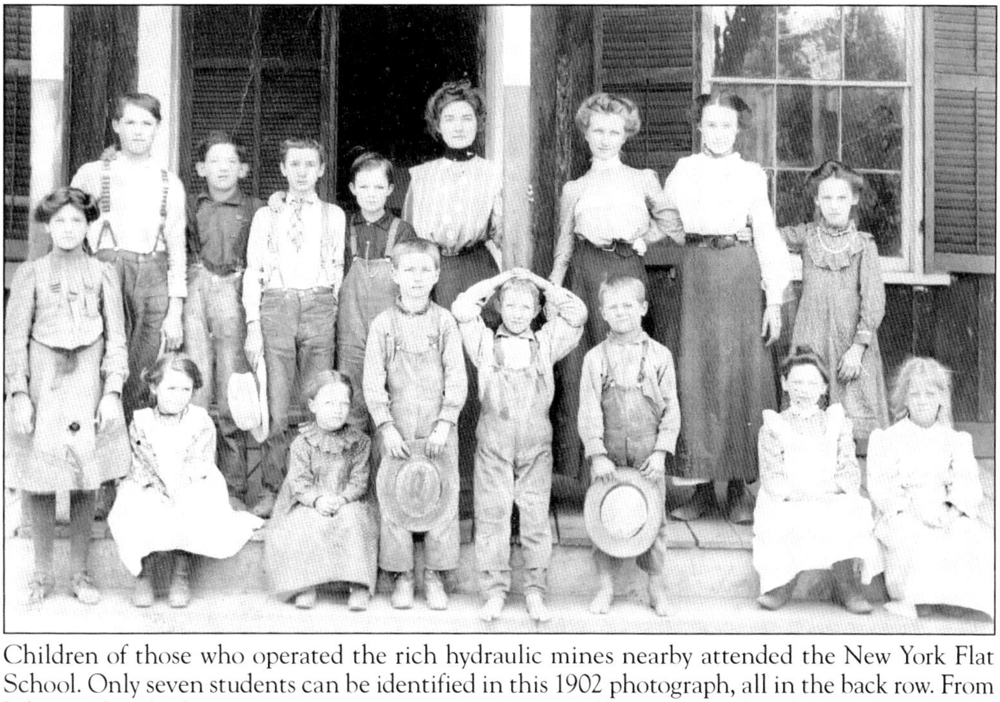

Children of those who operated the rich hydraulic mines nearby attended the New York Flat School. Only seven students can be identified in this 1902 photograph, all in the back row. From left to right, the boys are Harrison Lague, Joe King, and Warren Steele, who was later a Yuba County supreme court judge; and the four girls are Mabel, Vera, Alice, and Enid Foss. Teacher Ida Ruff is not in the picture. The school closed in 1908.

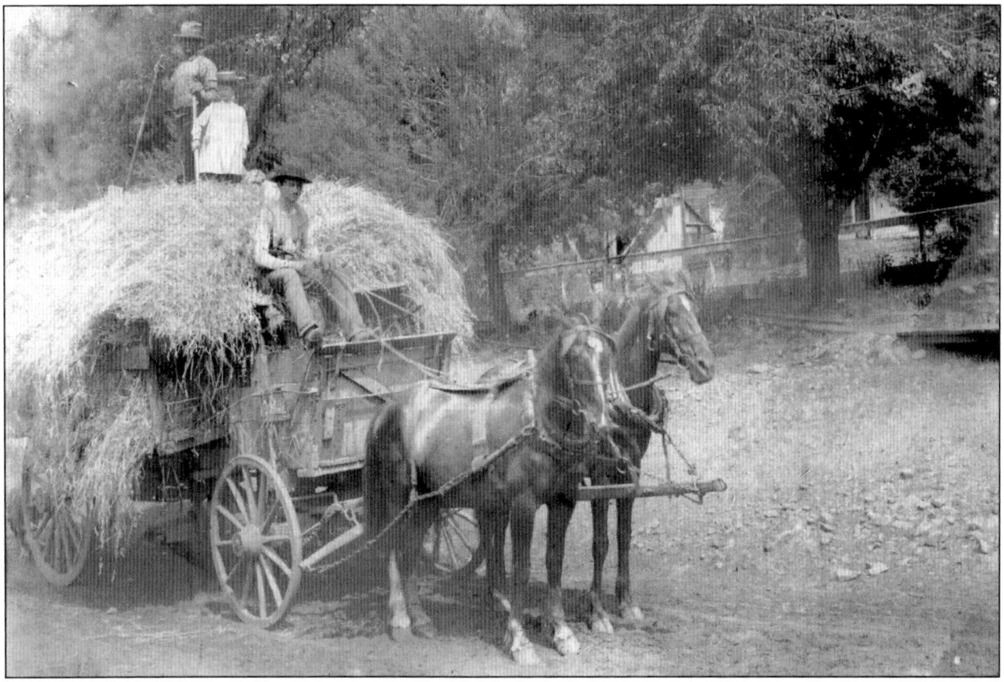

Most of the land in the hills was cleared of timber and planted in barley, wheat, corn, orchards, and vineyards. The crew is bringing in the hay at the Kloss ranch in 1890.

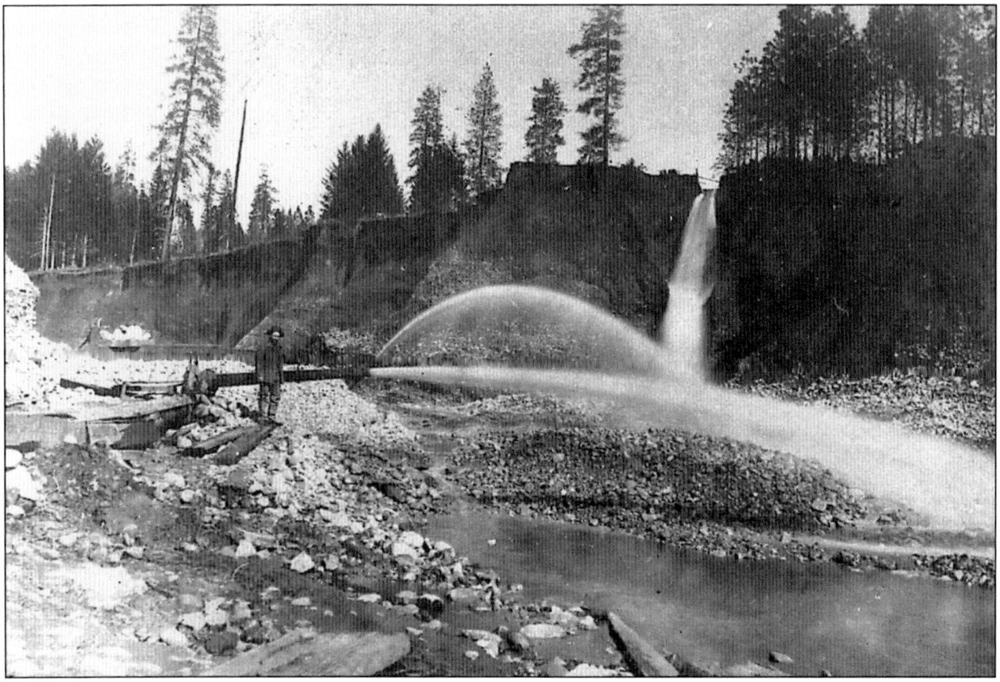

The Nevada Mining Company on New York Flat was owned by partners H. A. Conwell, the Foss family, Welcome Snow, L. T. Crane, J. L. Gibson, T. J. Lockwood, Mr. Richardson, and Daniel Greer. Their ledgers show that between 1863 and 1878 the hydraulic operations took out more than $250,000 in gold.

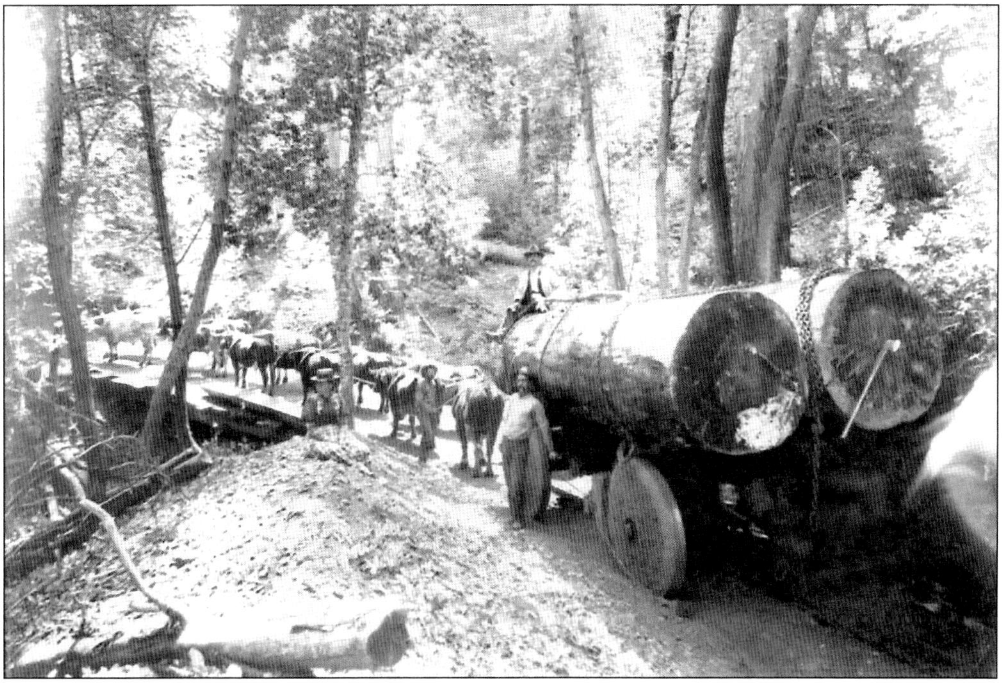

This team of oxen is hauling a load of logs over the bridge on New York Flat Road on their way to the Crane Mill. The Plaskett Mill in Forbestown was closer, but uphill, while the road to the Crane's ran downhill and was easier on the oxen.

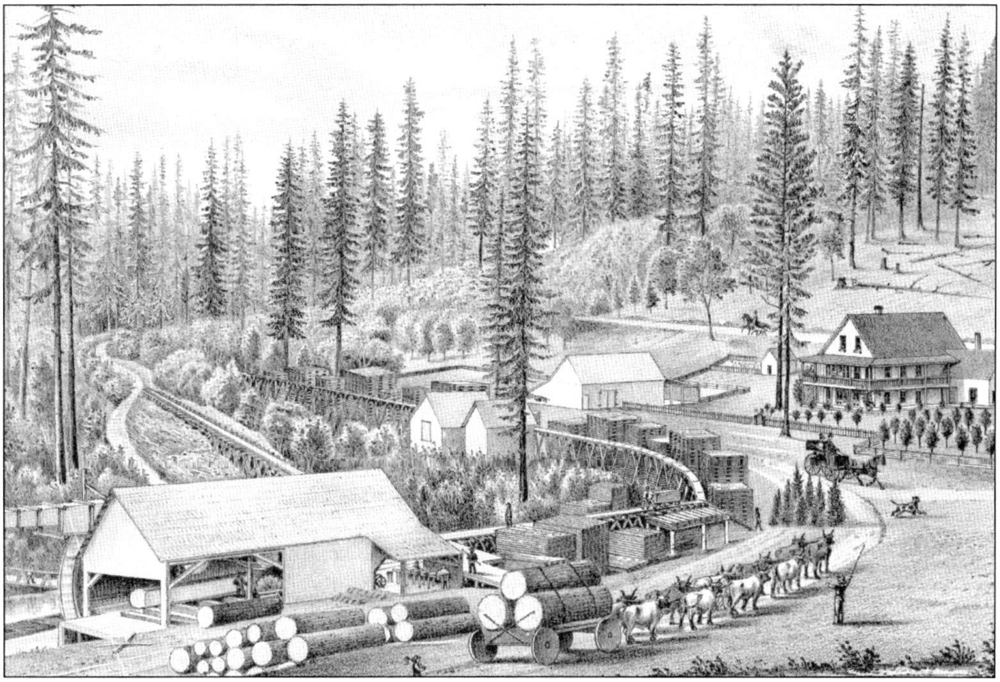

Lemuel Trescott and William M. Crane came to California from Maine. They built a steam- and water-powered mill at the junction of Challenge Cutoff and La Porte Road that produced 800,000 board feet per year. (*History of Yuba County*, Wells and Chamberlain, 1879.)

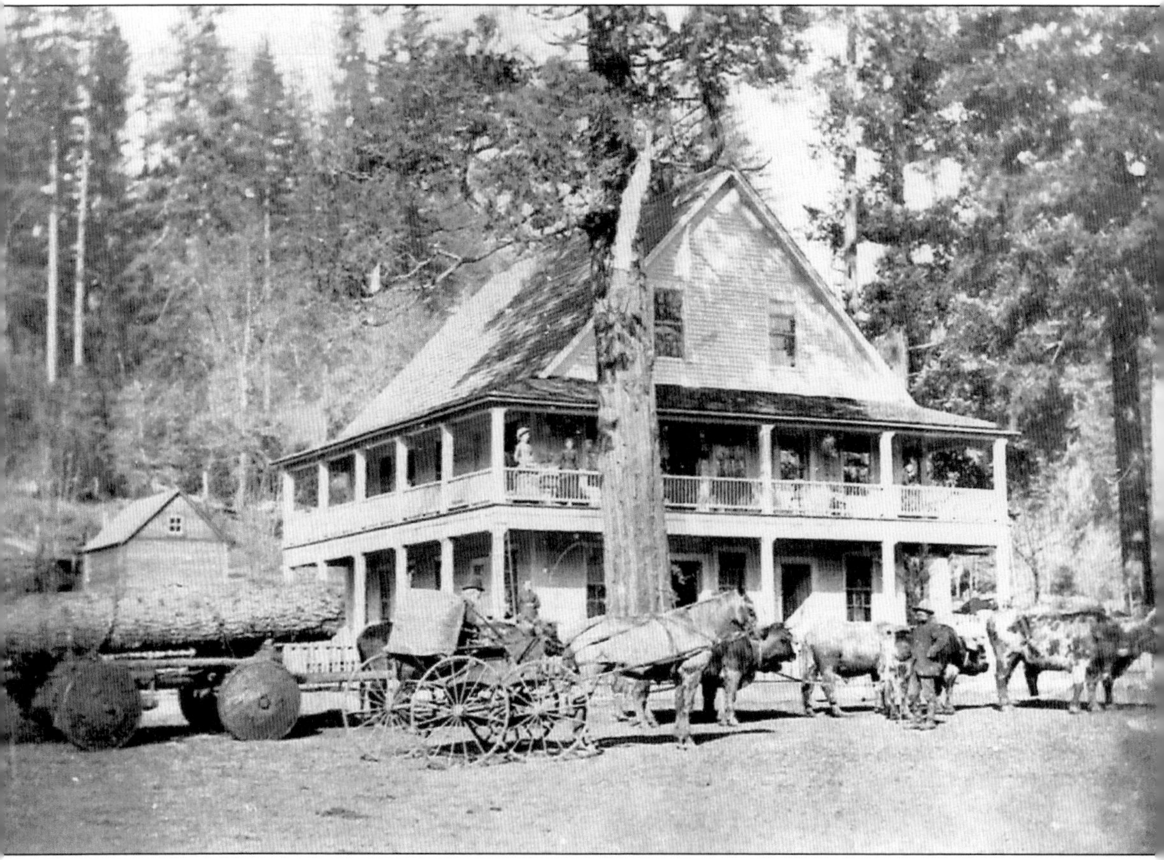

A team of eight oxen with a load of logs is stopped in front of the Sharon Valley Hotel before proceeding to the Crane Mill. A one-horse buggy is also parked at the hotel. The hotel had 16 rooms, 3 marble-faced fireplaces, and 2 staircases, one that was for the maids and cooks. There was also a large attic that was both the mill office and dormitory for the mill crew. The Chinese cook, King, ran the kitchen and was responsible for all the meals for the employees. After Lemuel and William died, William's widow continued to run the hotel. Her nieces, Annie and Lillian Lordly, came to live with her and help with the business. They carried on even after Sarah died in 1911 and had guests in the hotel in the 1930s. The house was dismantled after Annie died in 1956.

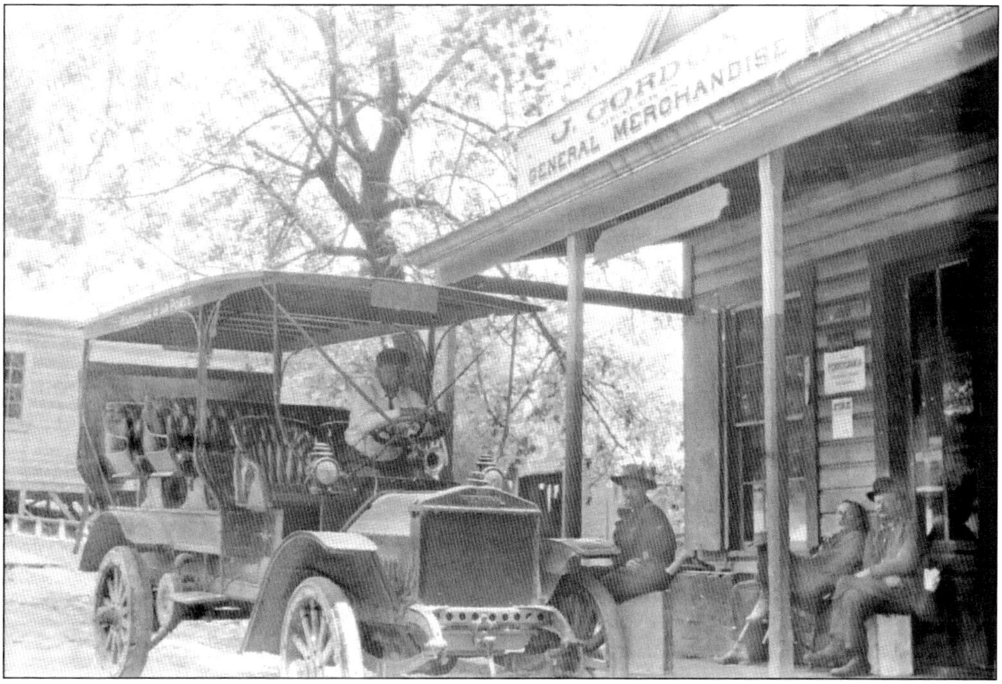


This new-fangled automobile, with seats for eight passengers, replaced the old stagecoach but was still known as the Marysville–La Porte Stage. The driver made regular stops at J. Gordon's general store.

Major Emil A. Hoeppner, at left, served in the Spanish-American War and was a construction superintendent in San Francisco after the 1906 earthquake. He bought the Knox property at Brownsville in 1916 and worked to develop a mine. It wasn't successful, but the chestnut orchard he planted produces to this day. He and his wife lived in a large house on the hill that was destroyed by fire in the late 1930s. Major Hoeppner and his friend Pete Mansell, at right, enjoy cigars in the afternoon sun.

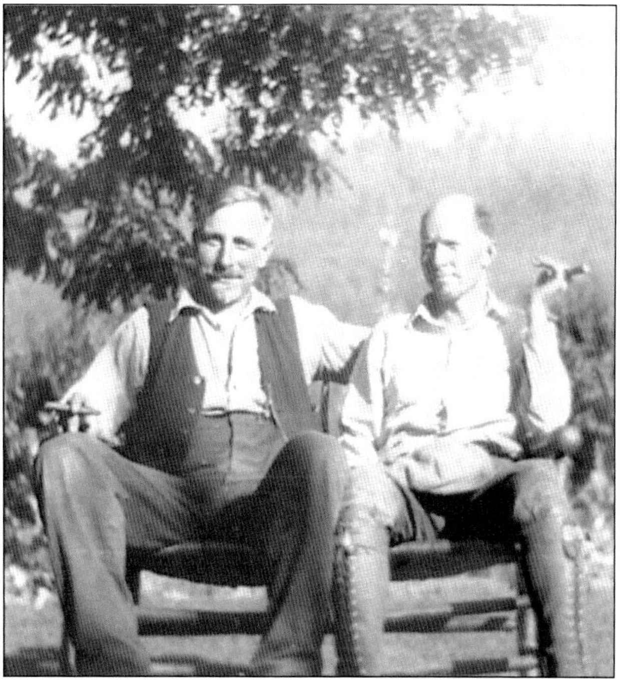

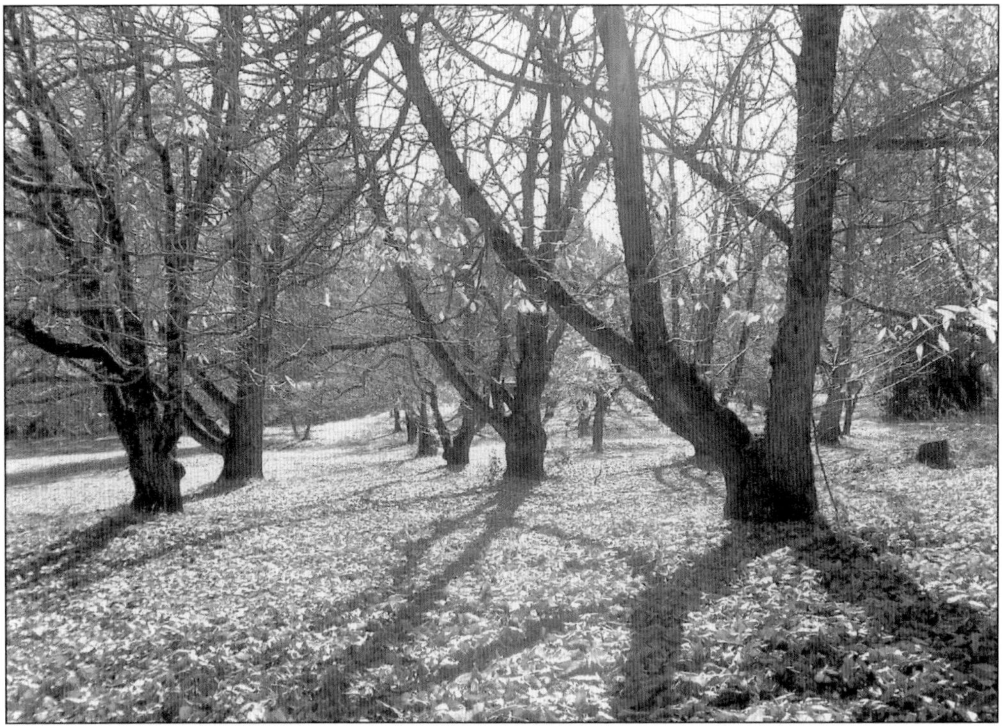

The chestnut orchard planted in the 1930s is one of only a few that survived on the West Coast and is a landmark in Brownsville, pictured here in 2006.

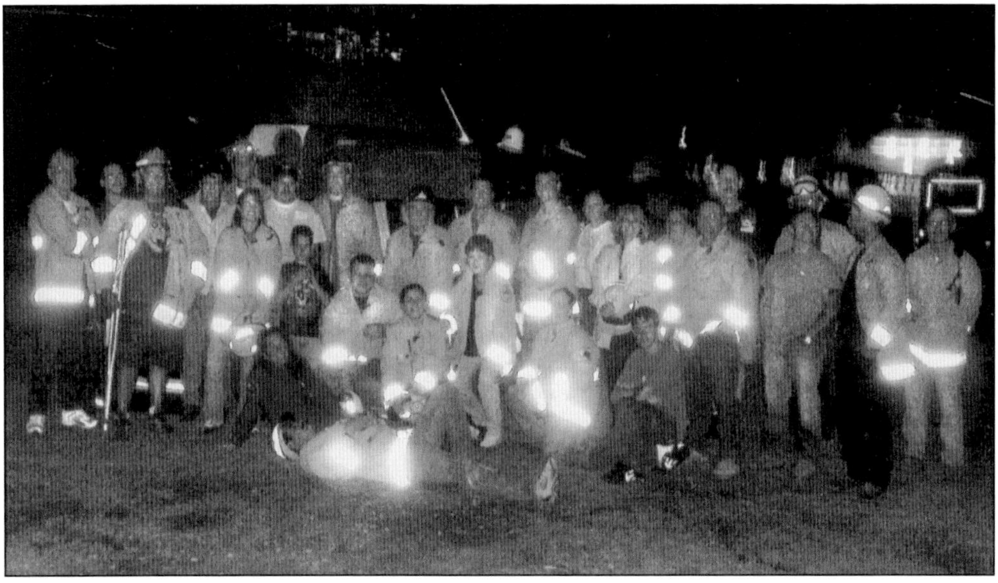

Some of the members of the Foothill Volunteer Fire Department gathered one night in 2005 to demonstrate their reflective gear. They are entirely supported by local residents, and their facility also houses the Yuba County Sheriff Substation. Located at the intersection of four main roads, Brownsville is the largest of the towns in present-day Yuba Feather Hills, with a medical center, a bank, five churches, an airport, restaurants, a grocery, a hardware store, and many other businesses. (Courtesy Foothill Volunteer Fire Department.)

# *Four*

# RACKERBY

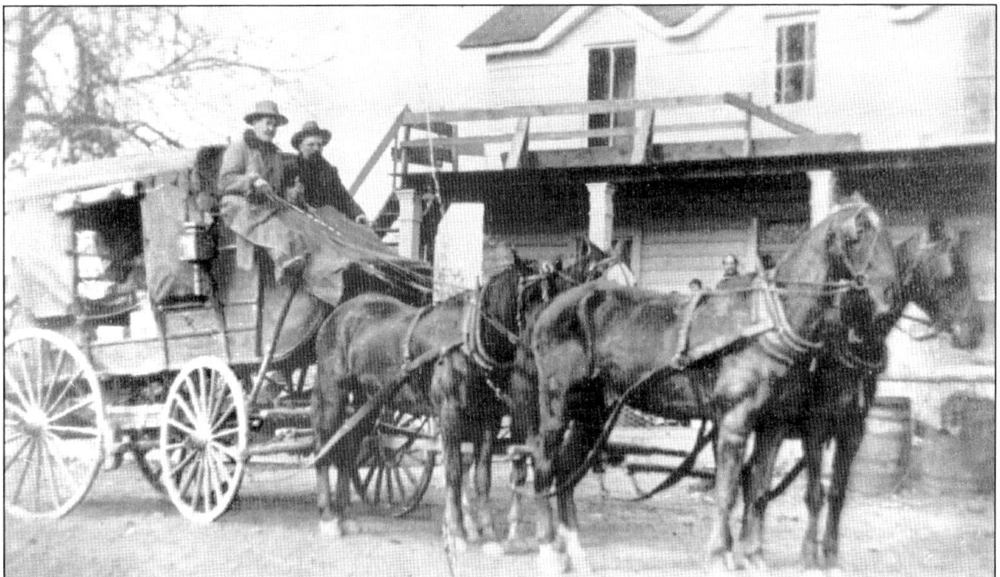

The Marysville–La Porte Stage, driven by George Guntry, stops around 1890 at the Rackerby Hotel, which is still standing. This town had many names, beginning with Natchez. Then, depending on who was postmaster, it was Hansonville (1851), Miller's Ranch (1862), Paulinville (1866), again Hansonville (1873), and Rackerby (1892). Within a year after it was settled in 1851, there were seven stores, eight hotels (each with its own bar), a bowling alley, gambling saloons, and a population of 1,000. Religious services were held in homes or barrooms, and the gamblers usually stopped long enough to hear the sermon. It was a rough place: when known as Natchez, the cemetery held 25 souls—none who died a natural death.

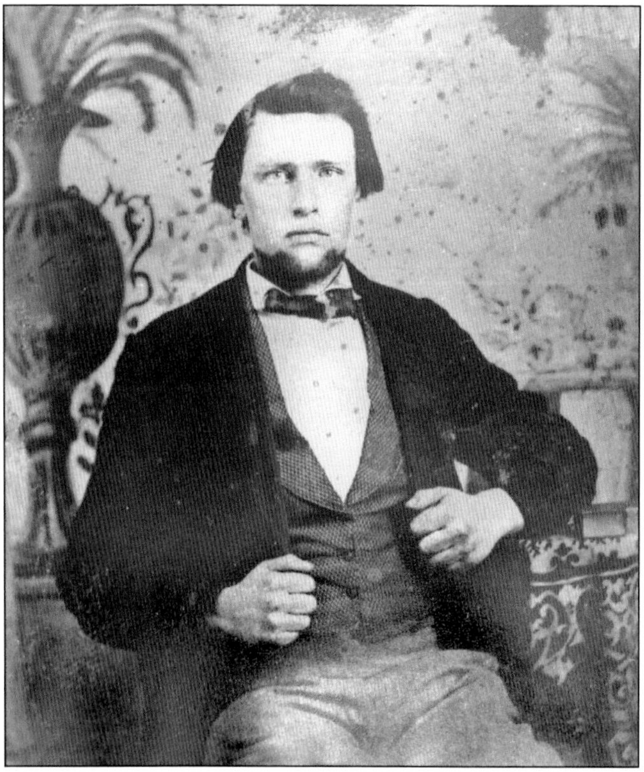

In 1851, Robert Monroe Johnson was a partner with James H. Hanson in their store and hotel. His likeness is captured on this early tintype around 1855.

When the post office opened in 1856, Hanson was the first postmaster. The climate was ideal for orchards, vineyards, and pastures for grazing livestock. Frenchman Paulin Rouzé built a wine cellar and distillery to process the grapes from his large vineyard. The remains of his stone building are still visible. When he was postmaster, the town was Paulinville. (Illustration from *History of Yuba County*, Wells and Chamberlain, 1879.)

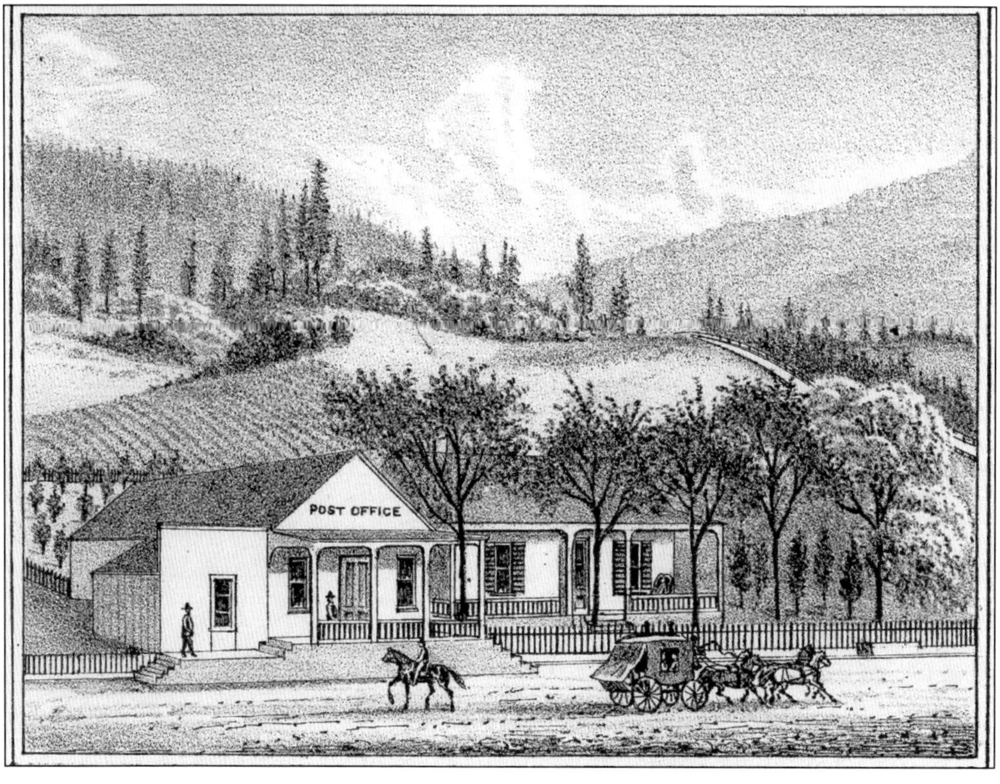

William Rackerby was 48 and single when he crossed the plains as a pioneer in 1849. He was 78 when photographed here at Wood's Studio in Marysville as a member of California Pioneers. He obtained a large tract of land, advertising it in newspapers across the country and selling parcels to settlers.

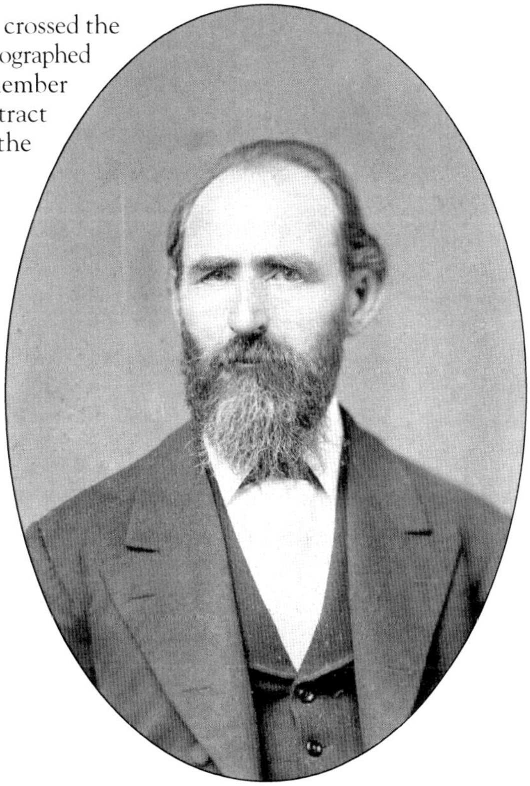

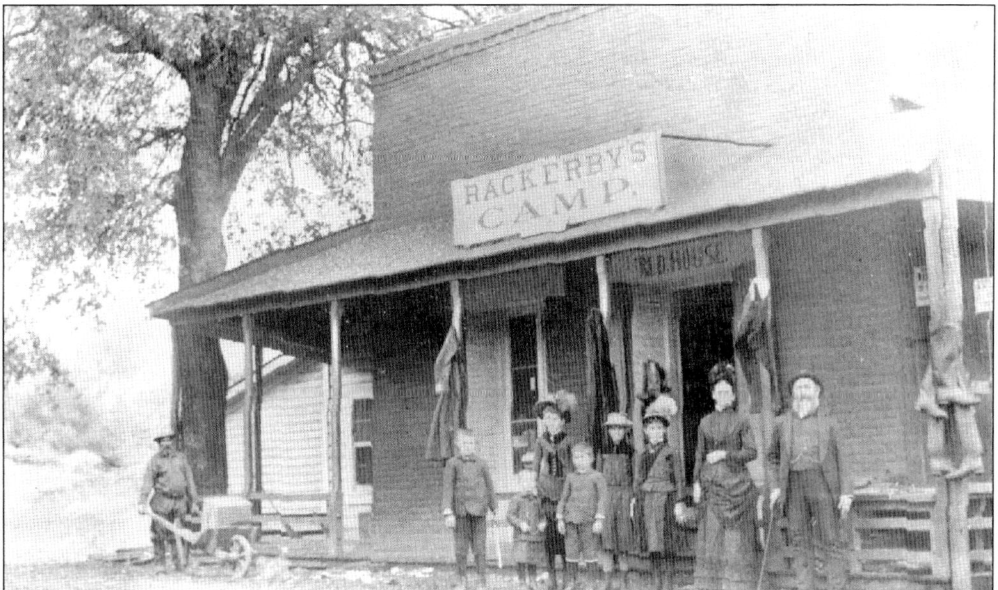


William and Ruth Rackerby stand in front of the Rackerby Camp Store with their children, Paul, Cleve, Undine, Wirt, Amy Johnson, and Vesta. All types of clothing and boots hang from the posts.

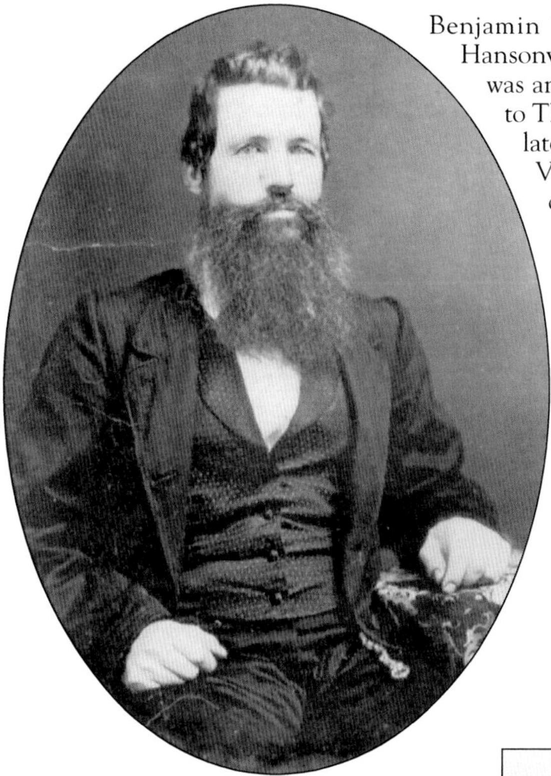

Benjamin Rodman built a store near the top of Hansonville Hill in 1852 that had no bar, which was an "exceedingly rare occurrence," according to Thompson and West's 1879 history. Rodman later acquired the property where Sir Henry Vere Huntley spent some $5,000 to build a quartz mill for Anglo-American Gold and Silver Company in 1851. The venture failed and Sir Henry, who lost about $40,000 of his own money, returned to his home in England in 1852.

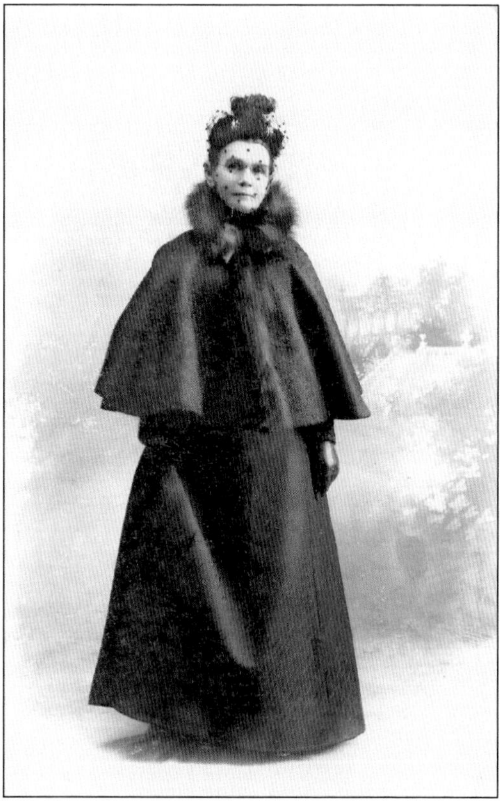

After Rodman's wife died in 1891 he created a bit of a stir when he married her maid, Katie McMannas of Ireland. In a magnificent cape and hat, Katie's portrait was taken here in San Francisco in 1897.

This is a bill for extensive wagon repairs done at Birdsley's blacksmith shop in Bangor, a town west of Rackerby. Birdsley also had a blacksmith shop in Forbestown for many years.

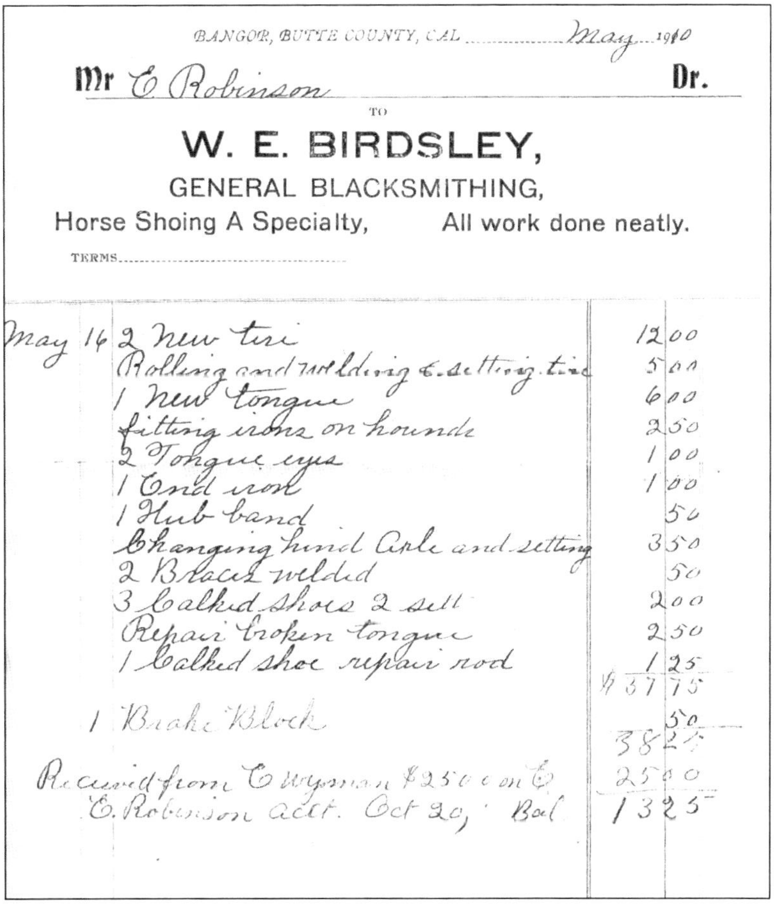

BANGOR, BUTTE COUNTY, CAL ............ May 1910

Mr E Robinson Dr.

TO

W. E. BIRDSLEY,

GENERAL BLACKSMITHING,

Horse Shoing A Specialty, All work done neatly.

TERMS............

| | | |
|---|---|---|
| May 16 | 2 New tire | 12 00 |
| | Rolling and welding & setting tire | 5 00 |
| | 1 new tongue | 6 00 |
| | fitting irons on hounds | 2 50 |
| | 2 Tongue eyes | 1 00 |
| | 1 End iron | 1 00 |
| | 1 Hub band | 50 |
| | Changing hind Axle and setting | 3 50 |
| | 2 Braces welded | 50 |
| | 3 Calked shoes 2 sett | 2 00 |
| | Repair broken tongue | 2 50 |
| | 1 Calked shoe repair rod | 1 25 |
| | | $37 75 |
| | 1 Brake Block | 50 |
| | | 38 25 |
| | Received from C Wyman $25.00 on E. Robinson Acct. Oct 20, Bal | 25 00 |
| | | 13 25 |

Lewis W. Clark's blacksmith shop, photographed in 1915, was equipped to build and repair all types of wagons. Clark also had a lively business shoeing horses, mules, and oxen.

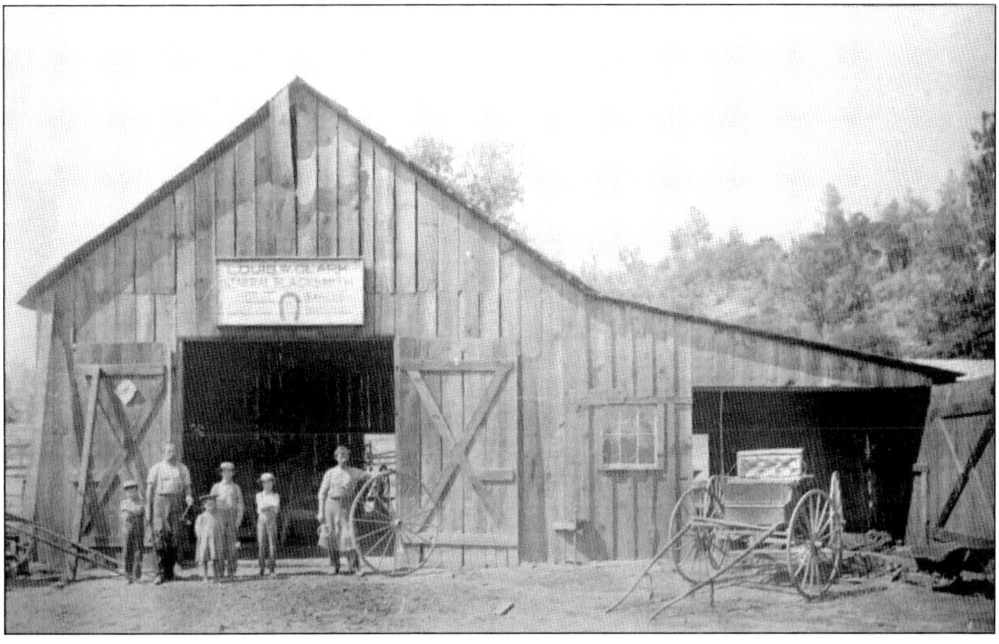

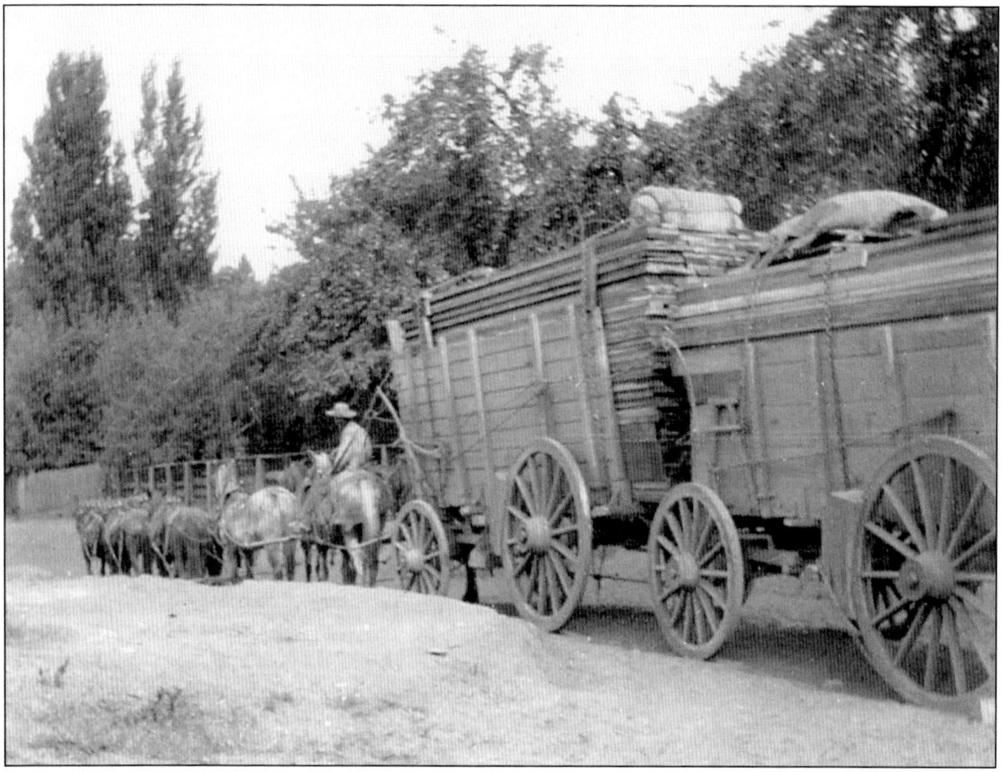

One of T. V. Clark's teams hauls two freight wagons on the road near Rackerby in 1910. There were many teamsters in the freighting business, transporting huge loads of supplies into the foothills.

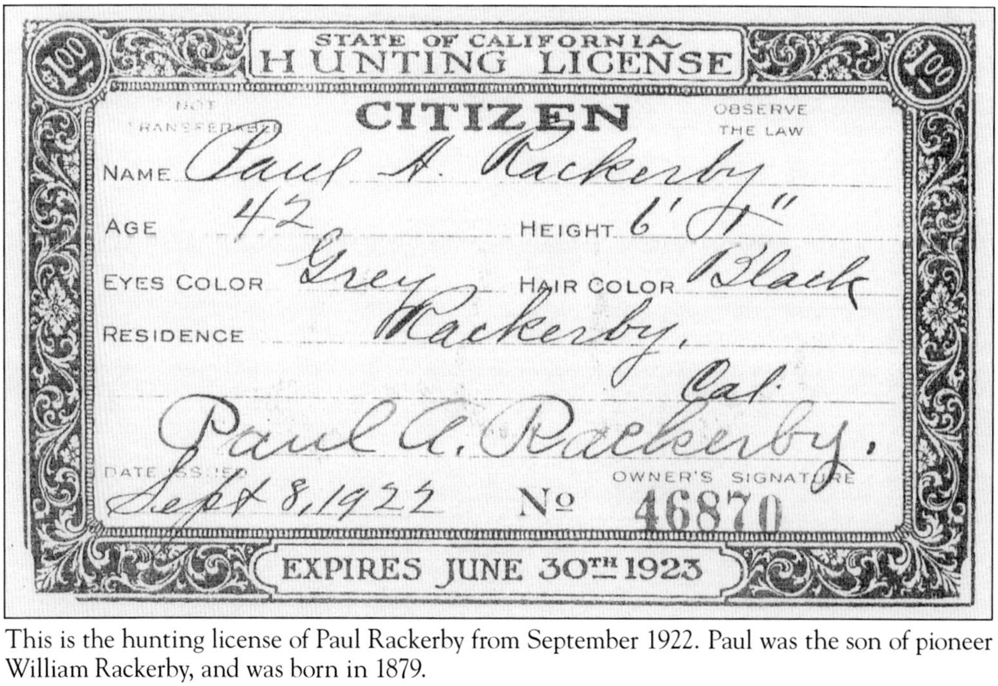

$1.00 STATE OF CALIFORNIA HUNTING LICENSE $1.00

NOT TRANSFERABLE

CITIZEN

OBSERVE THE LAW

NAME Paul A. Rackerby

AGE 42 HEIGHT 6' [illegible]

EYES COLOR Grey HAIR COLOR Black

RESIDENCE Rackerby, Cal.

Paul A. Rackerby.

DATE ISSUED Sept 8, 1922

OWNER'S SIGNATURE

No 46870

EXPIRES JUNE 30TH 1923

This is the hunting license of Paul Rackerby from September 1922. Paul was the son of pioneer William Rackerby, and was born in 1879.

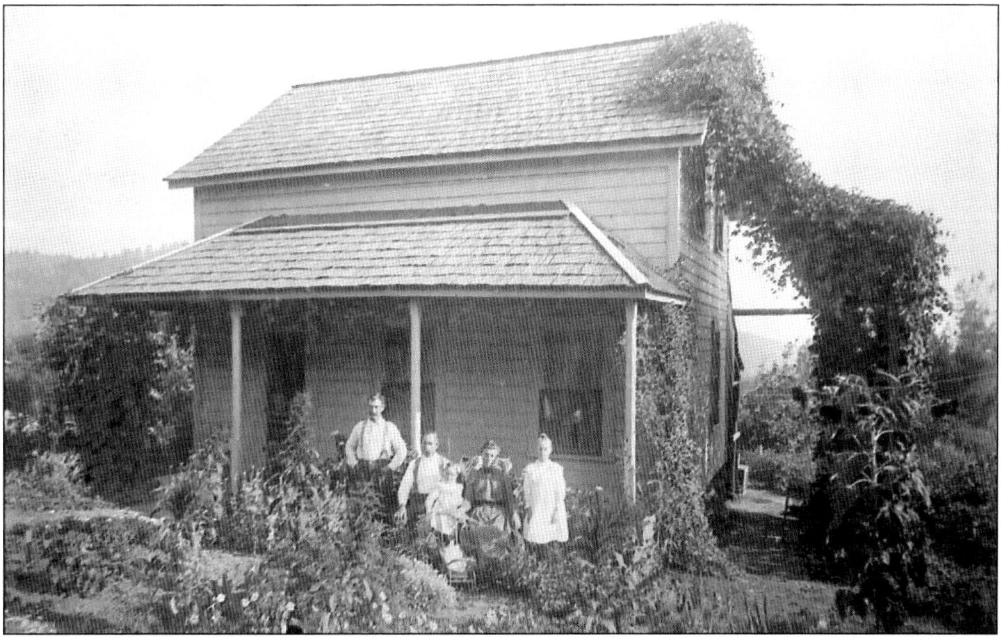

The Louis W. Clark family stands in front of their home, *c.* 1915. Although Louis was a blacksmith, he also had mining interests in the hills nearby. He was recalled as very fit, and that it "was not unusual for Louis to ride his bicycle to Marysville and back in one day."

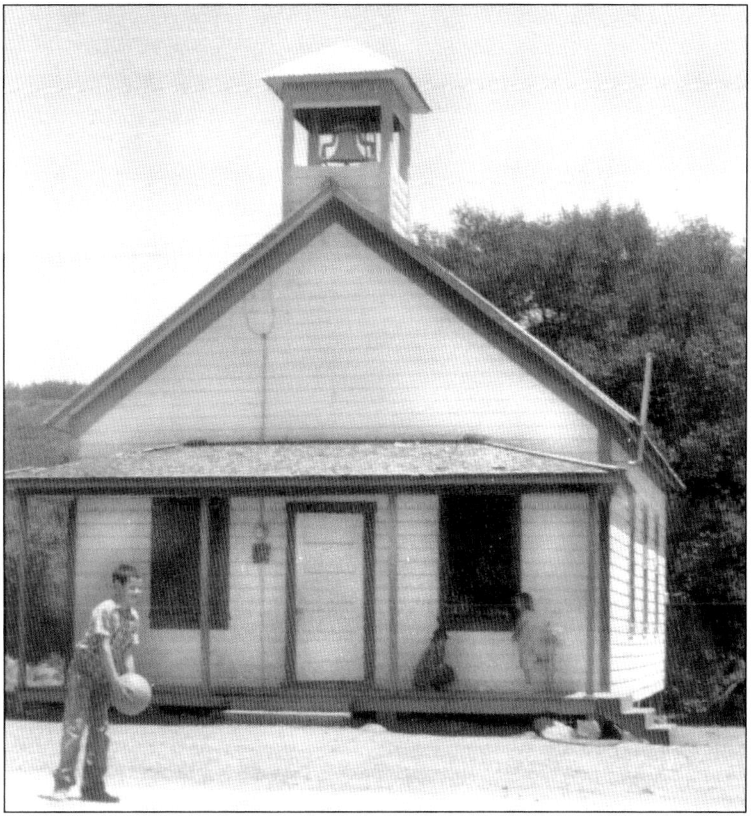

Although the town's name changed, the school, pictured here in 1940, was always known as Hansonville School. It became part of Yuba Feather School District in 1963. The property was sold and the building was remodeled for use as a private home and is still in use today.

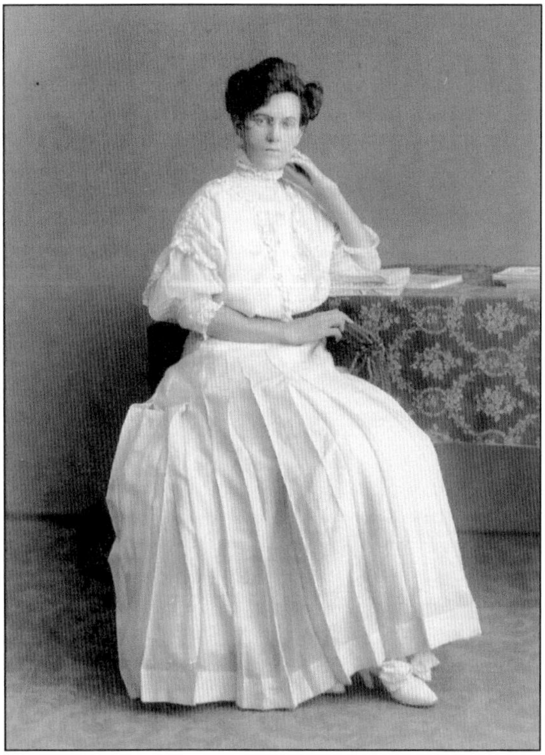

Edythe Lemmon grew up in small towns in the hills, determined to be a teacher. She picked berries, did housework, and took many other jobs to work her way through school. Edythe taught school in the Yuba Feather Hills from 1901 to 1907, and then in Turlock, Modesto, and Albany, and was principal at schools in Yolo and Stanislaus Counties.

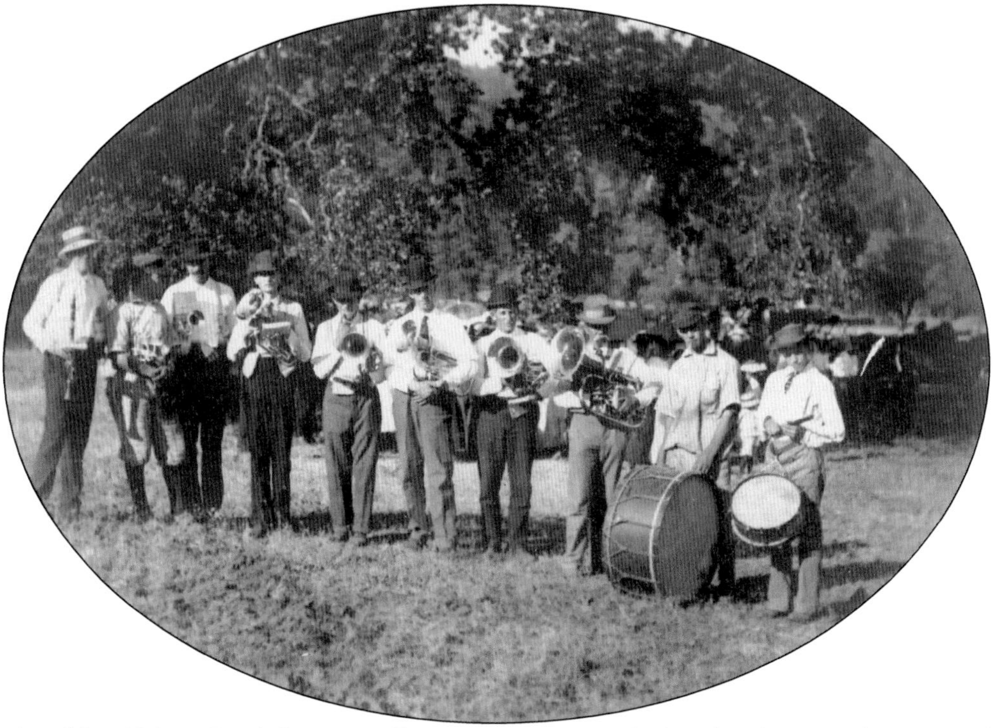

The all-boy Upham Band, from a small community near Rackerby, played at special events and parades. Upham also had its own school from 1862 to 1930.

This photograph of Marjorie Osgood as child is endearing. The Osgoods were a family of cattle ranchers and, along with other ranchers in the foothills, drove their herds to the high country around La Porte and Gibsonville for summer grazing.

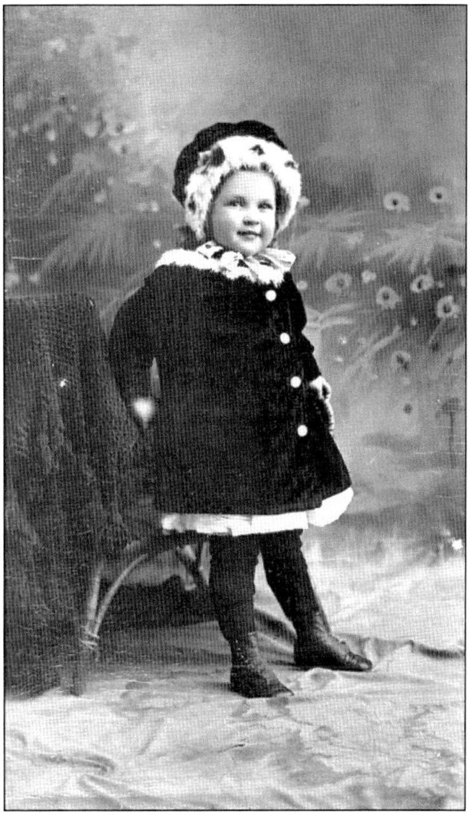

At the A. L. Andrews Feed Store, south of Rackerby, someone with a dandy roadster has purchased a bale of hay and loaded it into the back seat. The store was the major source for ranching supplies in the surrounding hills.

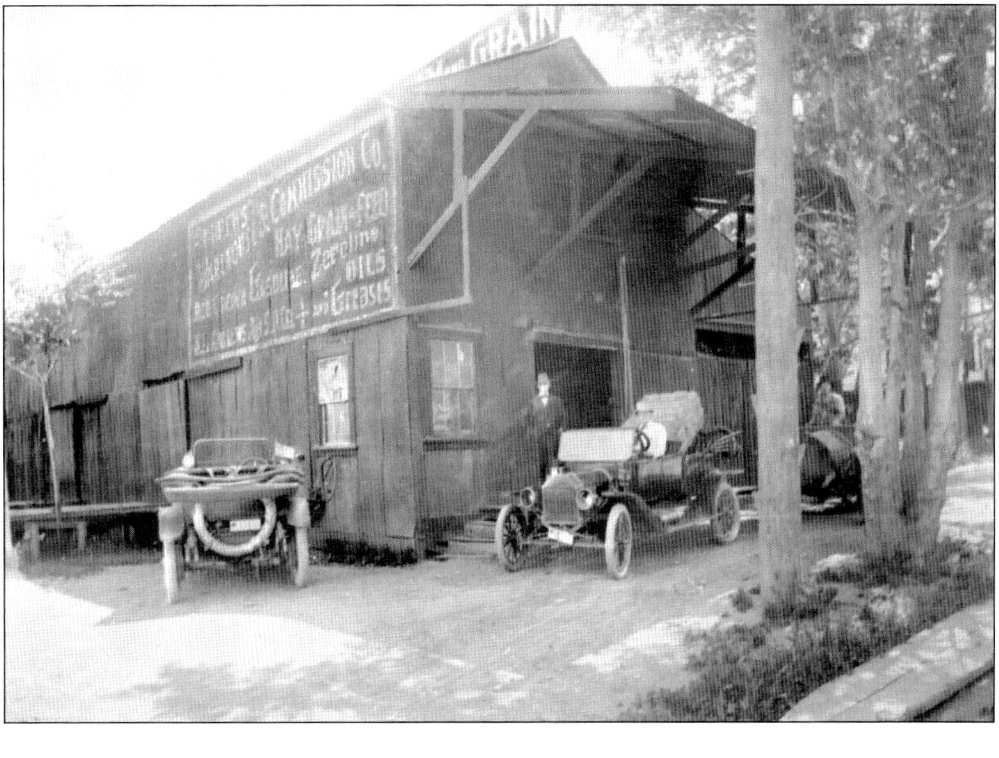

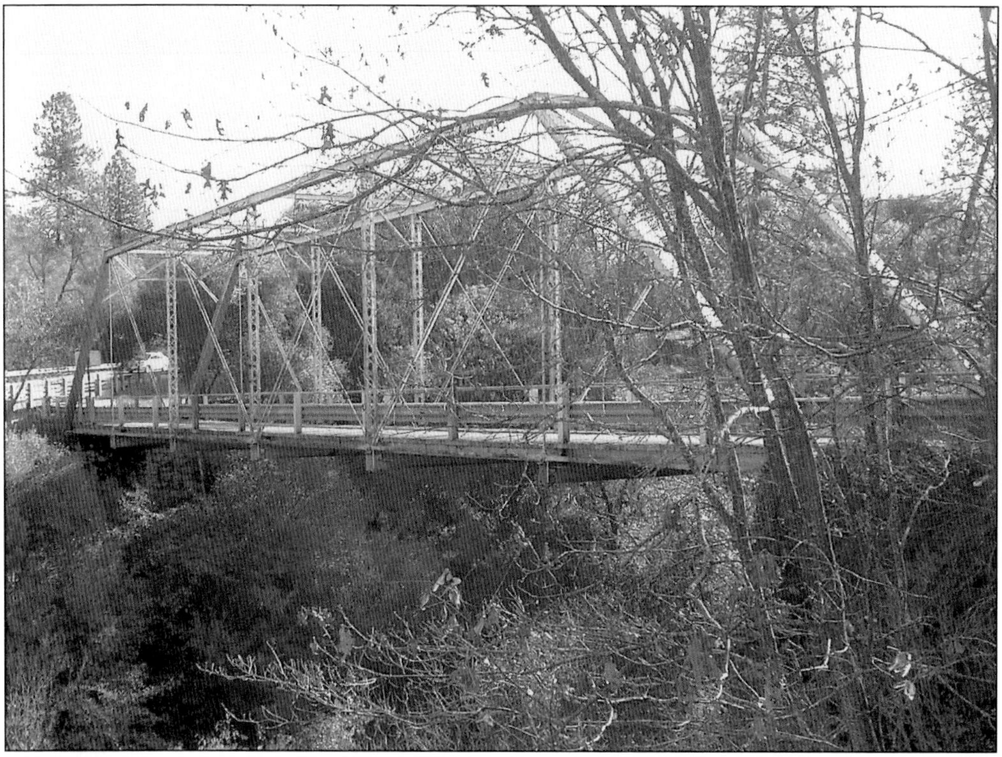

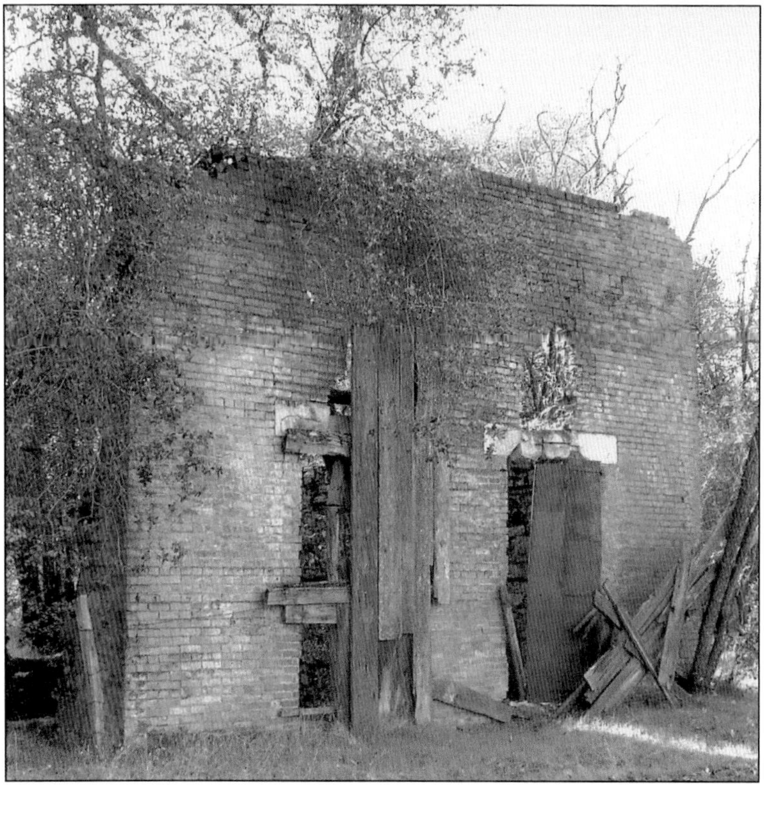

Honcut Bainbridge Crossing, built in 1908, has been preserved as a footbridge alongside the new bridge, at left, photographed in 2006.

Rackerby today is a quiet town with a church, post office, and private businesses tucked away here and there. One of the few reminders of Rackerby's early days is the remains of the stone-and-brick building on La Porte Road, which was Paulin Rouze's distillery and wine cellar of the 1850s.

# *Five*

# Challenge

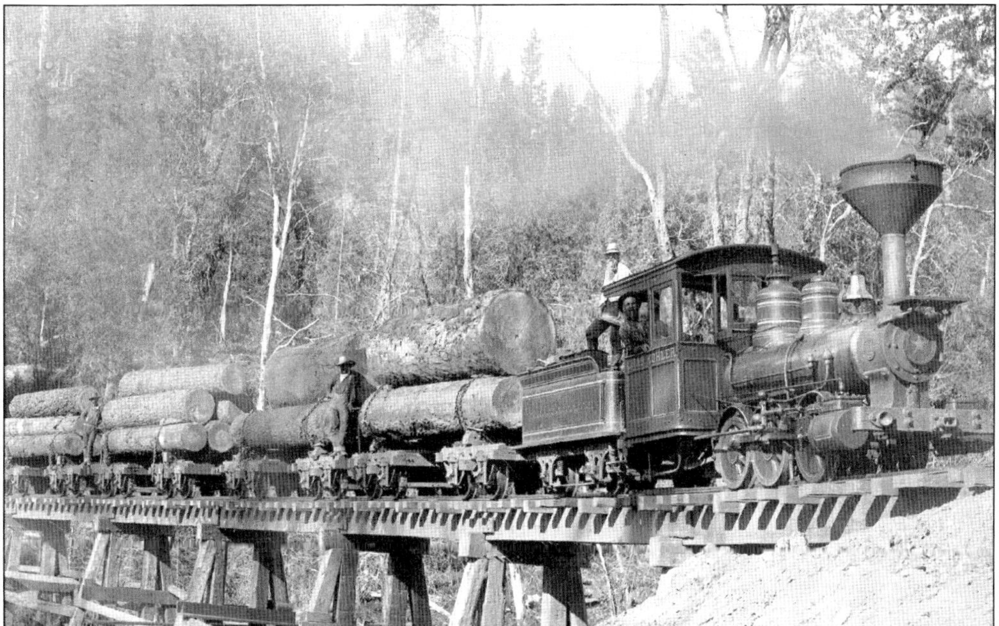

Lumbering was at the heart of Challenge's beginnings in 1856 when Cook and Malory built the first sawmill. A. P. Willey moved his lumber mill from Strawberry Valley six years later, and the place became known as Challenge Mills. Andrew M. Leach made the biggest changes, however, when he bought the entire operation from the Union Lumber Company in 1874 and increased production to 40,000 board feet per day. Fifty men were employed, and they were some of Leach's first customers, buying lumber to build homes for their families. In 1884, Leach built a narrow-gauge rail line from Beanville to Challenge Mills to haul logs.

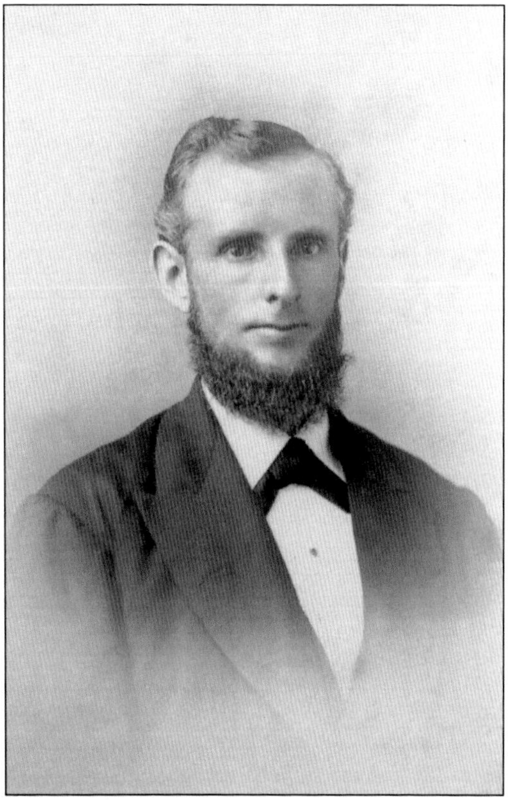

Andrew Martin Leach came to California from Vermont in 1863. He soon acquired more than 3,500 acres of timberland in the Yuba Feather Hills and the cutting rights to many thousands more. The magnificent trees of the Sierra Nevada became known as Green Gold as the demand for lumber increased, fueled by growing towns throughout the region. (Courtesy Yuba County Library.)

Challenge Mills was Leach's headquarters, and the operations included a company store, office, blacksmith shop, boiler house, a warehouse 200 feet long, barns for the oxen and horses used in logging, and Leach's family home. The logging wagons were built in the shop, and the axles, frames, U-bolts, and metal-rimmed wooden wheels were manufactured on-site. (Illustration from *History of Yuba County*, Wells and Chamberlain, 1879.)

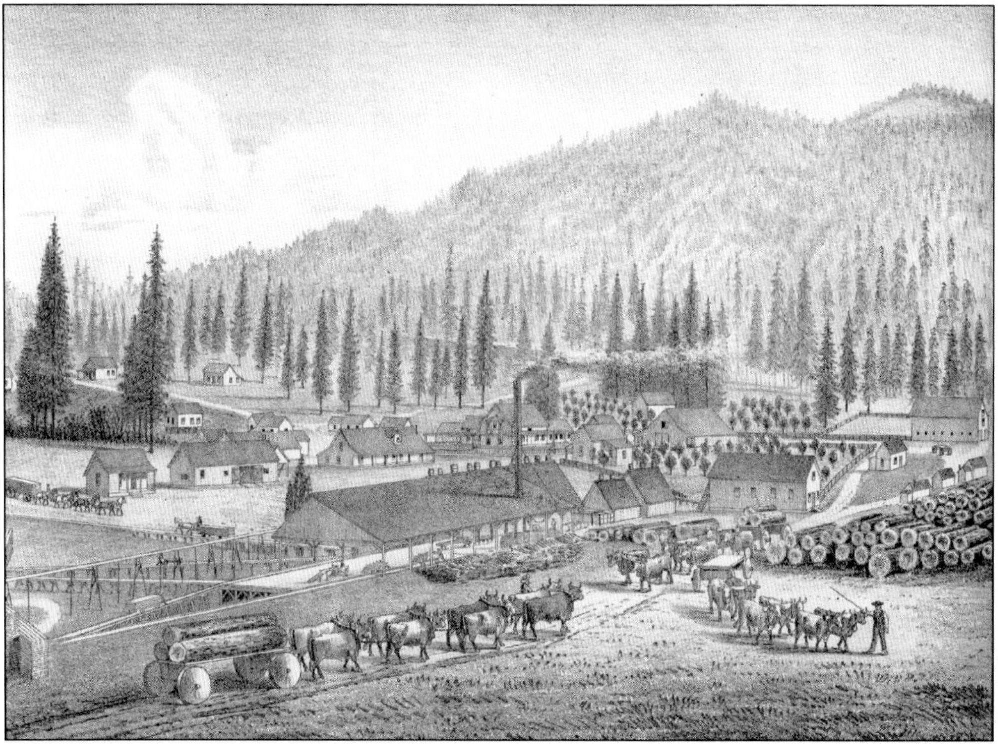

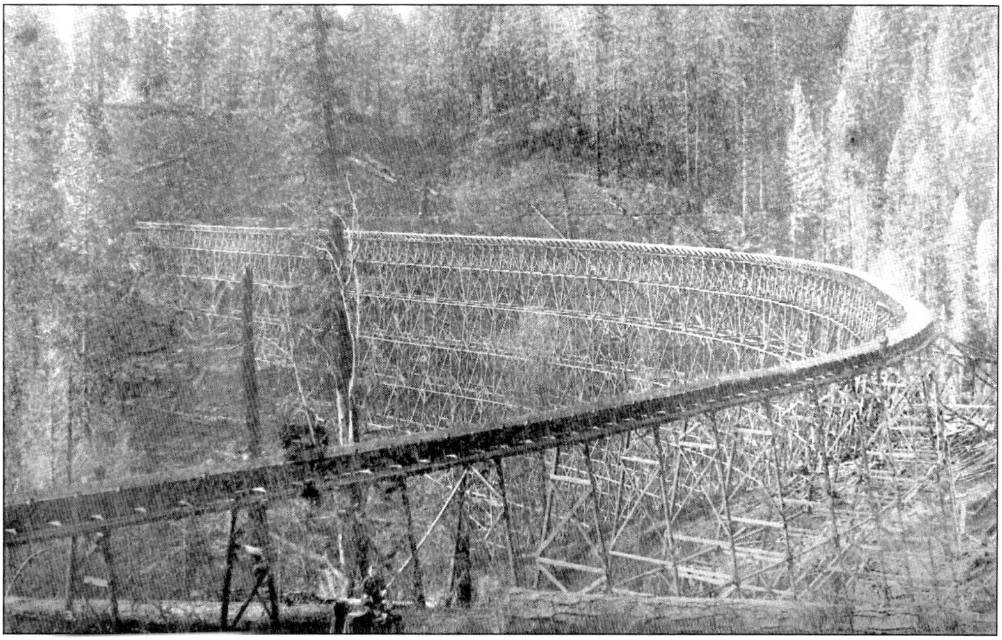

To speed lumber to market, Leach built flumes from his mills to the California Northern Railroad at Honcut, a distance of about 80 miles. Flumes used an average of 135,000 board feet of lumber per mile, and cost nearly $320,000—a fortune in 1879. The trestles soared 166 feet high across some ravines and through 20-foot-deep ditches in other places. Some sections were so steep, the water sped along at 50 miles an hour. In an emergency, a sick or injured person was sent flying down the lumber flumes for medical treatment, but they surely were treated for shock once they arrived. A few took the hair-raising trip on a dare were drunk, but they finished the trip "soaking wet, shivering, and stone-sober," according to early accounts.

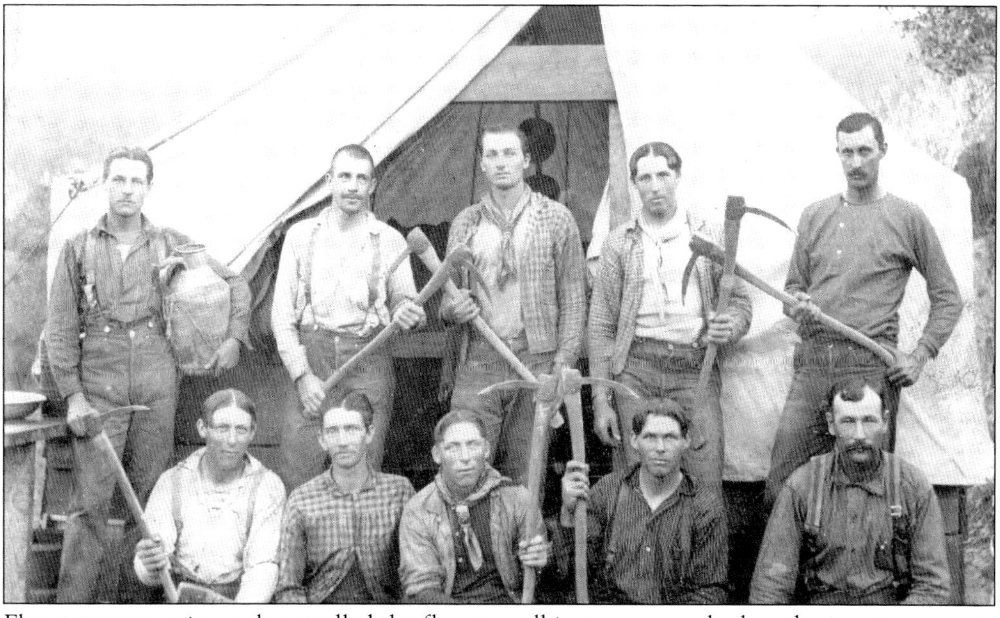

Flume crews continuously patrolled the flumes, walking a narrow plank and using picaroons to clear lumber jams. They stayed at camps set up along the route of the flume.

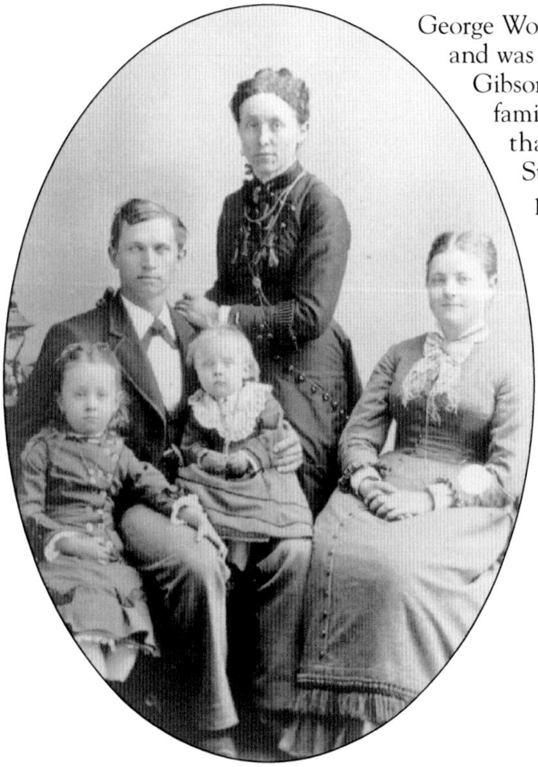

George Wolters came to America from Prussia in 1866 and was the Wells Fargo Express Company agent in Gibsonville before moving to Challenge with his family. His grandson, Martin B. Smith, revealed that George once carried $10,000 in gold to Strawberry Valley on snowshoes. Wolters was a partner in the Wolters Brothers Store and was also a butcher. After a horrible accident, he had to use his butcher tools to amputate the crushed leg of a miner. The man recovered and was walking around on a peg leg by spring. The family also lived at Whiskey Diggings for a time during the 1870s. They moved to Challenge in 1883.

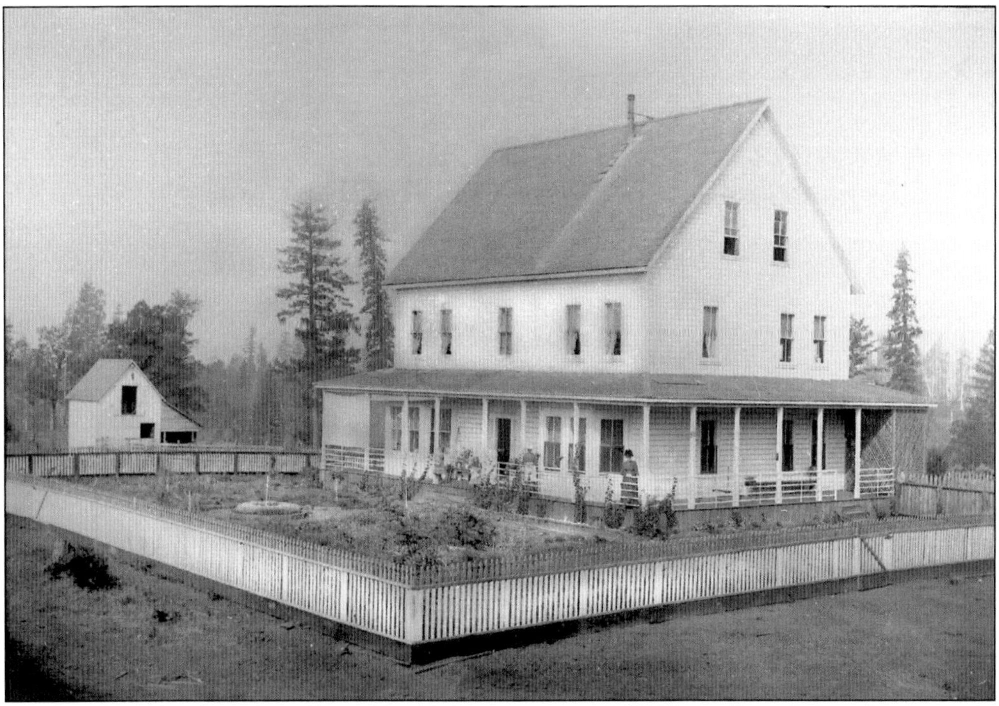

Wolters worked for A. M. Leach and built this home surrounded by well-tended gardens in 1883. He moved to San Francisco in 1890 where he was in business with his brothers.

Besides lumber, Leach produced shakes, shingles, posts, firewood, and poles. He had mills at Woodleaf, Owl Gulch, and Beanville, along with those listed in this 1879 advertisement.



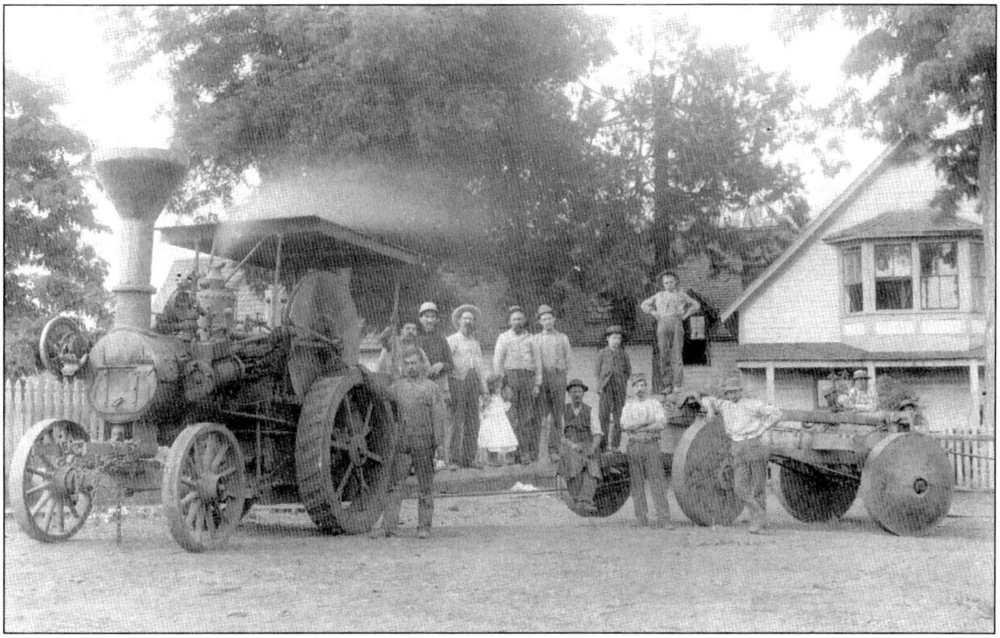

Leach's family and some of the mill crew gathered to see the new steam tractor, a wood-burning contraption that could replace oxen to haul logs to the mill in areas not accessible by the railroad. Leach was the largest employer in the region, and his operations lasted 15 years. Forest fires were a constant terror. "A fearful fire at the Diamond Spring Mill," wrote the Woodleaf toll keeper, G. S. W. Twogood in 1880, "Leach takes men from Challenge Mill to fight fire." In 1887, fire completely destroyed the Challenge Mill, Moore's Station planing mill and box factory, and the Woodville Mill. In 1889, many flumes collapsed in heavy snows, which measured 20 feet deep at Woodleaf. Leach tried to refinance and struggled on until 1893, in the midst of a severe depression in California. He paid many of his workers with parcels of land, until his creditors took over. He moved to Dunsmuir where he began a new and successful business venture as a building contractor.

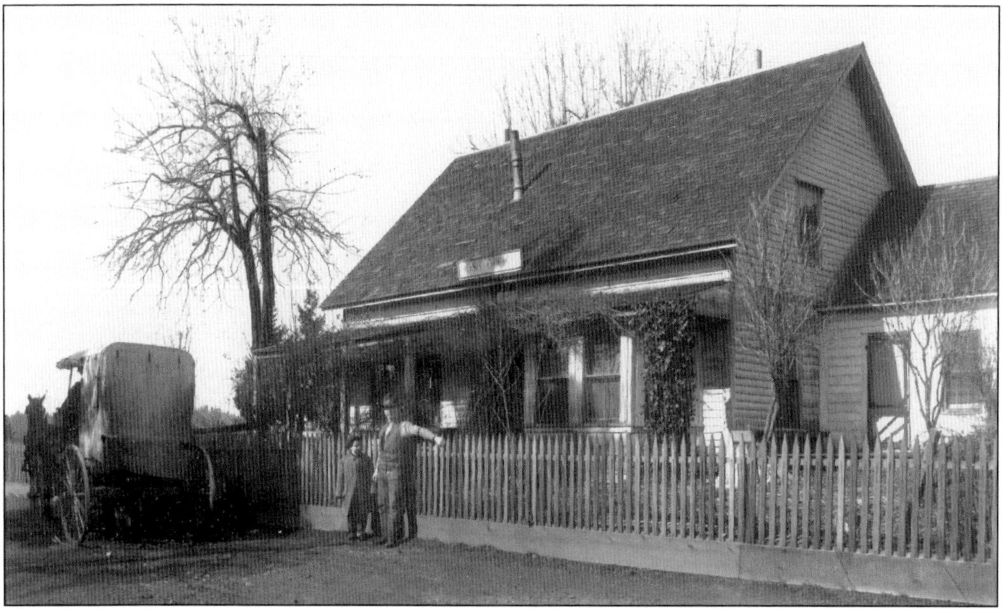

When granted a post office in 1895, the town's name was shortened to Challenge. Phillip Peterson and Mr. Kelly stand in front of the post office, and the Marysville–La Porte Stage waits at left. The writing on the original glass plate negative notes that "Mom, Lotta and Otto Peterson are on the stage, leaving for Marysville at 10:00 a.m." (Courtesy Ben Falck.)

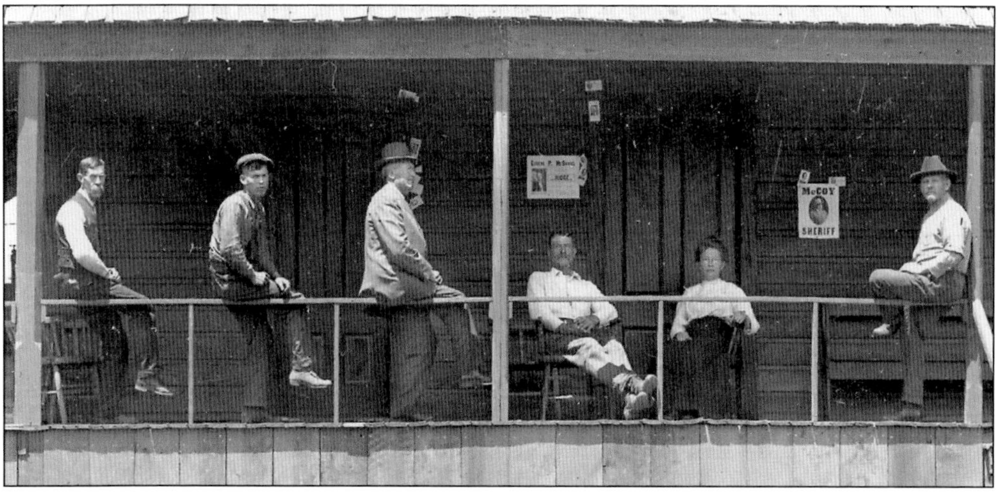


The Kelley family and friends gather on their porch. The Kelley ranch had a fine apple orchard and many of the trees still produce fruit today. The ranch was one of several around Challenge that also grew grain and hay and had fields where livestock grazed.

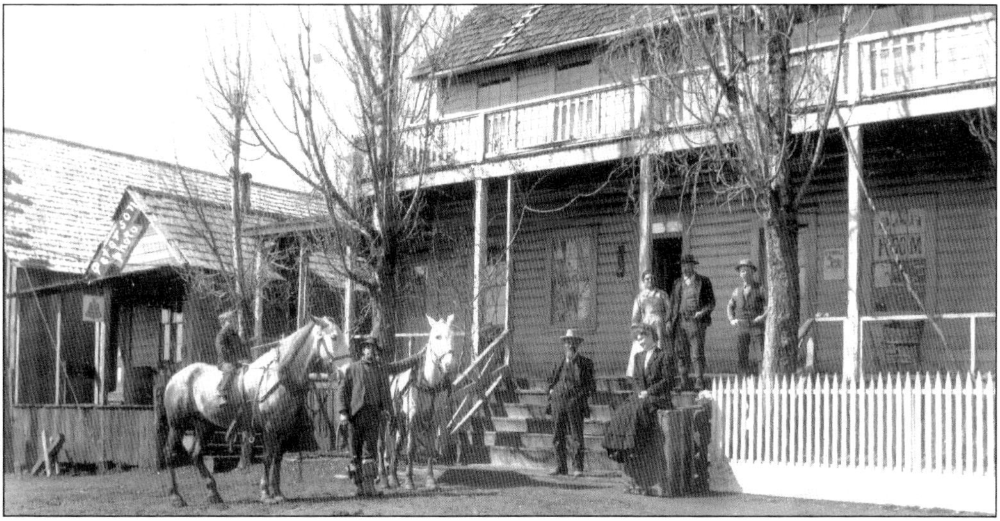


J. W. Ribble built the Challenge Hotel in 1886, where lumber merchants, gold miners, teamsters, and travelers of every kind could find rooms. Miss Loveless, the Clipper Mills school teacher, perches on her trunk and waits for the stagecoach. The hotel was owned for a few years by Dr. Van Male, and then by William H. Joy, who also bought the general store. The hotel was the site of many parties, grand balls, and celebrations, but it burned to the ground November 11, 1914. Joy, a member of the Owls Lodge and described as a "progressive businessman," then built summer cottages on his road, Joy Circle, and added 25 more cottages and a swimming pool in 1928. During the "Days of '49" in 1928 and 1929, 3,000 visitors came for the dances, games, and venison stew. The records don't tell us who washed the dishes.

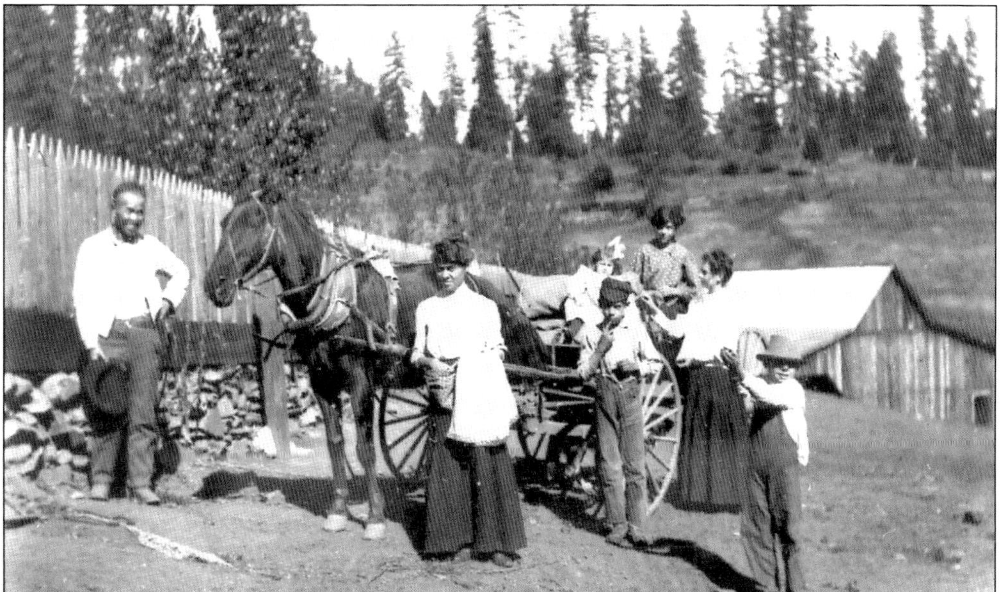

Challenge Mills had a large population of Chinese men who worked in the mills, as cooks, merchants, and miners. Jim Ah Wah and his wife and six children were the only Chinese family living there. One of the merchants, at left, is pictured with Mary Kloss, Ethel Ashburn, Ed Gomez, Kate Costa, and Lena Ashburn.

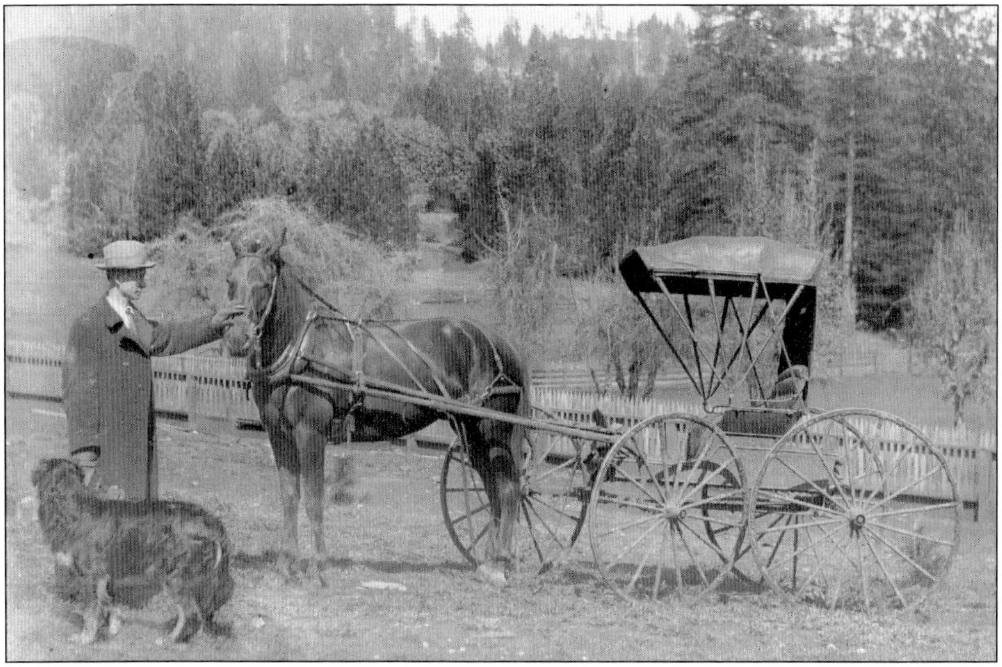

Dr. Gearheart made house calls in his buggy and also traveled to surrounding communities. Other medical doctors who lived in the region were Dr. Mansfield and Dr. Van Male.

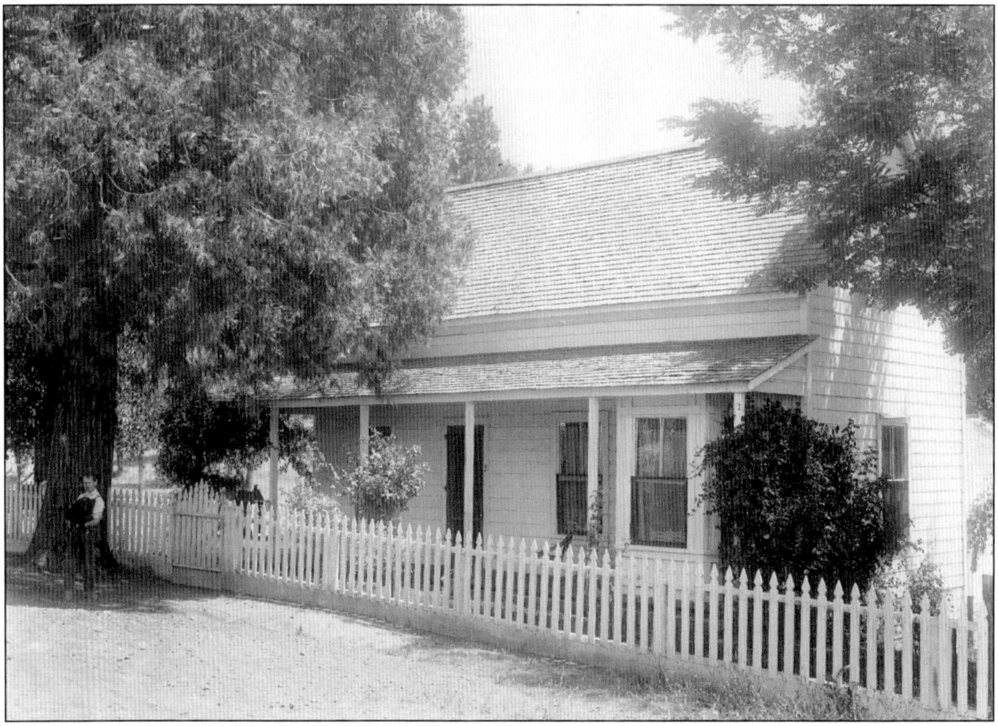

William J. Mellon served as Yuba County supervisor for more than 30 years after first being elected in 1895. His home, pictured here, was eventually purchased by the adjacent Catholic church, and after restoration was used (and still is) as a fellowship hall.

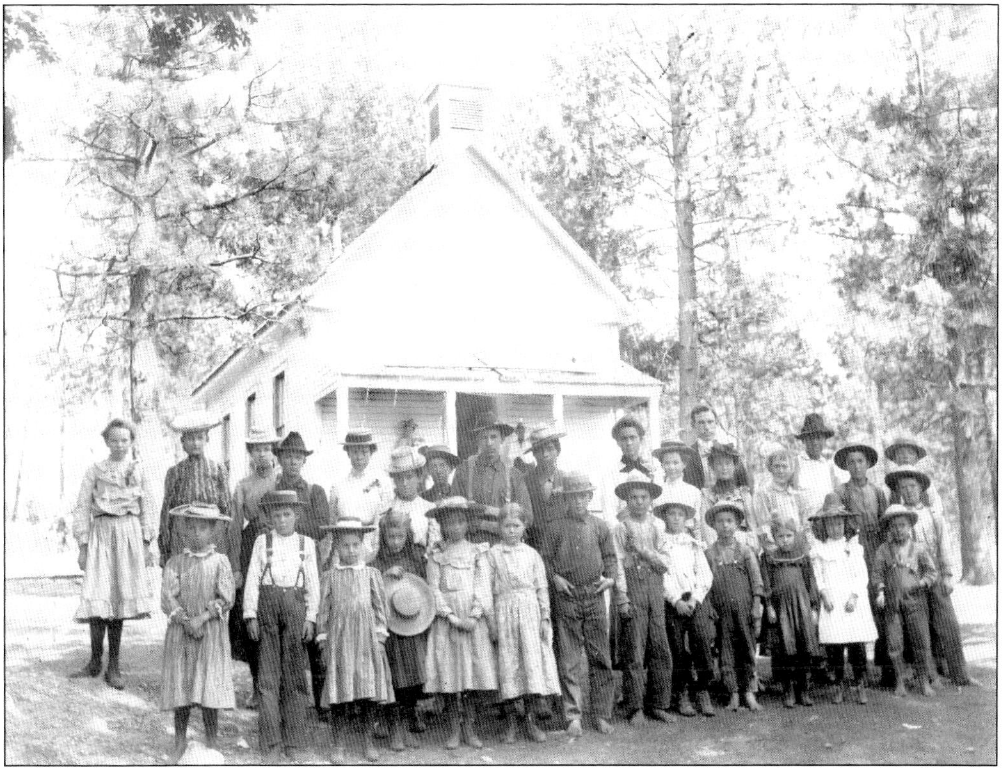

At Challenge School in 1905, nearly everyone was decked out in fashionable hats and outfits for the photographer. Students included Aileen Willey, Ernest and Edna Kelley, Margaret and Katherine Costa, George Thurston, Eva Pike, Nellie and Frances Hendricks, and Gertrude Mellon.

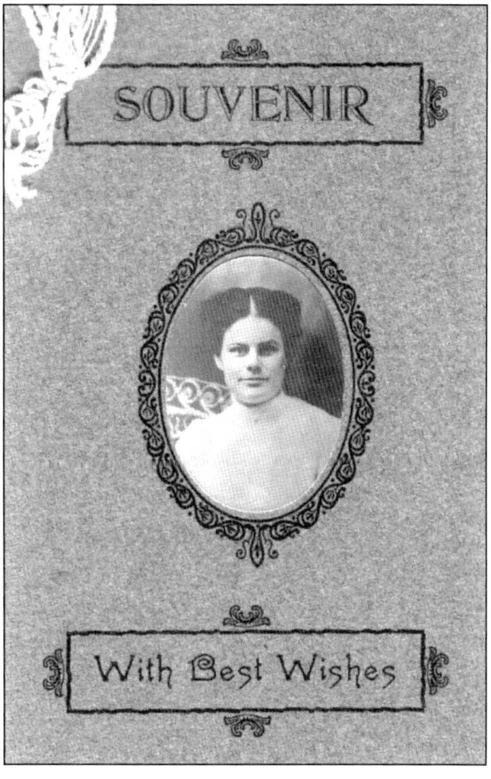


Mabel Kumle, who grew up in Brownsville, taught at Challenge School from 1906 to 1909, and was featured on the cover of the 1907 graduation program. She taught 30 pupils in eight grades, and her salary for the year was $664, a fine wage at the time. The school district superintendent was Challenge resident James A. Scott, and the clerk was A. C. Kelley, a Challenge ranch owner. The trustees were A. P. Mansfield, the local doctor, and E. M. Grubbs, a ranch owner. Mabel also taught at Dobbins School from 1905 to 1906 and at Strawberry Valley School from 1911 to 1913.

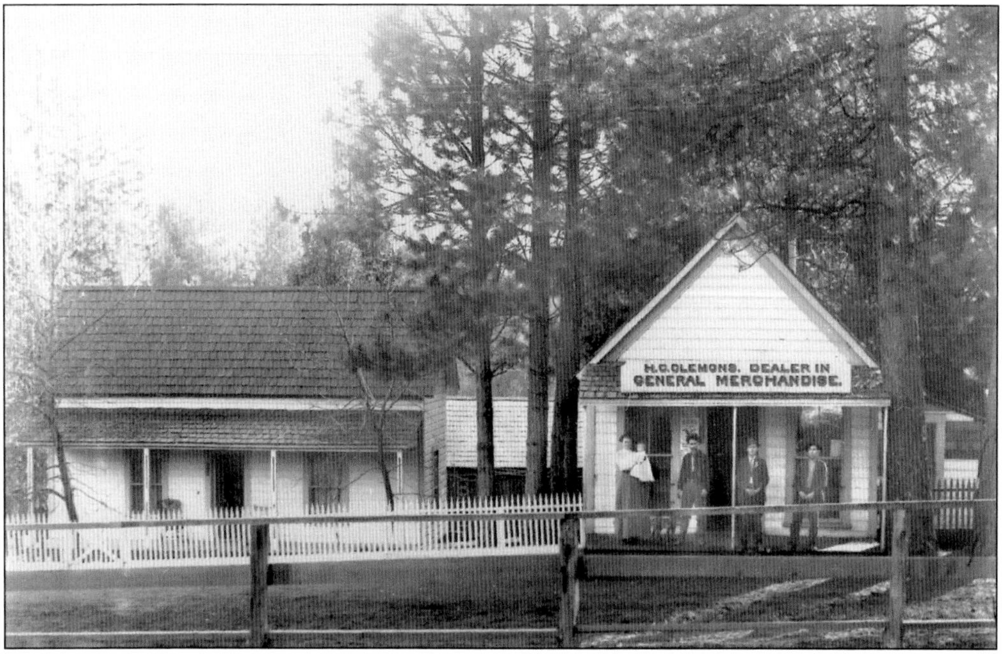


Mr. and Mrs. Clemons's store sold all the groceries and other goods needed by Challenge residents in 1890. The store and the Clemons home, at left, have had many additions since then, but one may still recognize these basic structures in today's buildings.

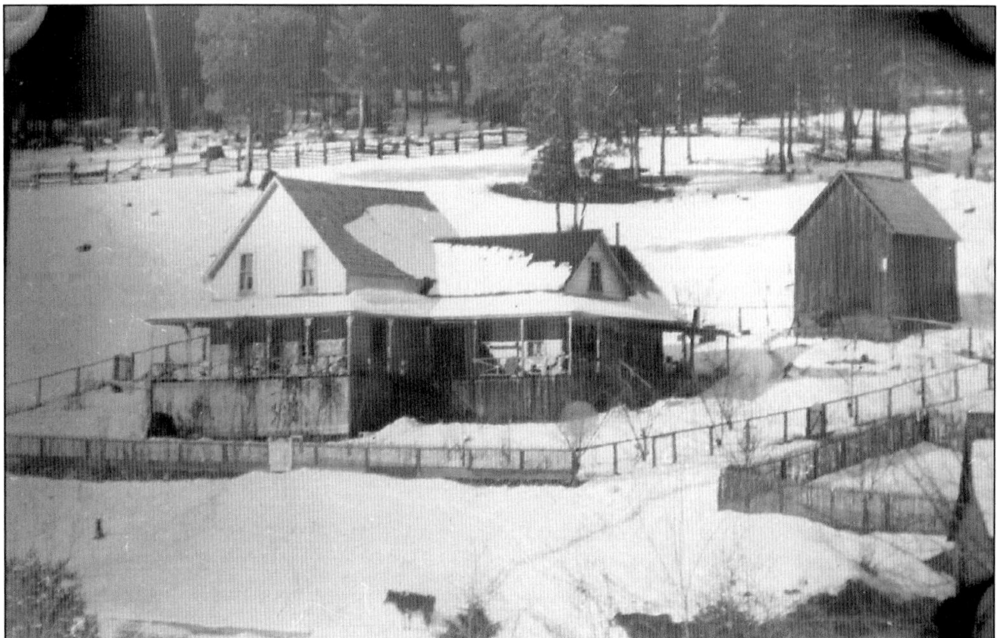

Martin Costa operated a gold mine and cattle ranch in meadows on each side of Costa Creek. The original house has been restored and is now a private home.

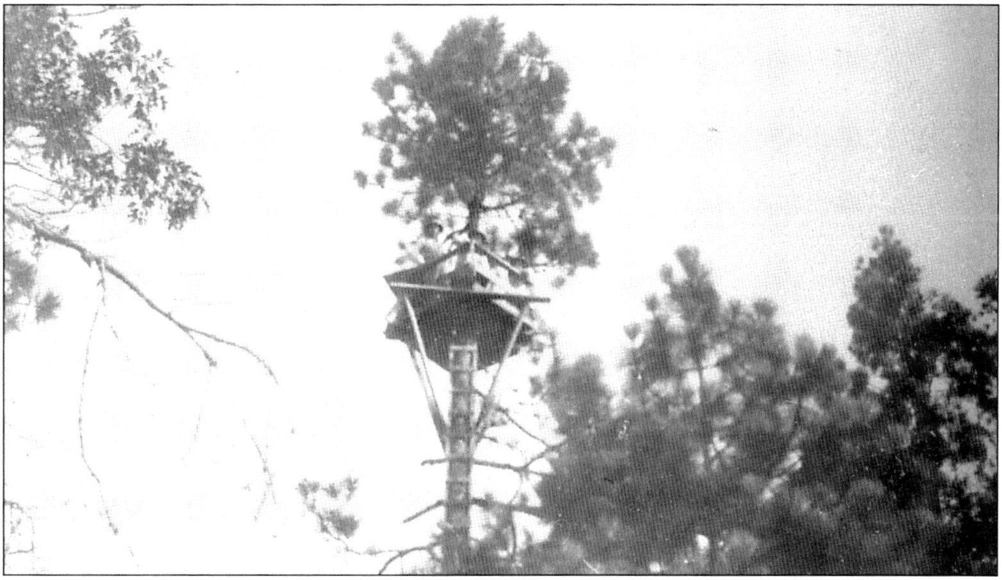

The first lookout on Pikes Peak was a tree platform built in 1914. Although quite rustic, some considered it a luxury because in other places, there was only a tall tree. Lookouts were required to climb up and check for smoke several times a day, and if any was spotted, they had to hike to the spot and put out the fire. Pikes Peak tree house lookout was replaced long ago by a modern, well-equipped tower. Plumas National Forest Service operates a station in Challenge during the summer, and maintains extensive reforestation programs.

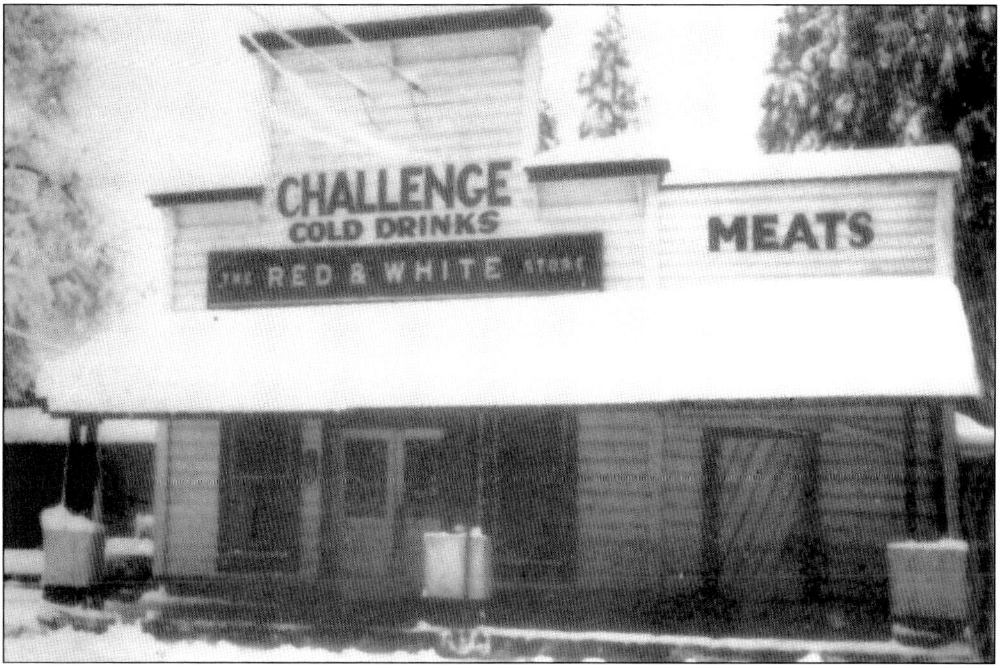


Besides groceries, the Challenge Store sold fabric, shoes, overalls, shirts, lanterns, tools, dishes, pots and pans, along with cable and rope. Local children, however, would tell you that the store's vast assortment of penny candy was the most important commodity. The business was known as the Red and White Store in 1938.

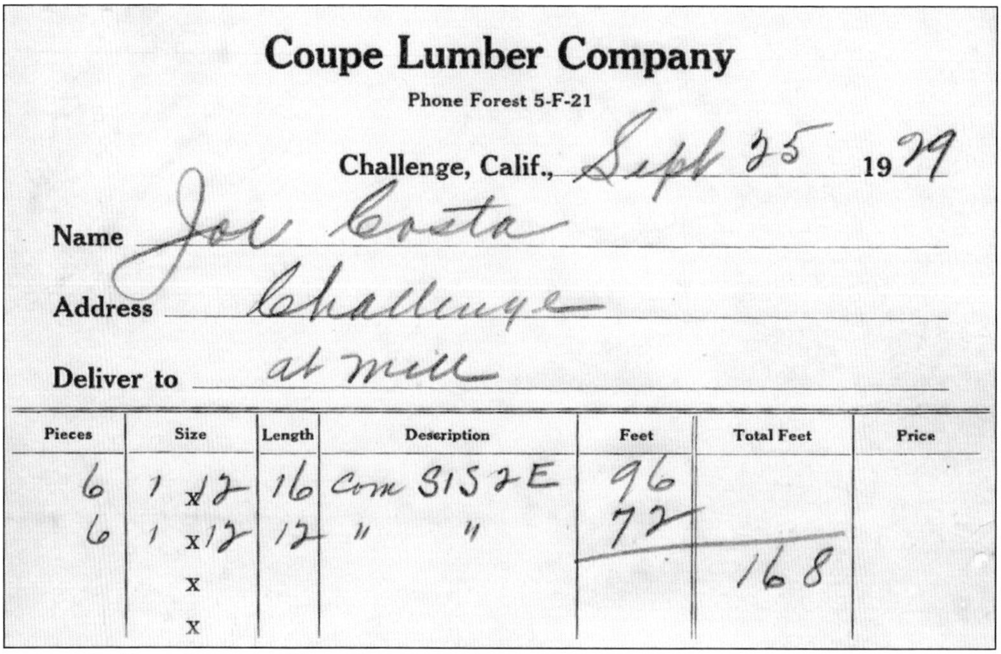

**Coupe Lumber Company**

Phone Forest 5-F-21

Challenge, Calif., Sept 25 1929

Name Joe Costa

Address Challenge

Deliver to at mill

| Pieces | Size | Length | Description | Feet | Total Feet | Price |
|---|---|---|---|---|---|---|
| 6 | 1 x 12 | 16 | Com S1S 2E | 96 | | |
| 6 | 1 x 12 | 12 | " " | 72 | | |
| | x | | | | 168 | |
| | x | | | | | |

Coupe's Mill on Oregon Hill Road near Challenge ran from the early 1920s to the early 1950s. The receipt is for lumber purchased by Joe Costa in 1929.

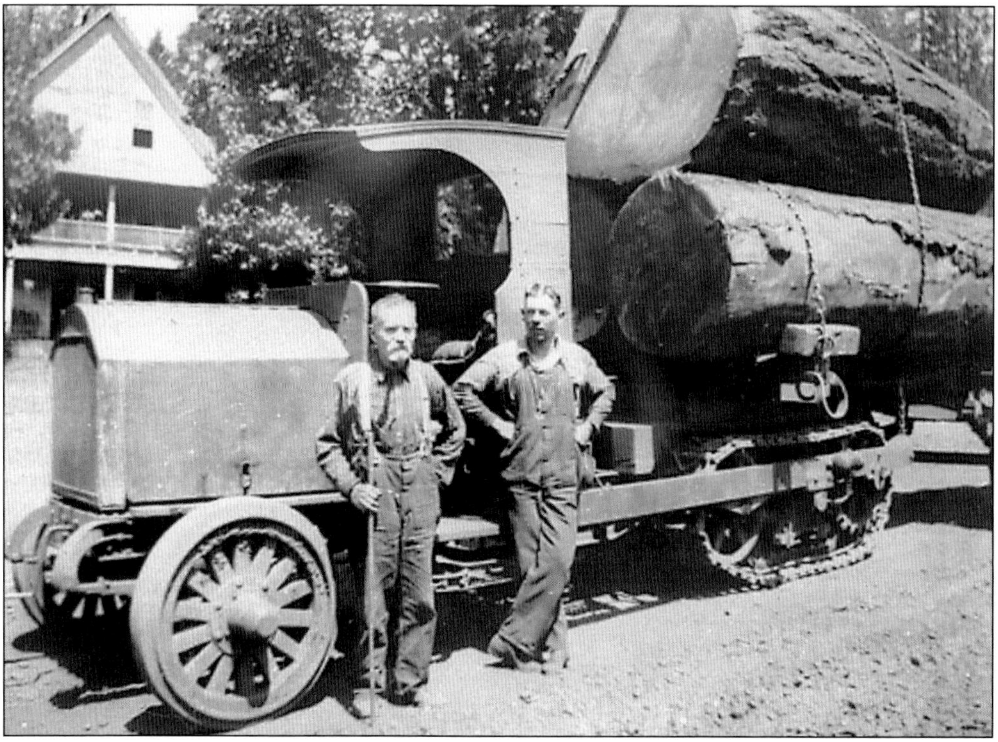

Marcus Weiss and Eddy Leal stand beside their logging truck below Challenge circa 1925. The truck had solid-rubber tires, and a track that helped navigate the rough roads. Weiss holds a scaling stick, used to determine the number of board feet in each log.

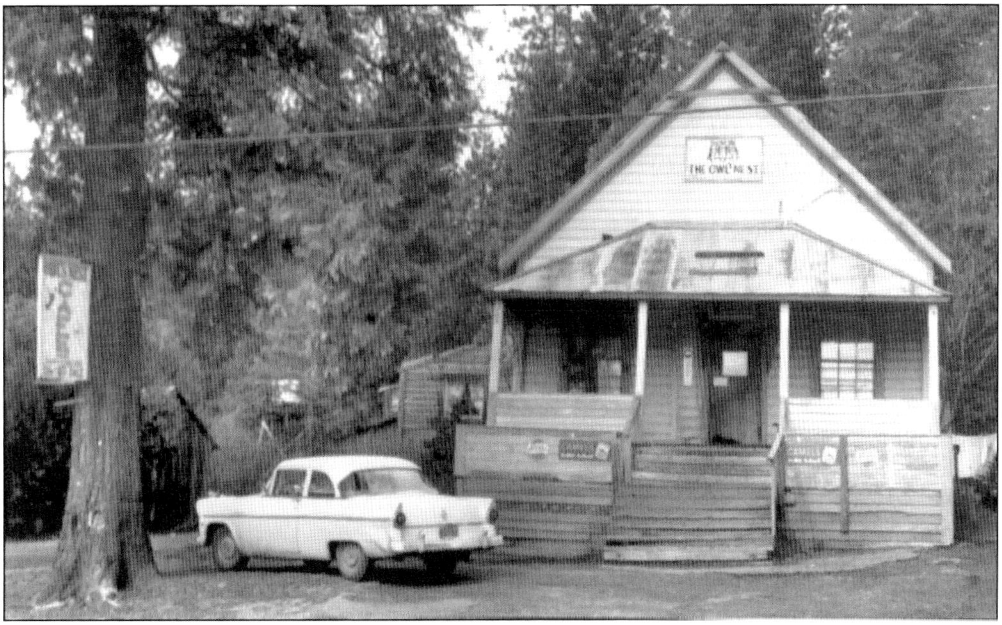

The Owls Lodge was a benevolent fraternal organization, but membership gradually dwindled until only one man remained. The story goes that he used the treasury's meager funds to stock up on liquor and food and turned the lodge into a saloon and cafe. The sign painter nearly forgot the "S" after Owl on the sign above the door, but he managed to squeeze it in. The building, photographed in the early 1950s, was destroyed by fire in the 1960s.

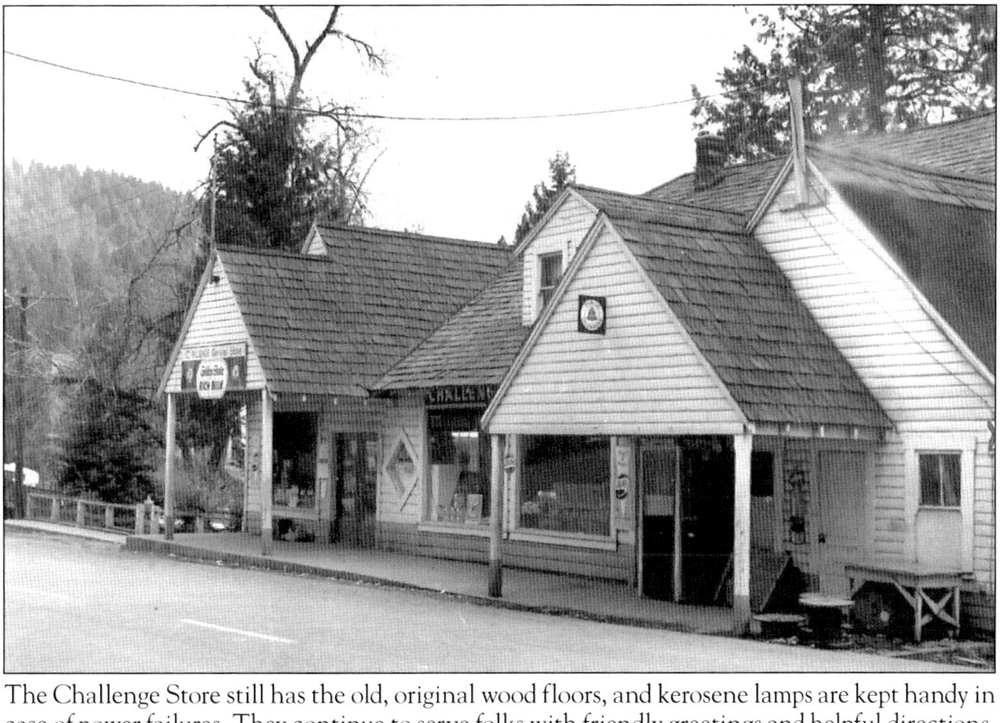

The Challenge Store still has the old, original wood floors, and kerosene lamps are kept handy in case of power failures. They continue to serve folks with friendly greetings and helpful directions, and can tell some interesting stories if you have the time.

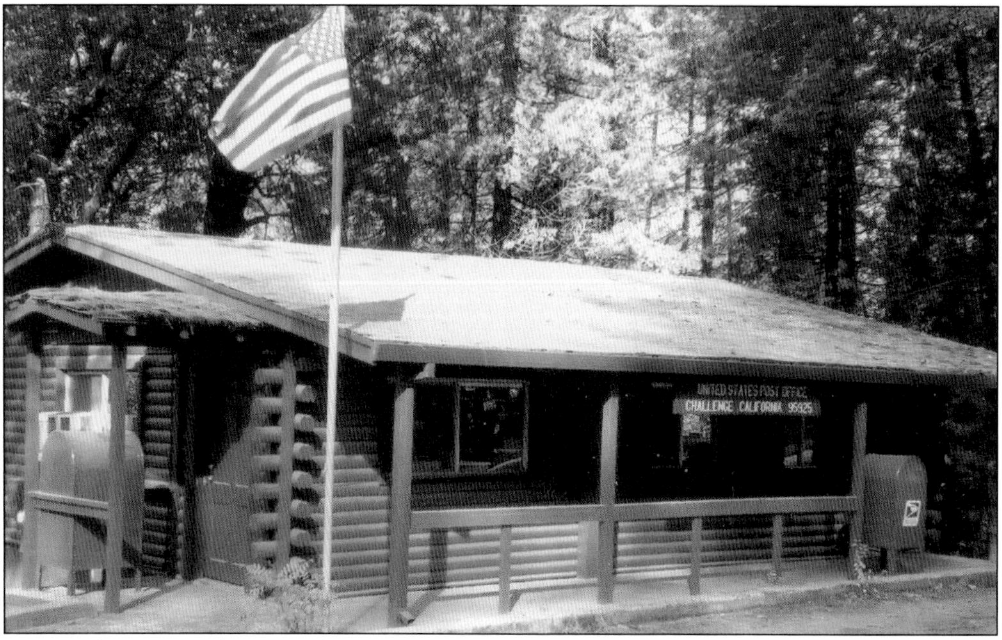


During the 1950s, when postal business grew too great to be housed in a corner of the general stores, local residents built the post office, a log building completed in a couple of days.

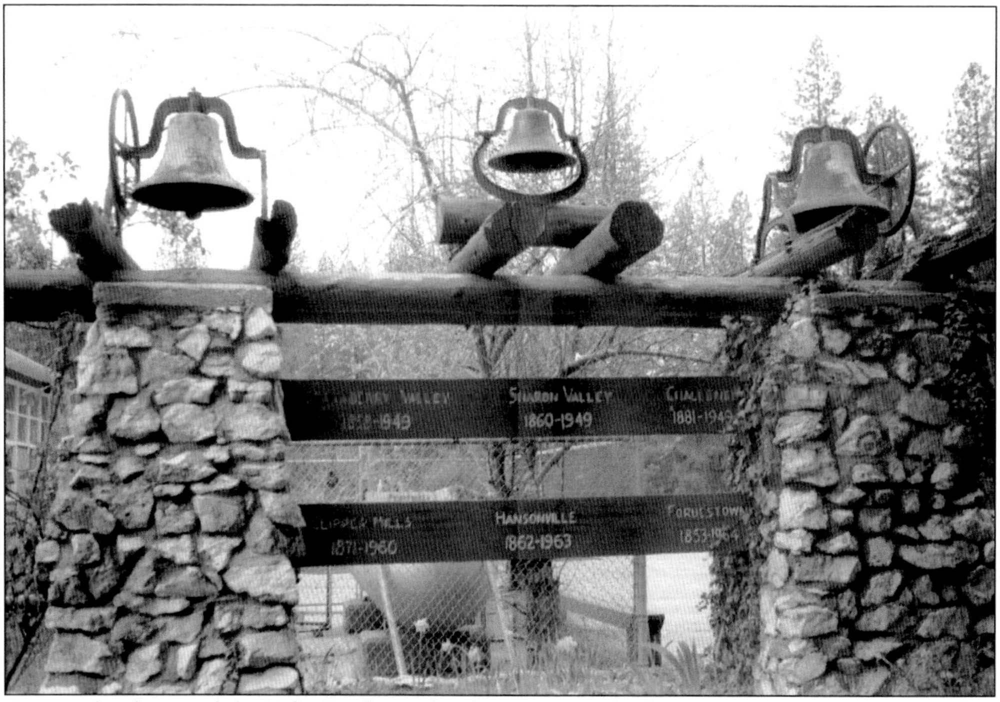


Seven schools joined the Yuba Feather School District at Challenge, and a new facility was built in 1952. Sharon Valley (Brownsville), Strawberry Valley, and Challenge joined the district in 1949, Clipper Mills in 1960, Hansonville (Rackerby) in 1963, and Forbestown in 1964. The bells from three of the schools are mounted in a tower, pictured here, and a fourth one was added later. Yuba Feather is now part of Marysville Joint Unified School District.

*Six*

# FORBESTOWN

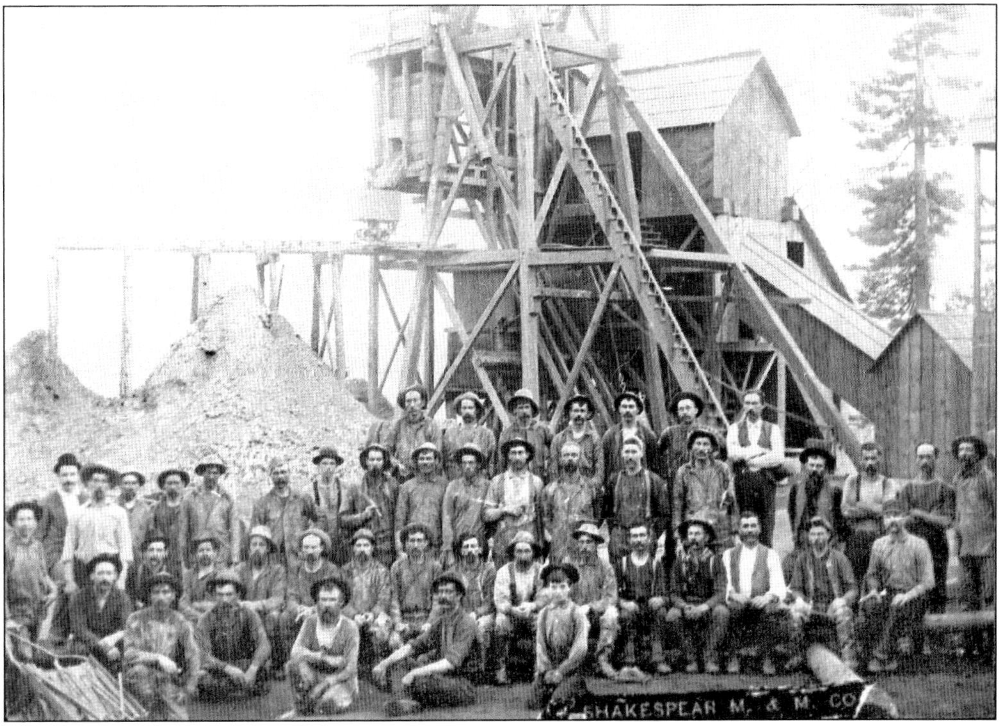


The town of Forbestown straddles the Yuba and Butte County lines where the Forbes brothers settled, beginning in 1849. Although they weren't the first to arrive, they had a notable impact. Ben opened a store and established the first post office, while James started a stage line to Ophir (Oroville), became justice of the peace, and with partner Nathaniel Plum built the United States Hotel. Jared Forbes operated Ben's stagecoach business, and W. C. Forbes opened a mercantile store. Within a few years, this was the second largest town in Butte County, with five hotels, five general stores, a sawmill, a livery, seven saloons, a shoe shop, a church, a barbershop, a water company, a brass band, a China house, restaurants, a Masonic lodge, a tin shop, a blacksmith, a stage office, a school, and a butcher. Supporting all this growth were rich mines such as the Golden Queen, Midas, Southern Cross, Carlysle, Denver, and the Shakespeare, pictured here with its crew. It was owned by Alvinza Hayward (1822–1904), who also mined in Amador County, taking out over $25 million from his Hayward Mine alone. He founded the first bank in Southern California and was reputed to be the richest man in California with an estate in San Mateo.

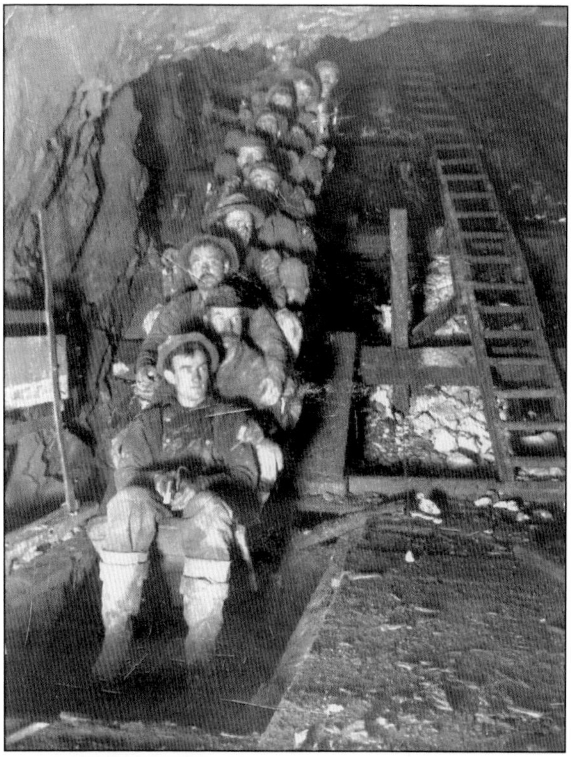

Miners in the Goldbank Mine skip, a car with seats that travels on an inclined track, prepare to descend into the 350-foot shaft; Dave Eddy is third from the bottom. The mine employed around 90 men and produced around $40,000 dollars a month. The manager was Harry P. Stow, son of W. W. Stow of San Francisco. The Stows also operated the nearby Monmouth, Church, and Pine Grove Mines.

Sam the mule hauled ore cars to the surface where stamp mills pulverized the quartz, around 1895. Mules were treated as pets by the miners and lived as long as 30 years before retiring to someone's pasture.

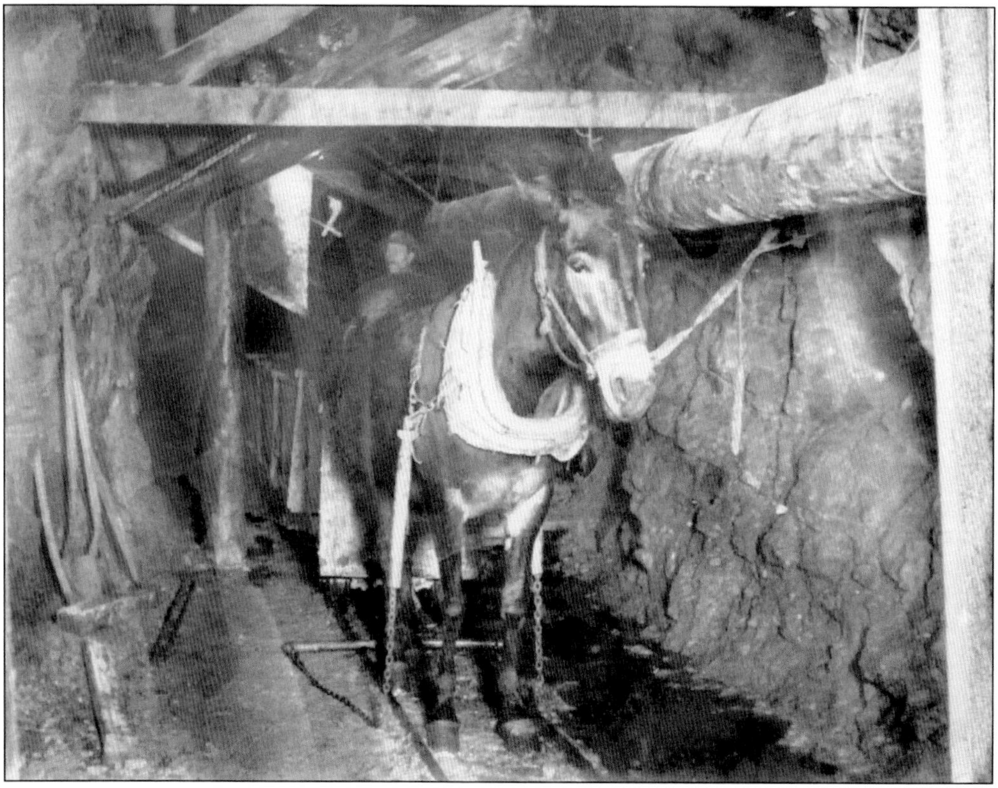

Wells Fargo Express Company opened an office in Forbestown in 1866. Eventually, more than 28 mines in the Forbestown area were operating. With so much treasure coming out of the hills, it was inevitable that some saw easy pickings. The La Porte Stage was robbed three miles west of Forbestown in 1875, and Wells Fargo express box was taken with a loss of a large amount of gold.

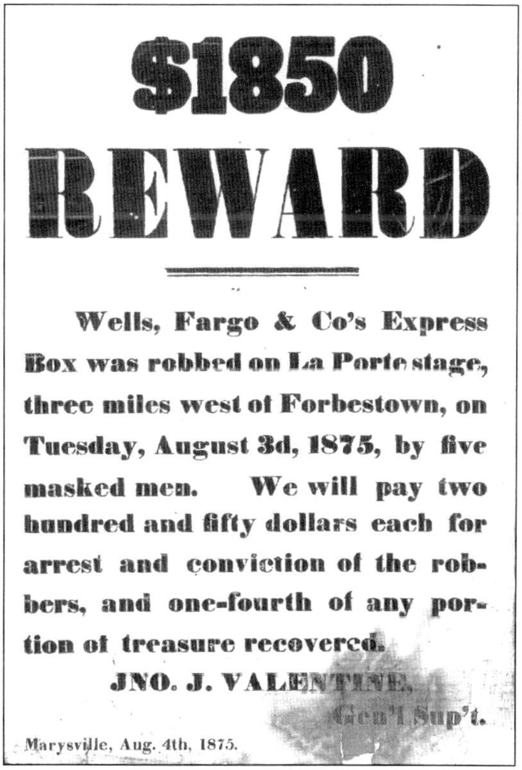

# $1850 REWARD

Wells, Fargo & Co's Express Box was robbed on La Porte stage, three miles west of Forbestown, on Tuesday, August 3d, 1875, by five masked men. We will pay two hundred and fifty dollars each for arrest and conviction of the robbers, and one-fourth of any portion of treasure recovered.

JNO. J. VALENTINE,
Gen'l Sup't.

Marysville, Aug. 4th, 1875.

The miners' hard and dangerous work included drilling holes in the hard rock, and then blasting the quartz loose with dynamite. By 1928, Goldbank Mine had produced nearly $3 million in gold.

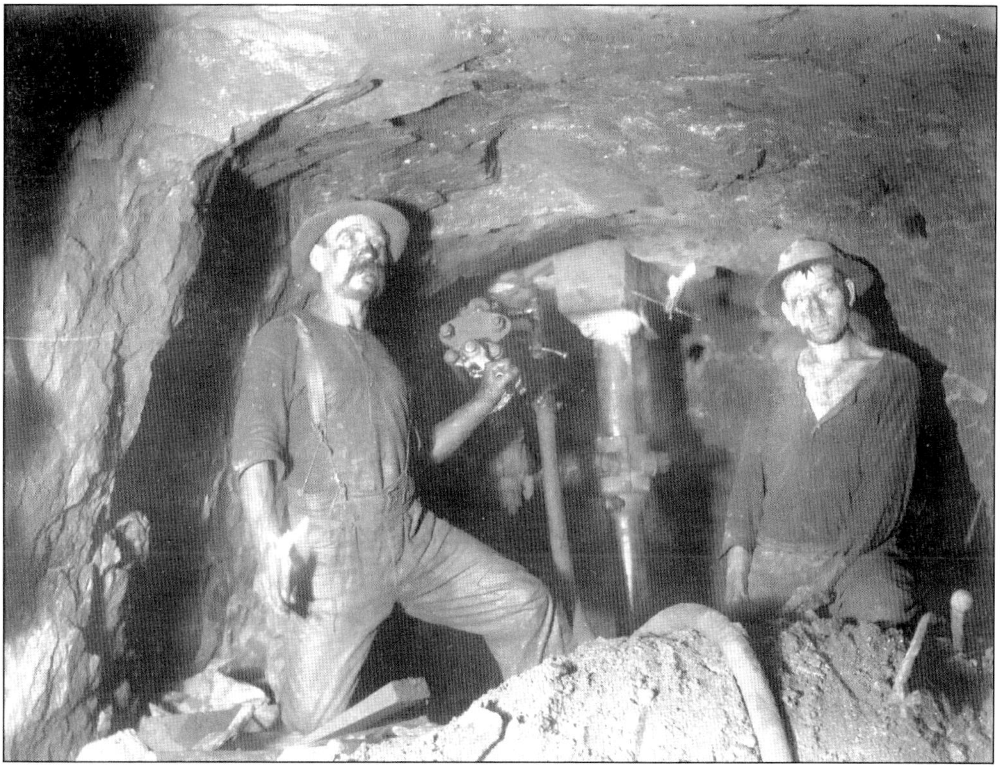

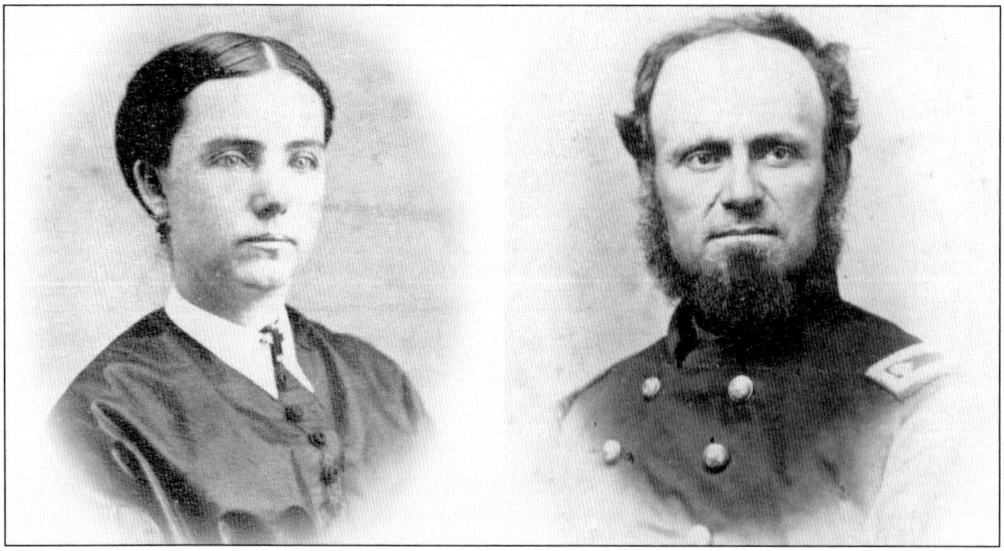

Dr. Horace T. Persons and his wife, Agnes Jane Fenton, left Wisconsin and came by wagon train to Forbestown in 1854. He practiced medicine there for four years before becoming a surgeon in the army during the Civil War. He was captured by the Confederates in 1863 and released a year later, but he never recovered his health. He brought his family back to Forbestown in 1868, this time by ship. Agnes wrote of the difficulties of traveling with their two daughters, but she was quite intrepid, bringing along a cage full of canaries on the three-week sea voyage.

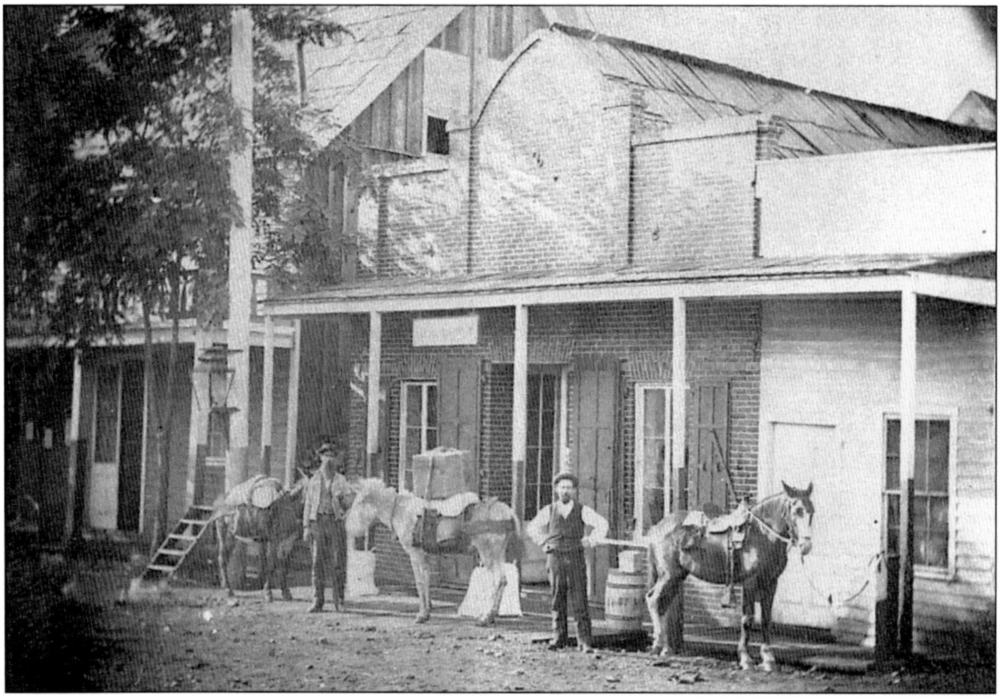

Pack animals are being loaded with provisions in 1855 in front of a fine brick store. The iron doors could be closed in the event of a fire and sometimes saved a building from destruction. Street lights were mounted on posts throughout the town during this prosperous time, and one is visible to the right of the stairs. At left is one of the town's five hotels.

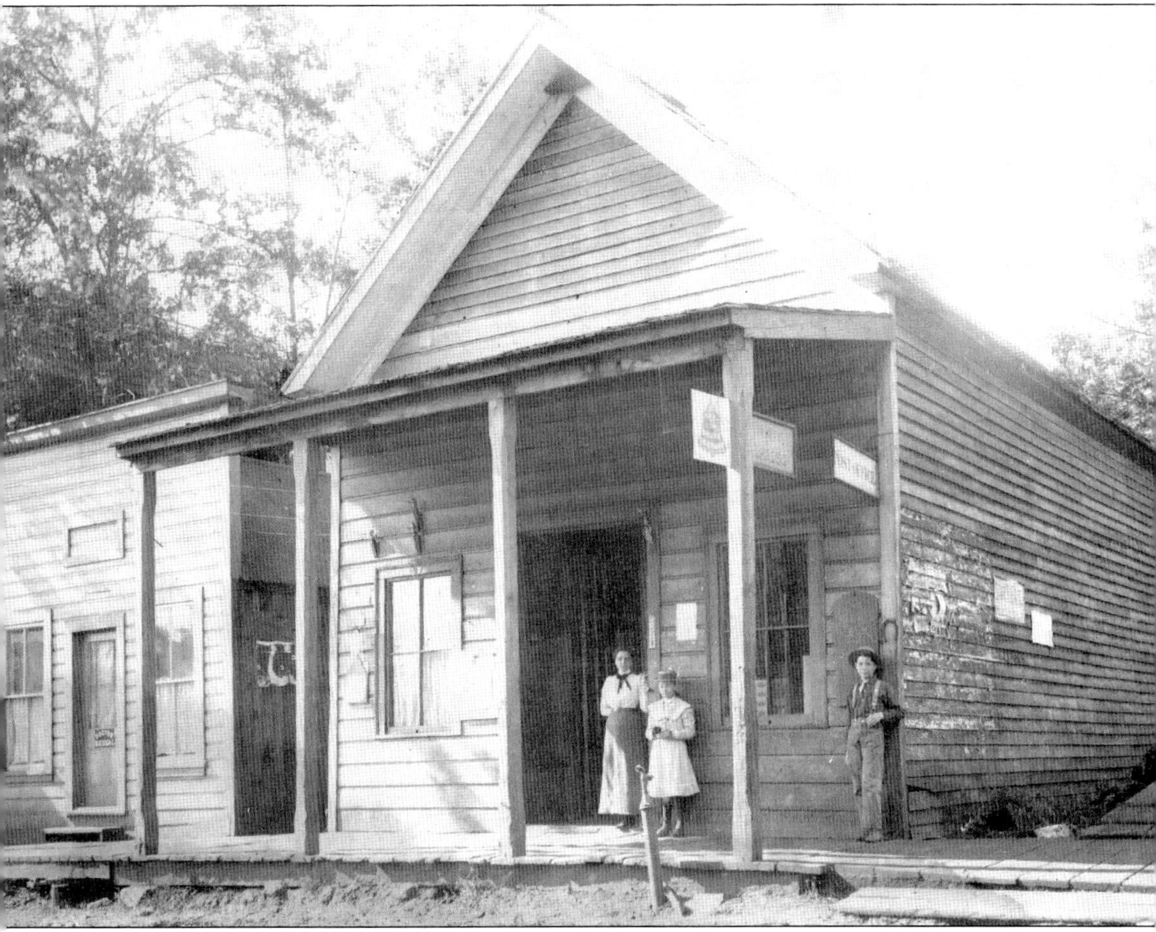

Emma Joslyn and her children, Mamie and Walter, stand in front of the post office in this 1880 photograph. Dr. Gibson's office at left. He later moved to Oroville and continued his practice as both a medical doctor and dentist. The telephone lines were brought into the region in 1878, and the sign on the post indicates the new device was just inside. The charges to call were 50¢ for 10 words and 3¢ for each additional word. Someone was also on the line to count words as a person spoke. G. S. W. Twogood wrote, "I talk to Emmerson through the telephone—first experience in such witchery."

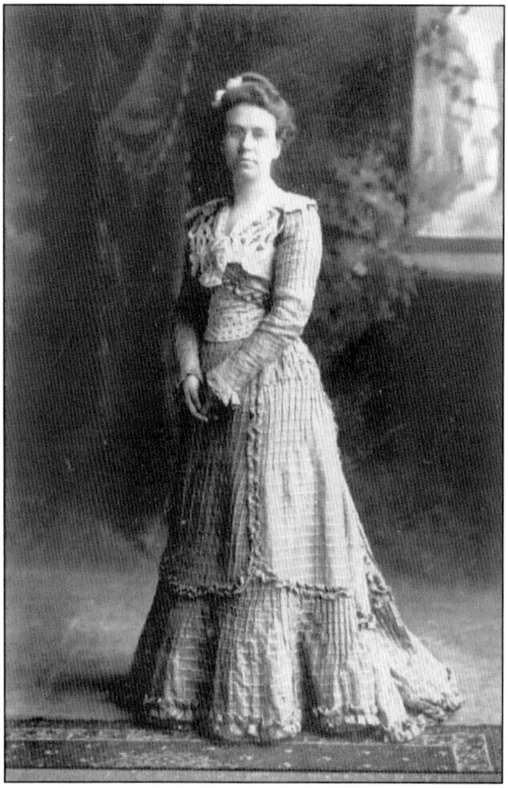

Mrs. Harry P. Stow, wife of the owner of Goldbank Mine, was active in the Ladies Library Society, which provided books for the townspeople. Many of the young men and women missed the cultural activities they were accustomed to, so music classes were started and groups gathered at homes for sing-alongs. Sunday services were held in the community hall or the school. If no preacher was available, sermons by H. W. Beecher were read from a pamphlet followed by singing and prayer.

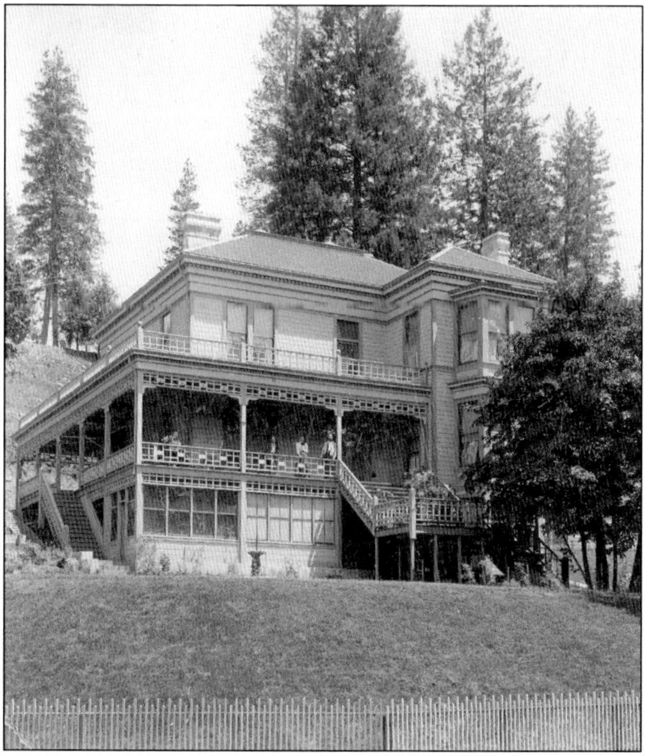

The 20-room Stow mansion on Golden Gate Avenue was heated with steam, and boasted a wine cellar and a large ballroom where dances and community social events were held. Ten-foot-wide verandas surrounded the upper floors. It was destroyed by fire in July 1930.

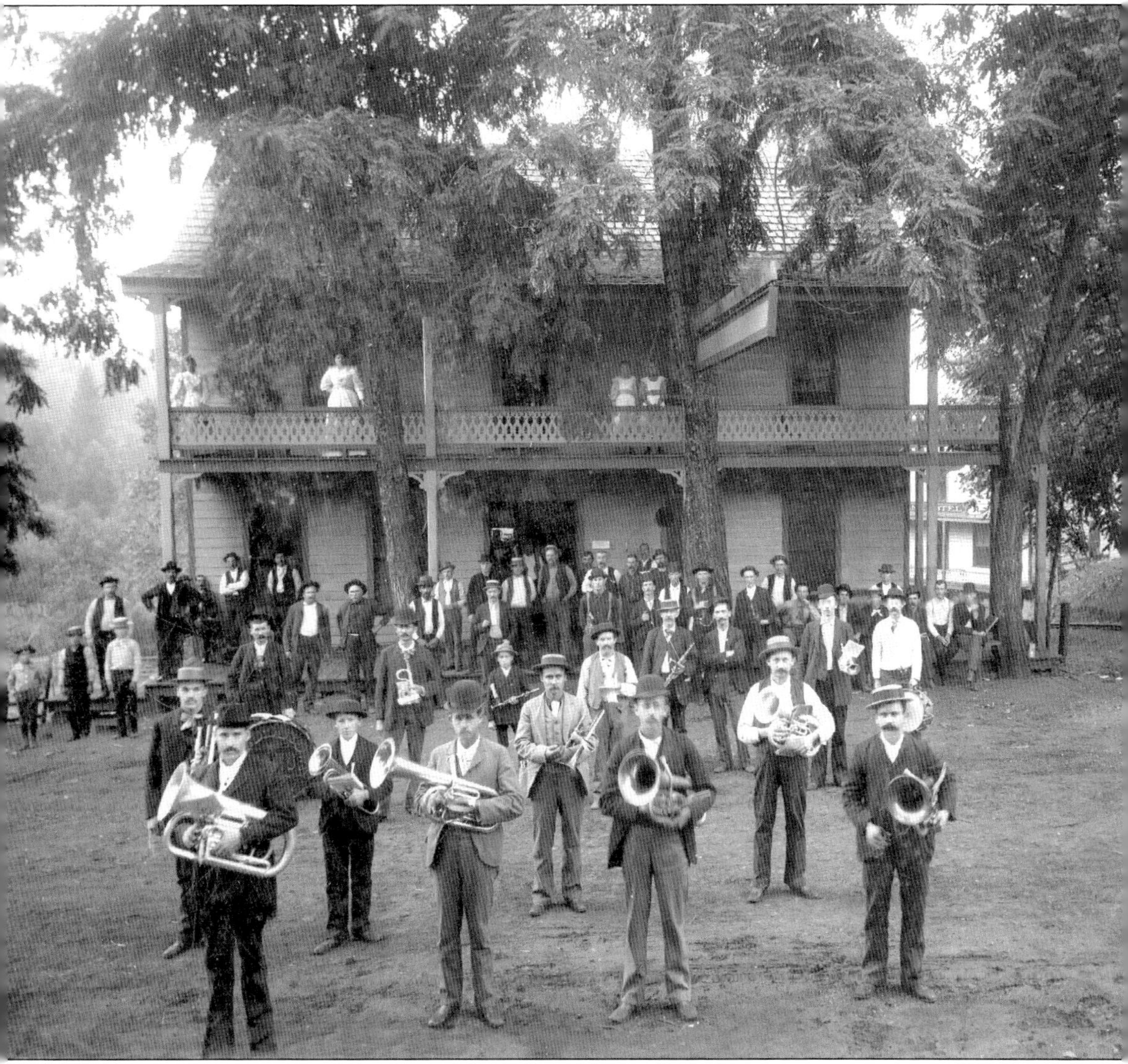

The members of the Forbestown Band in front of the Exchange Hotel in 1893 are identified only by the instrument they played: A. L. Moore (clarinet), John Peller (cornet), John Gribbens (baritone), Charles Roberts (cornet), Dr. York (cornet), Charles Bovier (clarinet) E. S. Dealey, (tuba), Tom Thurston (baritone), George Beik, (tenor), Julius Rosenthal (alto), James Martin, (alto), Frank Wilkie (bass drum), and Charles Leyval (snare drum). Unfortunately, there are more than one of some instruments, so the names can't be matched to the individuals in the photograph. William Whipple was the band leader, and according to Harry L. Wells's *History of Butte County*, he "practiced the tonsorial art for a livelihood."

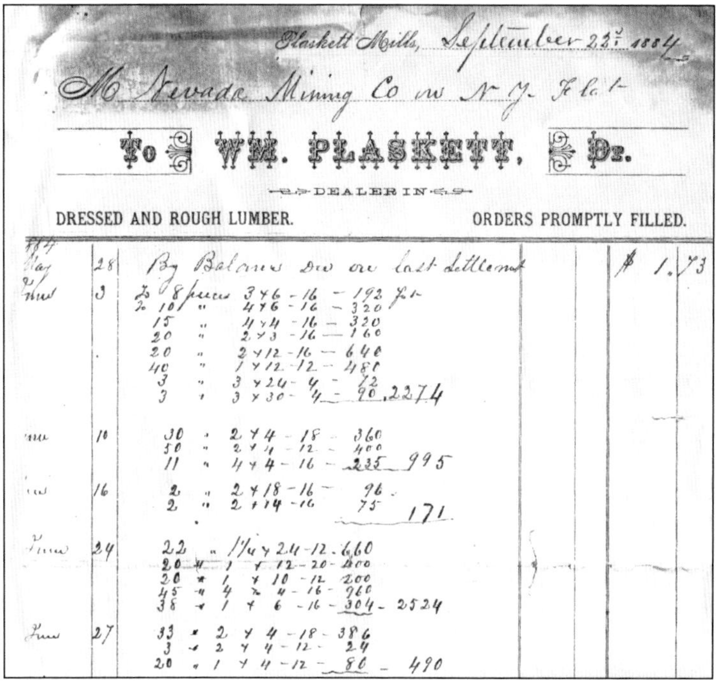

Plaskett Mills, September 22nd 1884

M Nevada Mining Co on N. Y. Flat

To WM. PLASKETT, Dr.

DEALER IN

DRESSED AND ROUGH LUMBER. ORDERS PROMPTLY FILLED.

| 1884 | | | |
|---|---|---|---|
| May | 28 | By Balance due on last settlement | $ 1.73 |
| June | 3 | To 8 pieces 3×6 - 16 - 192 ft<br>10 " 4×6 - 16 - 320<br>15 " 4×4 - 16 - 320<br>20 " 2×3 - 16 - 160<br>20 " 2×12 - 16 - 640<br>40 " 1×12 - 12 - 480<br>3 " 3×24 - 4 - 72<br>3 " 3×30 - 4 - 90 2274 | |
| June | 10 | 30 " 2×4 - 18 - 360<br>50 " 2×4 - 12 - 400<br>11 " 4×4 - 16 - 235 995 | |
| June | 16 | 2 " 2×18 - 16 - 96<br>2 " 2×14 - 16 - 75 171 | |
| June | 24 | 22 " 1¼×24 - 12 - 660<br>20 " 1×12 - 20 - 400<br>20 " 1×10 - 12 - 200<br>45 " 4×4 - 16 - 960<br>38 " 1×6 - 16 - 304 - 2524 | |
| June | 27 | 33 " 2×4 - 18 - 396<br>3 " 2×4 - 12 - 24<br>20 " 1×4 - 12 - 80 - 490 | |

This receipt is for lumber purchased from the Plaskett Mill on September 22, 1884, by the Nevada Mining Company at New York Flat, a hydraulic operation.

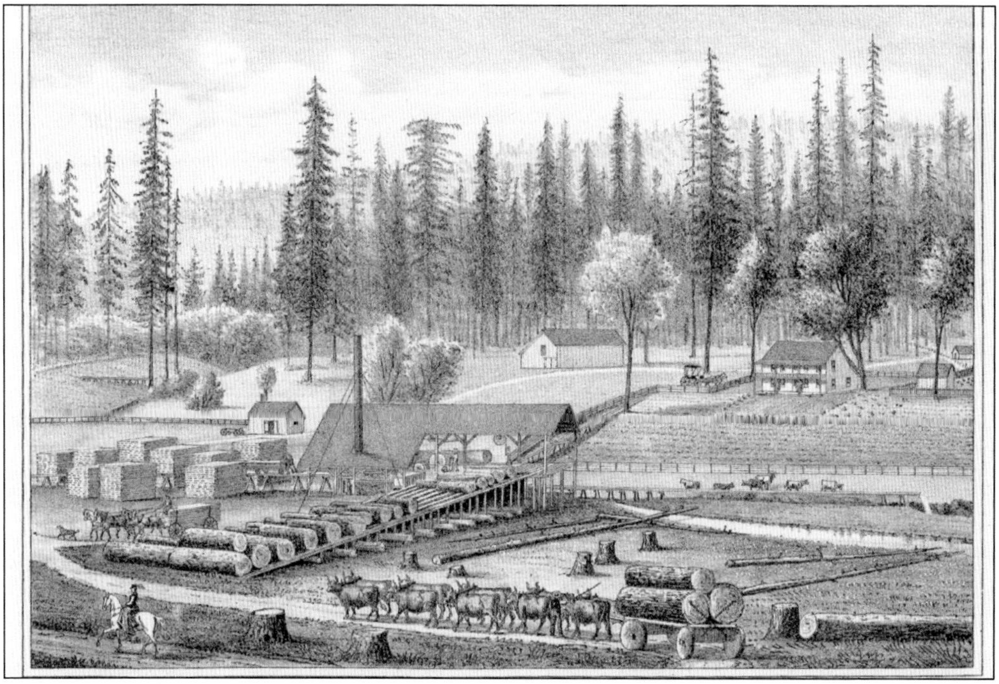

Maj. William Plaskett came west to join his brothers after the Civil War and received a land grant. He cleared the land, built a home for his family, and planted prunes, apples, quince, peaches, and berries. The sawmill machinery for his steam-powered mill was shipped around Cape Horn. The major died at age 81 after he dashed across the street in San Francisco and was hit by an electric streetcar. Descendents of his family still live on the original property. (Illustration from *History of Yuba County*, Wells and Chamberlain, 1879.)

An elaborate drama production at Forbestown included Lillie Liebhauser, Charlie Lynds, Ed Graham, Christine Liebhauser, and Harry M. Liebhauser (holding the wheel).

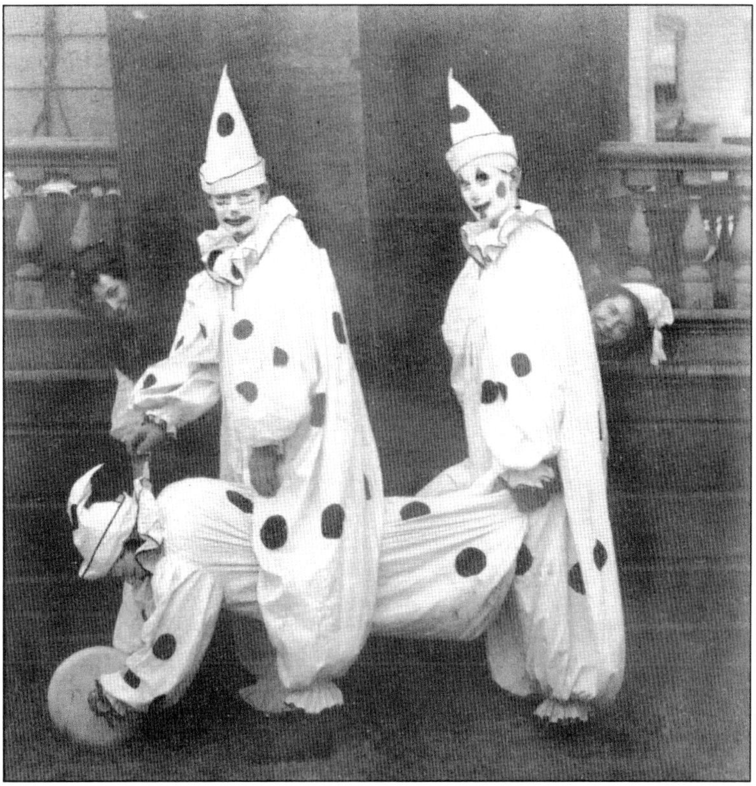

The steadily producing gold mines brought comfortable lifestyles, as evidenced by the many homes surrounded by gardens and white picket fences like this R. B. Fry home in 1890.

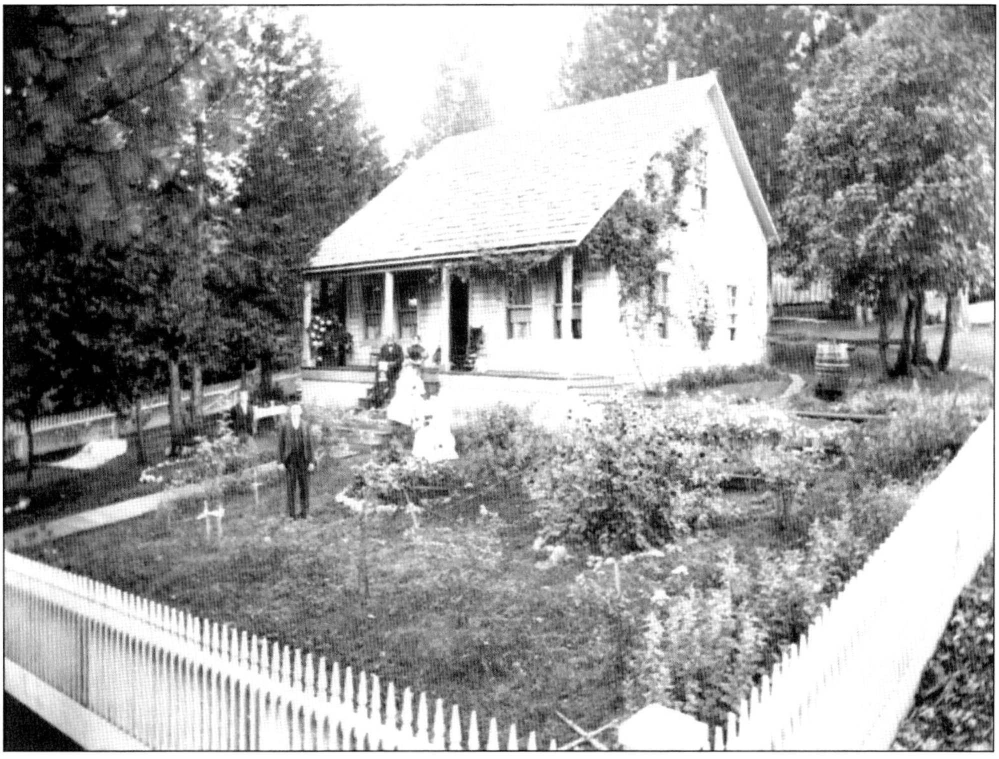

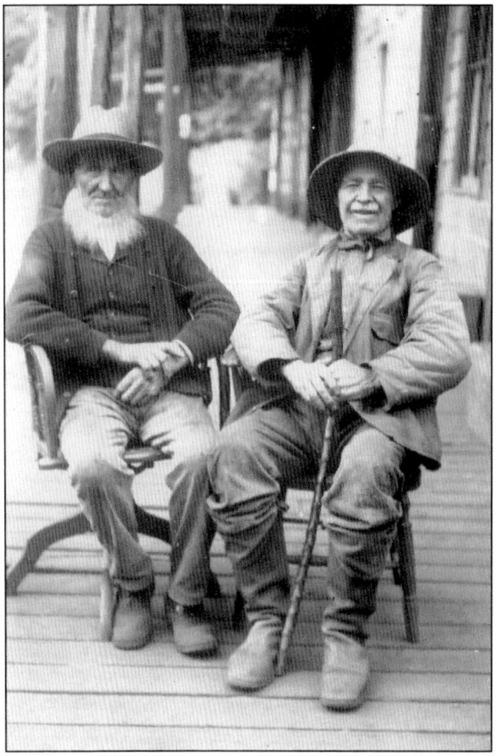

Judge Jack Price and Ben Wilkie sit on the porch of one of the town businesses in 1890, no doubt swapping stories. Judge Price was a constable for many years and Ben Wilkie was a rancher. They could keep residents, especially children, enthralled with their tales of the old days when there were seven saloons in a row down the street. Bears and rattlesnakes abounded—some serpents were of the two-footed kind—and the good guys always won.

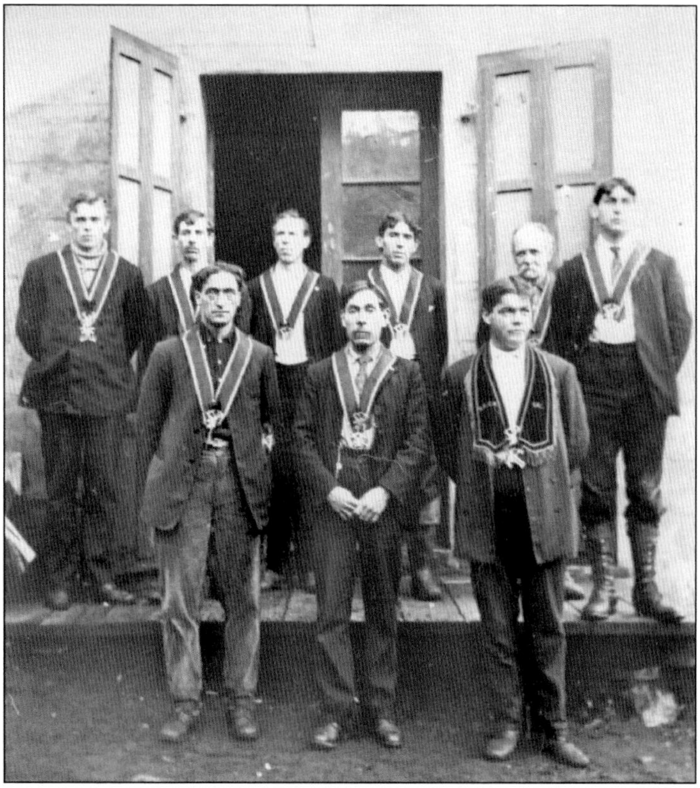

Pictured in front of the Masonic lodge in 1900, from left to right, are Forester Lodge members (first row) Andy Arbucco, Martin Costa, and Frank George; (second row) John Beik, Manuel Fernandez, Alvin Beever, Joe Costa, Joe Liebhauser, and Frank Costa. Masonic Lodge No. 50 F&AM was established in 1854. Forbestown has suffered from at least six fires, and the hall is one of only a few of its original buildings that survives.

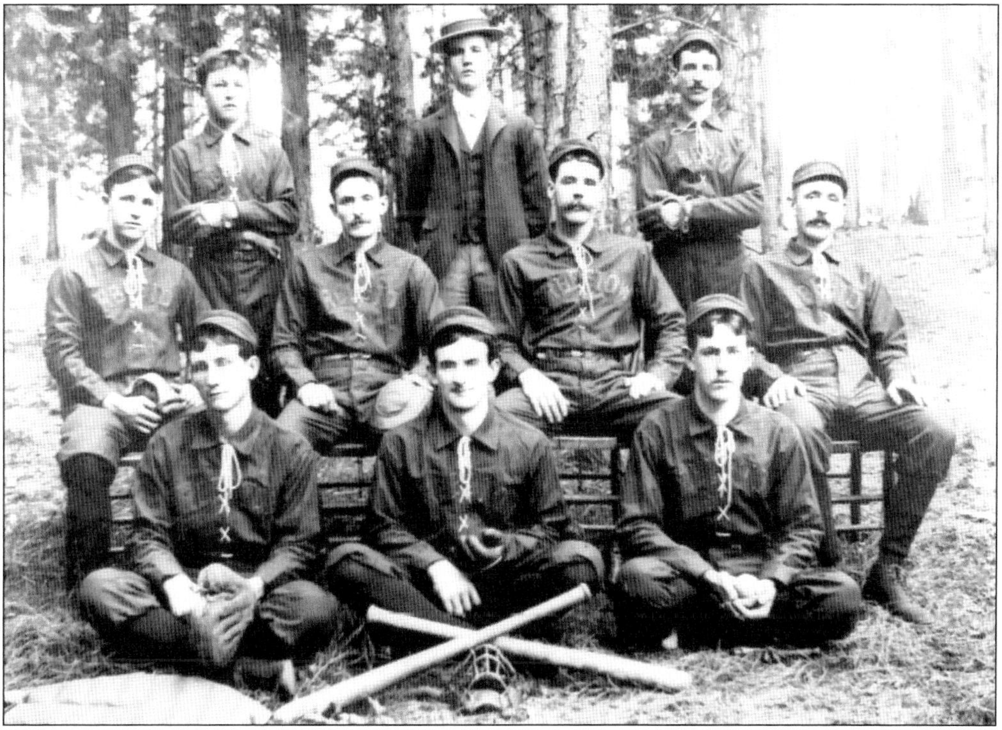

The Forbestown baseball team in 1900, from left to right, included (first row) Jim Bennett, Will Eddy, and Charles Harding; (second row) Oscar Fry, ? McCabe, John Edwards, and Tom Clemo; (third row) Elmer Fry, Cecil Burroughs, and William Wilkie.

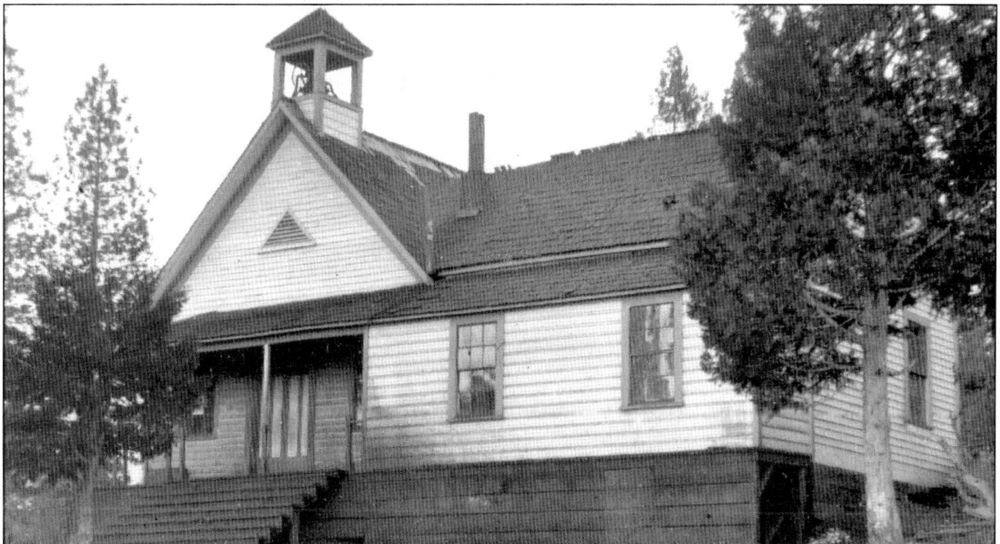

When the gold ore in local mines ran out or became too costly to work, the mines shut down and Forbestown lost most of its population. The post office closed in 1925, and the Forbestown School, in the above 1907 photograph, was abandoned in 1930. The lumber industry brought new revenue and residents in the mid-1930s. The post office reopened in 1936, and a new school was built on New York Flat Road in 1948.

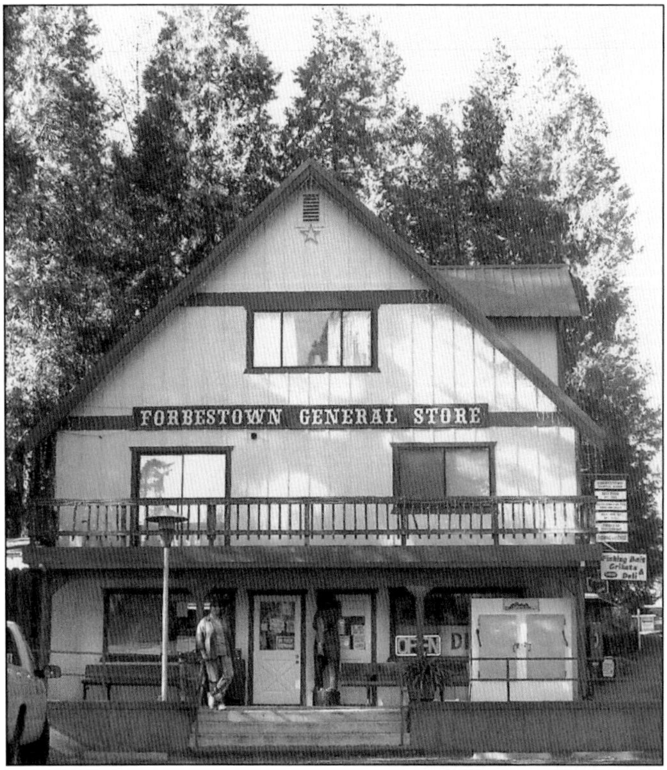


As of 2006, Forbestown has around 1,000 residents and the church, park, and community center serve people throughout the region. Clerk Karla Thompson is pictured on the porch of the general store.

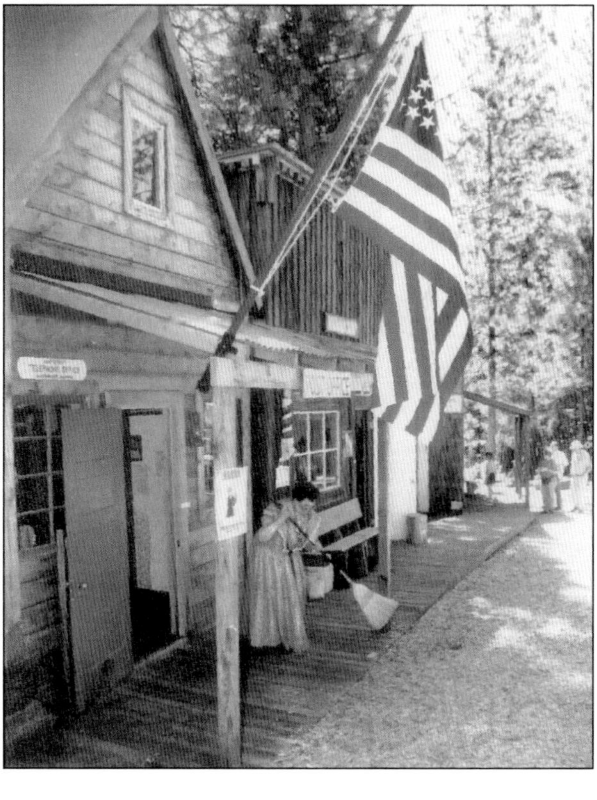

Yuba Feather Museum represents all the towns in the Yuba Feather Hills, past and present. The replica village of Gold Trader Flat includes 16 buildings where living history events are held during the summer. Here, retired postmaster Geraldine Sheehan sweeps the porch of the post office.

# *Seven*

# WOODLEAF

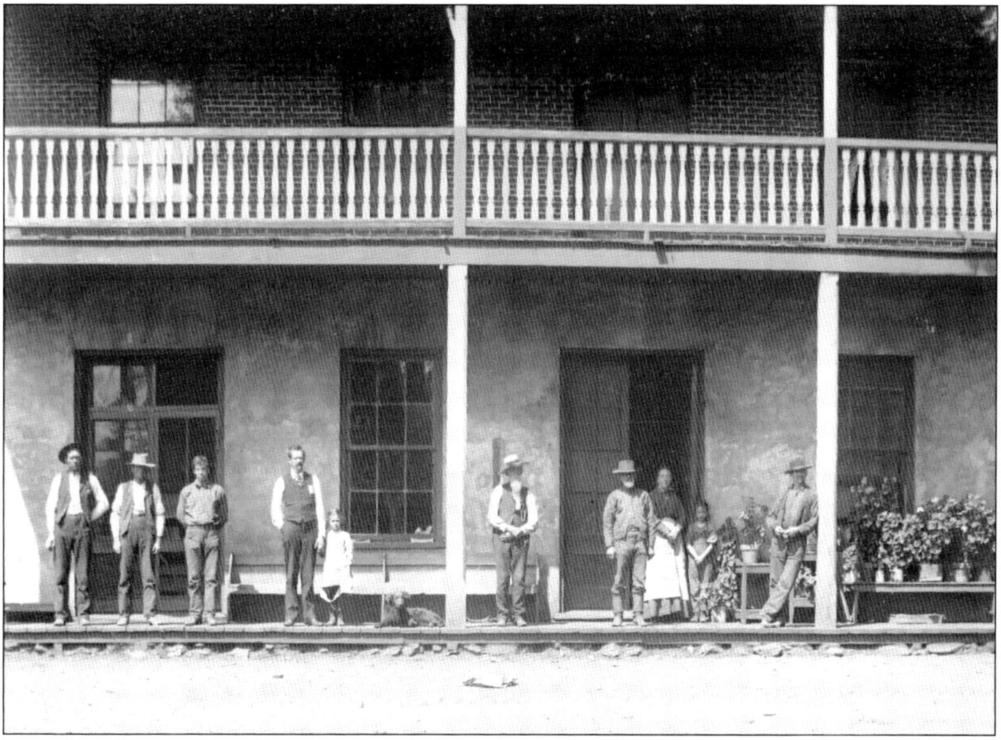

Woodleaf was known by many names in the past, including Abbott House, Barker House, Woodville, and finally Woodleaf. The first post office was granted in 1858 as Woodville, and it became Woodleaf in 1898. Joseph Wood built the grand old hotel from brick made on the spot. Double fireplaces flanked both gable ends, and there were four upstairs and downstairs. "That's me, in the torn dress, holding my father's hand," said Helen Falck Dunning of this photograph taken in 1905. "I was into every wagon . . . there was always something exciting coming into Woodleaf." The others, pictured here from left to right, are Deputy "Zack," stage driver Dan Boland, hosteler Will Coupe, proprietor Charles Falck, his daughter Helen, MacManus, Dan Sevey, Mrs. Agnes Falck, daughter Berenice Flack, and George Coppack.

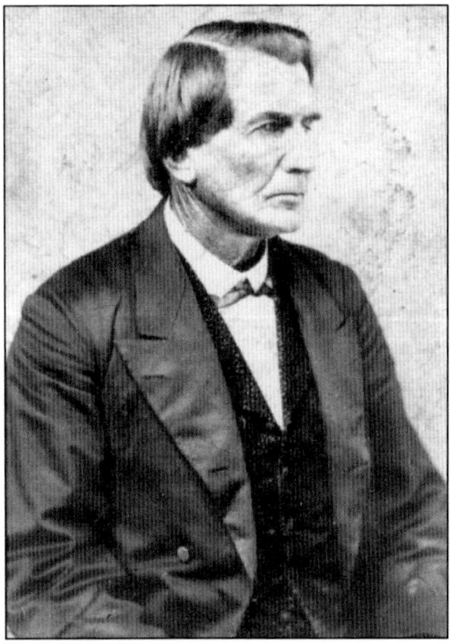

Joseph Wood first arrived in California in 1845 before returning east after his entire family died. He married again, made a third trip overland in 1853, and bought Abbott House and 160 acres for $3,500. He built a freight barn measuring 50 by 80 feet, with mortise-and-tenon joints that stood until the 1950s. The hotel was completed in 1857, furnished with mahogany furniture and velvet draperies. A spring on a nearby hill furnished water, brought in with wood pipes.

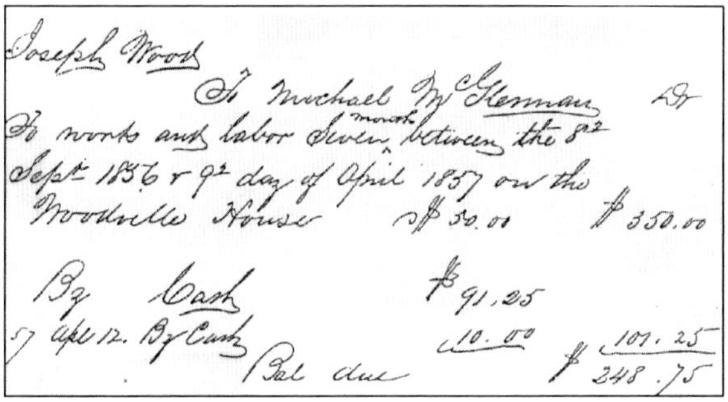

Joseph Wood
To Michael McGlennan Dr
To work and labor Seven month between the 8th
Sept 1856 & 9th day of April 1857 on the
Woodville House $50.00 $350.00
By Cash $91.25
57 Apl 12. By Cash 10.00 101.25
Bal due $248.75

Michael McGlennan's bill documented his work on the hotel from September 1856 to April 1857, worth a total of $550. Many others worked to hand-plane all the wood trim and finish the lathe-and-plaster interior walls.

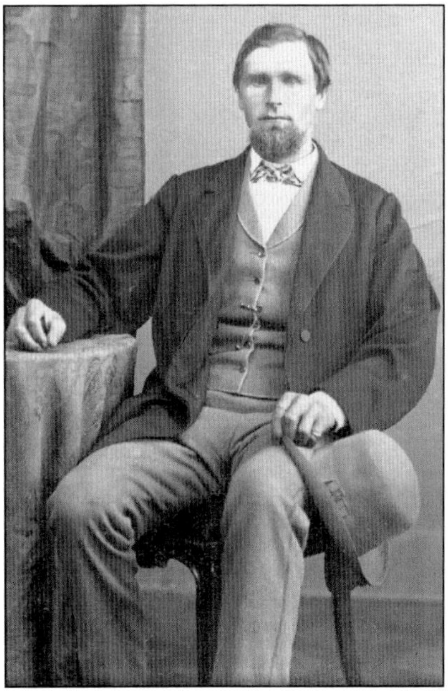

This photograph of John C. Falck was taken in his homeland of Sweden. He was a mate aboard a ship when he heard about the gold rush, and jumped ship when it docked in San Francisco. He bought Woodville in 1878 with the profits from selling his interest in the Buckeye Mine in Sawpit Flat, above La Porte. Falck built the large ballroom next to the hotel, carriage barn, and a store where he made custom-fitted coffins.

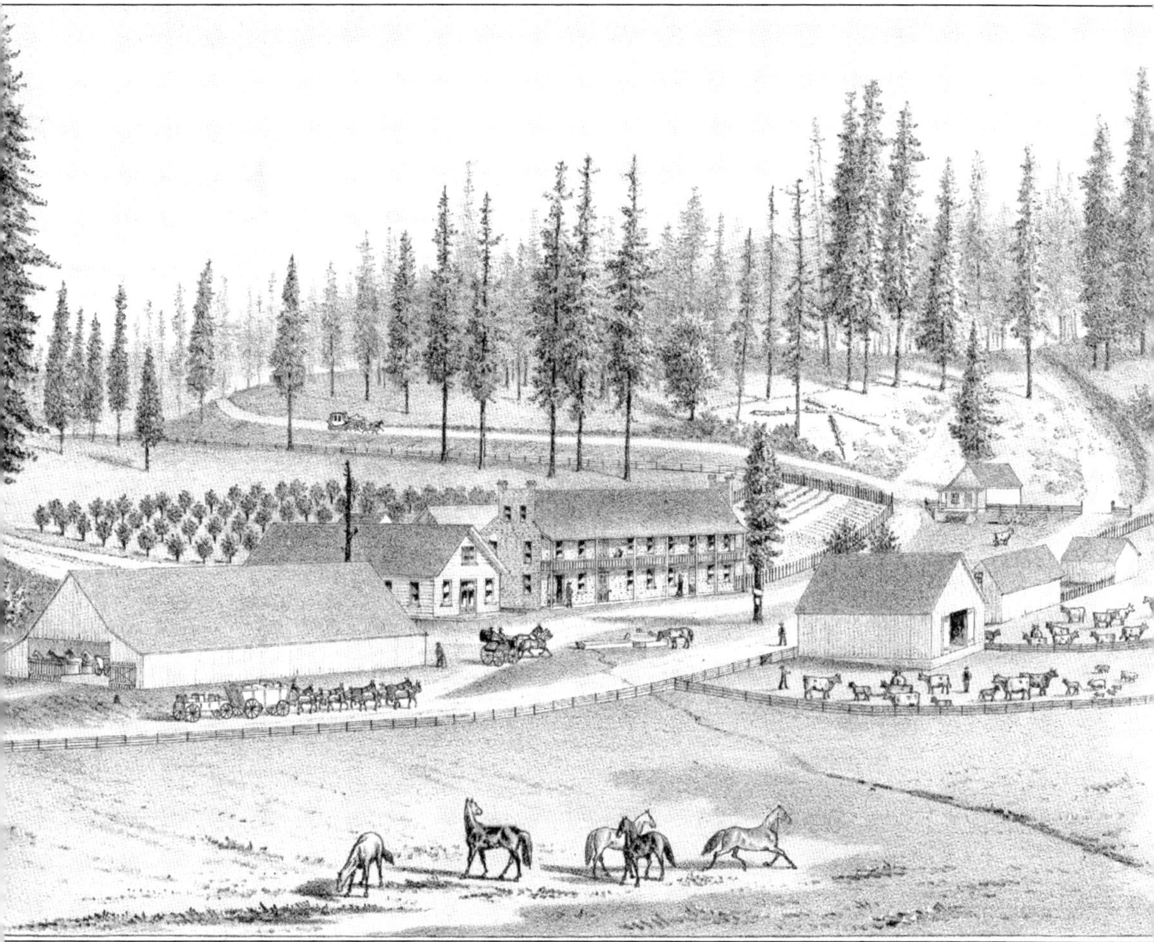

In this 1878 lithograph, the freight barn, ballroom, hotel (the bath house and the old Abbott House and wood shed in the rear), the stage barn across the road, and the tollhouse and gate at upper right can be seen. Behind the hotel are orchards and gardens. A mule team with freight wagons approaches the water trough, and a stagecoach nears Woodville, coming downhill toward the tollhouse. (Illustration from *History of Yuba County*, Wells and Chamberlain, 1879.)

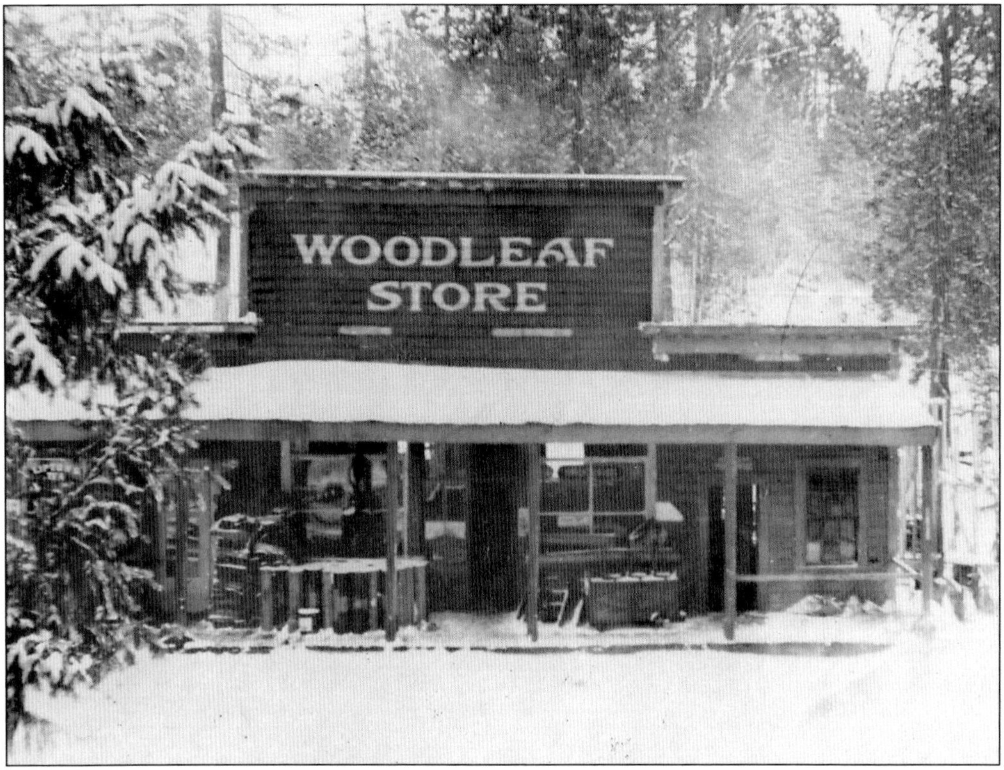


The Woodleaf Store was built in the 1870s and carried all kinds of hardware and groceries. It was still in business around 1950 when it burned to the ground. The store then moved into the hotel, along with the post office that had also been destroyed by the fire.

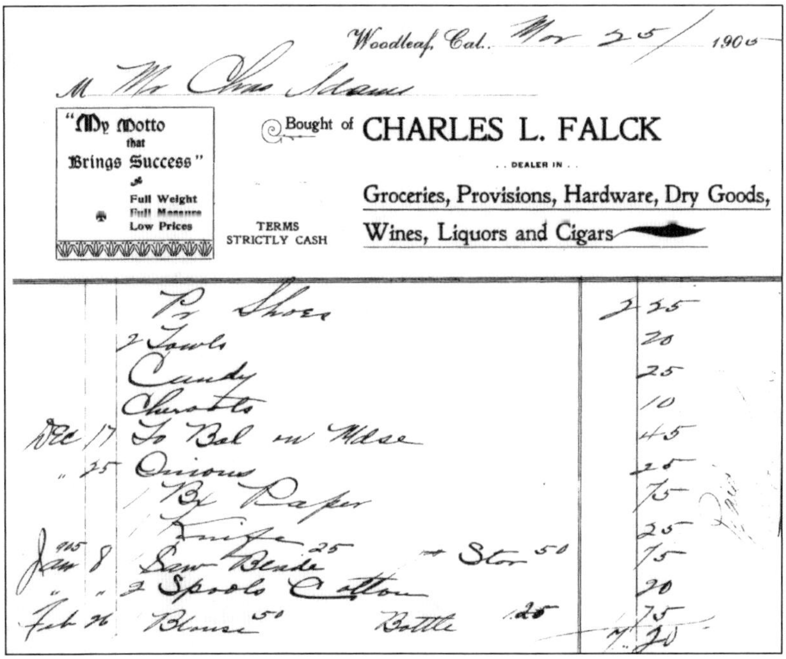

Woodleaf, Cal. Nov 25/ 1905

M Mr Chas Adams

"My Motto that Brings Success"
Full Weight
Full Measure
Low Prices

Bought of CHARLES L. FALCK

. . DEALER IN . .

Groceries, Provisions, Hardware, Dry Goods, Wines, Liquors and Cigars

TERMS STRICTLY CASH

| | | |
|---|---|---|
| | Pr Shoes | 2 25 |
| | 2 Towels | 20 |
| | Candy | 25 |
| | Cheroots | 10 |
| Dec 17 | To Bal on Mdse | 45 |
| " 25 | Onions | 25 |
| | 1 Bx Paper | 75 |
| | Knife | 25 |
| 1906 Jan 8 | Saw Blade 25 + Stor 50 | 75 |
| " " | 2 Spools Cotton | 20 |
| Feb 26 | Blouse 50 Bottle .25 | 75 |
| | | 7.20 |

A 1905 bill from the Woodleaf Store shows that Charles Adams of the nearby settlement of Oro Lewa bought shoes, candy, cotton thread, cheroots (cigars), onions, paper, knife, saw blade, two towels, and a blouse for a grand total of $7.20.

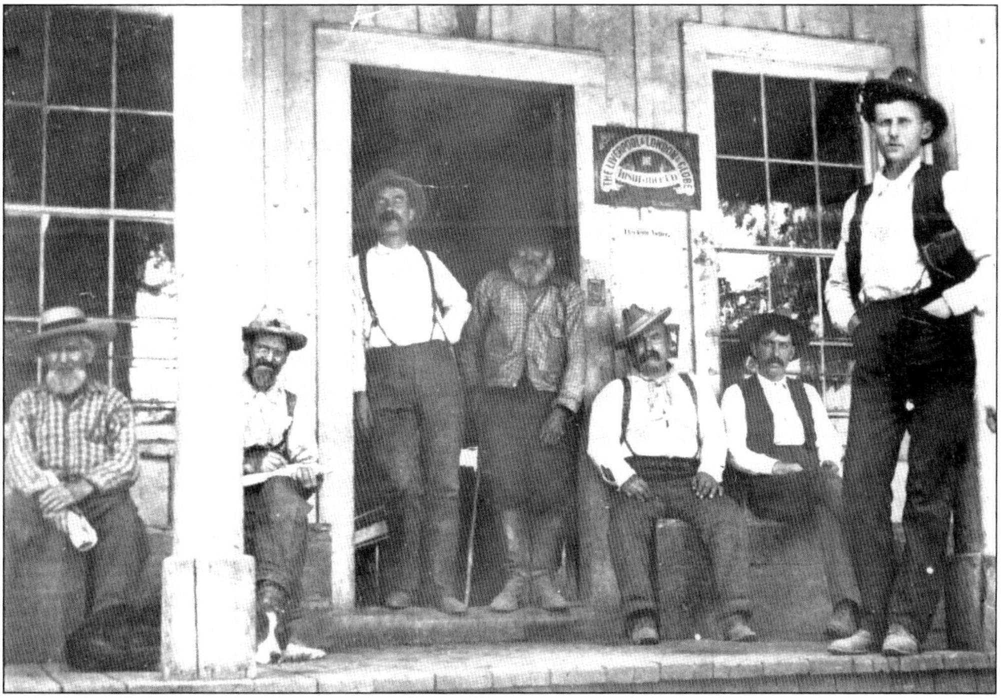

Local characters gathered on the porch of the Woodleaf Store to wait for the mail. Among them were ranchers, stagecoach drivers, and a wainwright. The man standing in the doorway on the right was miner Bill Kimball, whose mine was on Slate Creek. The two gold mines near Woodleaf were Mount de Oro and Mount Hope.

These Maidu baskets made by Nellie Johnson were collected by John C. Falck in the late 1800s and early 1900s. Falck traded valuable goods, such as a sewing machine, shoes, or clothing, for each one. The tray at the back was used to separate grain from chaff. Nellie was born at or near Woodleaf and lived there some of the time, but she made her home in Strawberry Valley after their tribe was granted property in 1916.

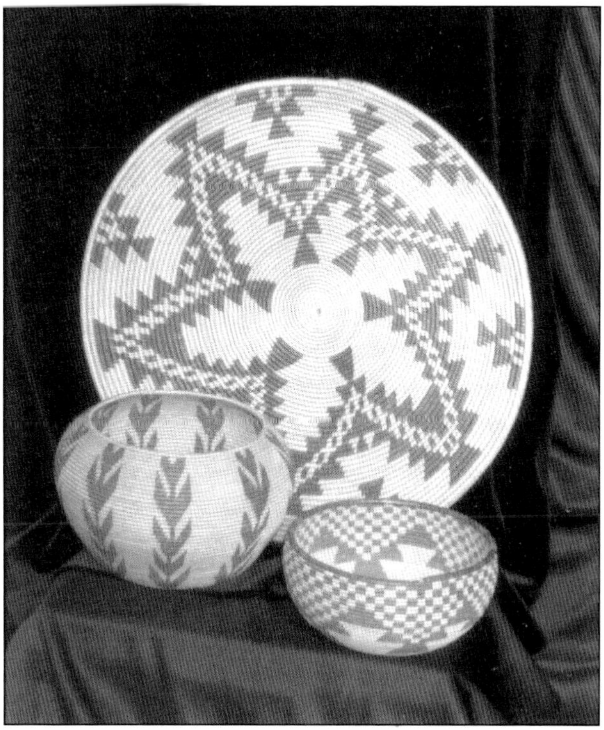

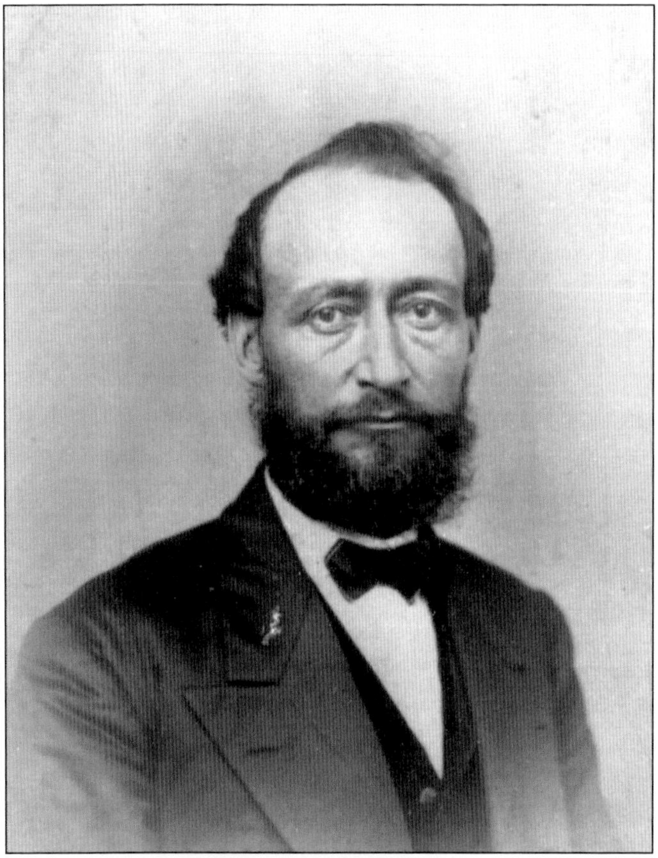

From his post during the summers at the Woodleaf Tollhouse, G. S. W. Twogood noted daily events in his journals from 1873 to 1906. He was also the proprietor of a store in Brownsville, where he and his family lived in the winter.

The La Porte Stage is stopped in front of the Woodleaf Hotel to pick up passengers. To the left of the hotel a portion of the ballroom is visible. The stage used on these roads was called a mud wagon, which was much sturdier than the Concord coach and able to navigate rough roads. Louis Stellman, a well-known photographer, made the image on one of his trips through the region.

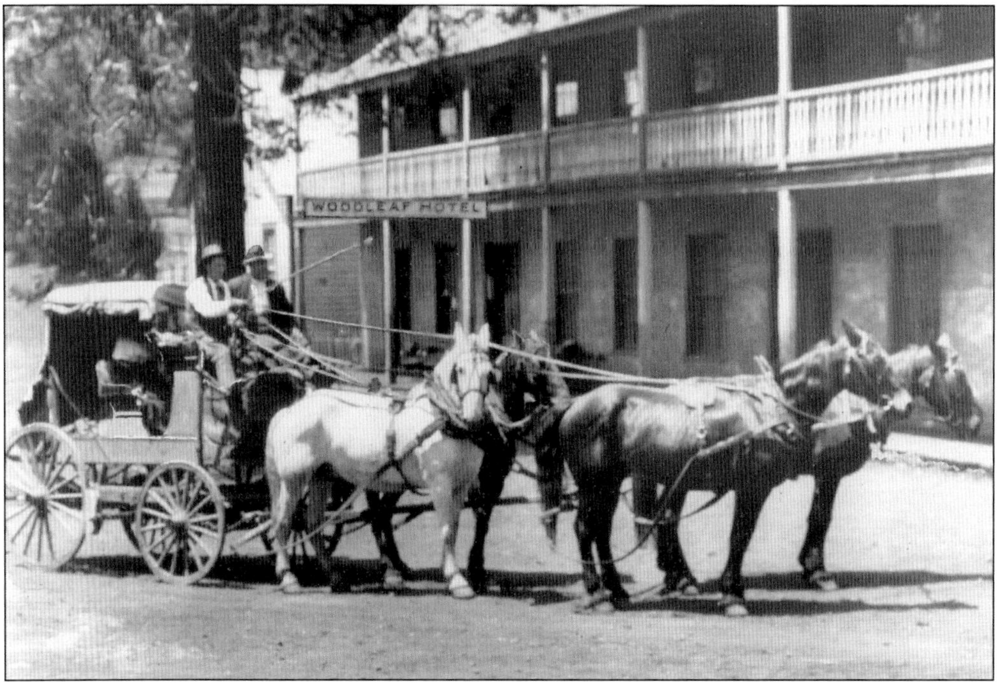

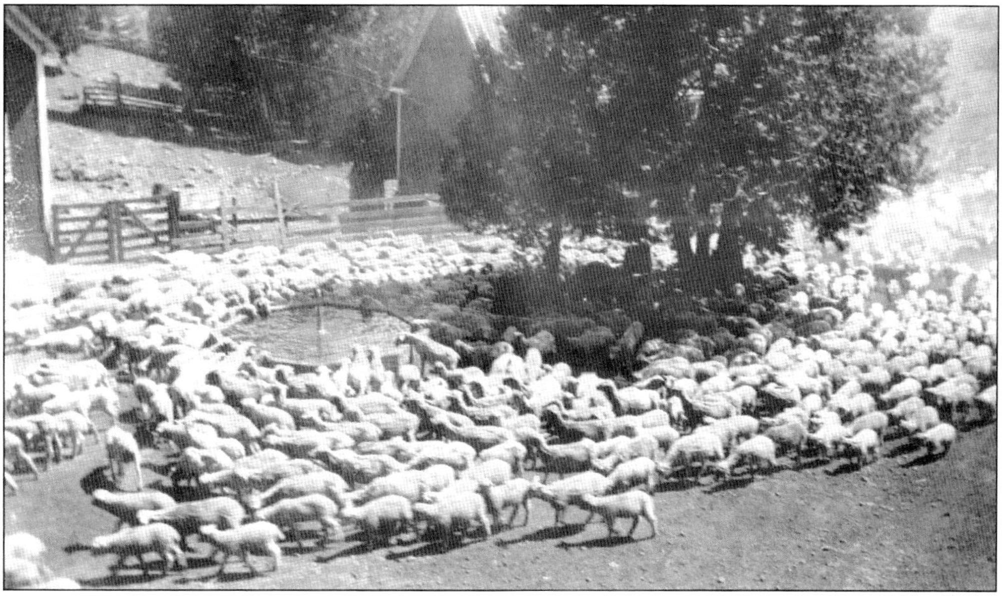

Livestock was herded through on the way to summer grazing in the high country, such as this flock of sheep surrounding the water trough and fountain. Toll keeper Twogood wrote on December 5, 1871, "A drove of turkeys came along, driven by two La Porte men, 96 turkeys in all."

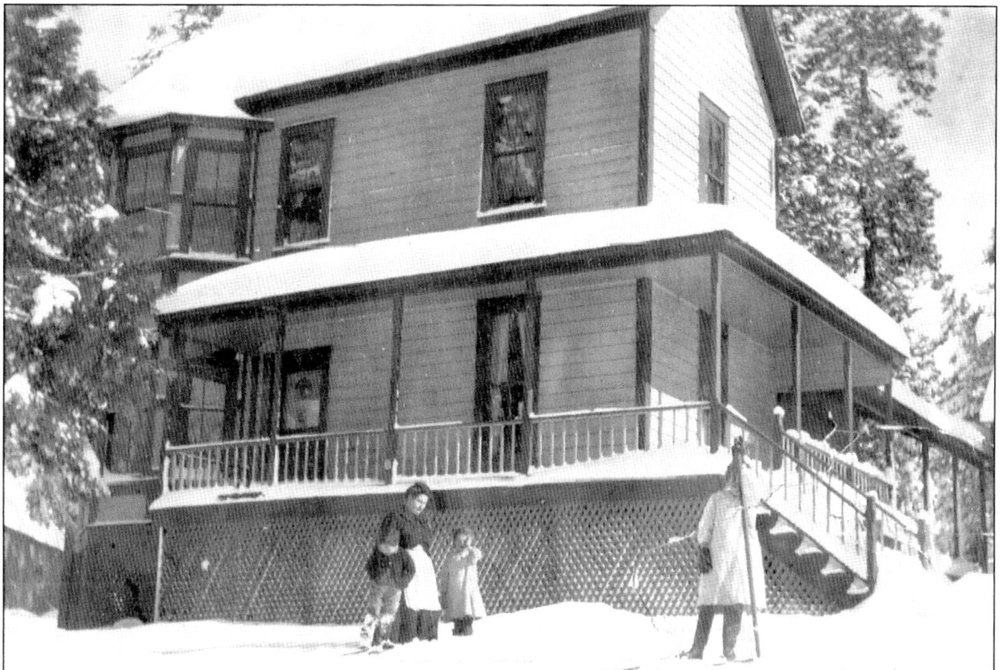

Falck added the two-story home to the front of the old tollhouse where he raised his family. His wife, son Wilbert, and daughters Berenice and Helen played in their snowy front yard. The house is still in use today.

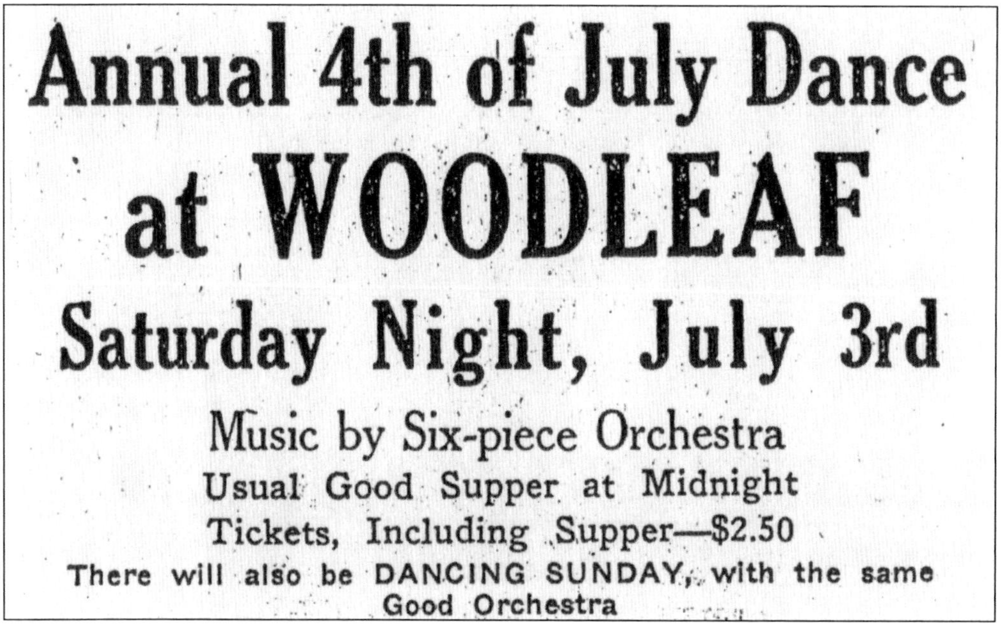


A ticket to the Fourth of July ball cost $2.50 and included a midnight supper of fried chicken and all the trimmings. "All the beauty of the neighborhood can be found at the Woodville Ball," noted Twogood after one of the dances.

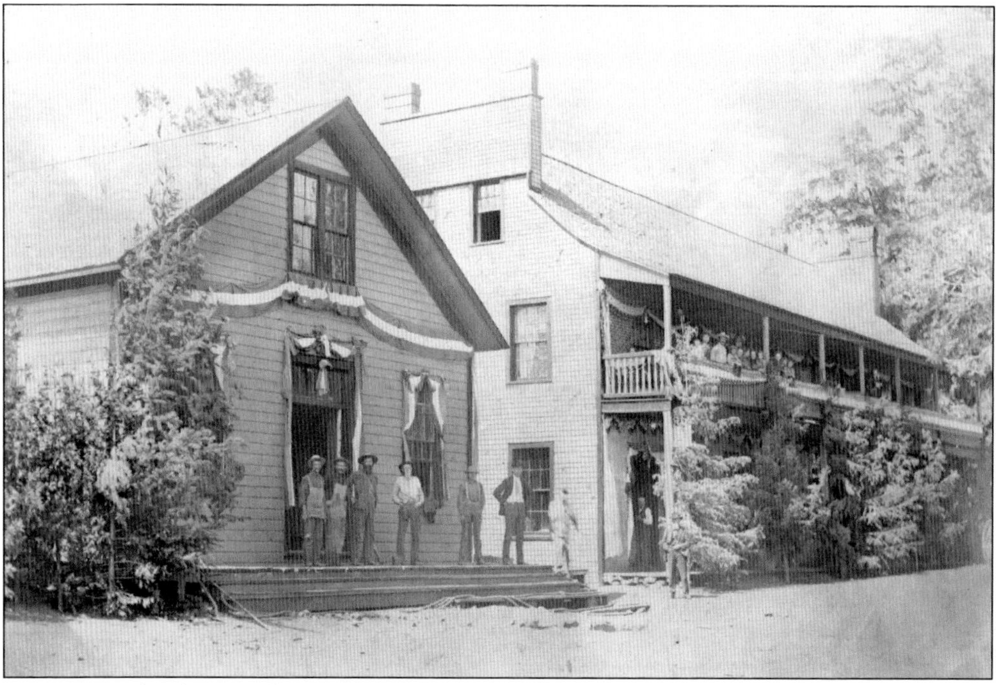

Decorations for the Fourth of July Ball and celebration included swags of red, white, and blue bunting and freshly cut evergreen trees placed along the buildings. More trees were set up inside, trimmed with small flags, paper rosettes, and strings of firecrackers that were set off outdoors after dark. Guests line the upper veranda of the hotel. Andy Arbucco, with a hammer at left, "was the most marvelous dancer," according to Helen Falck Dunning.

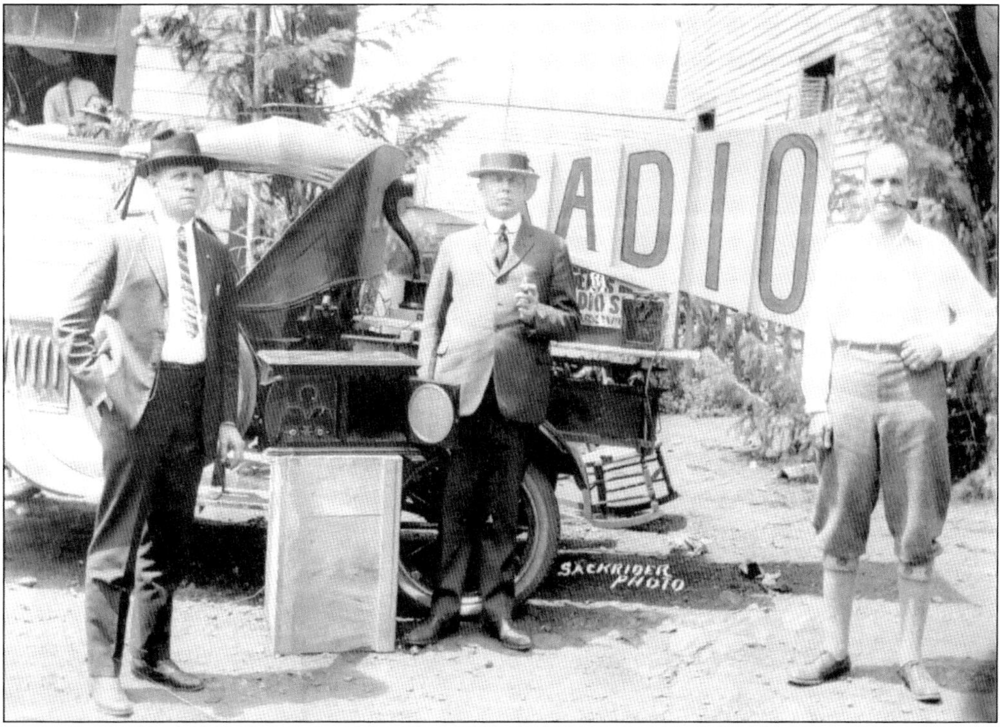


The Hoot Owl Picnic was sponsored by a radio station to celebrate its opening in the 1920s. The station broadcast its program from Woodleaf and provided food and drinks for an all-day party. In the evening, guests danced to the music from the latest records played over the radio.

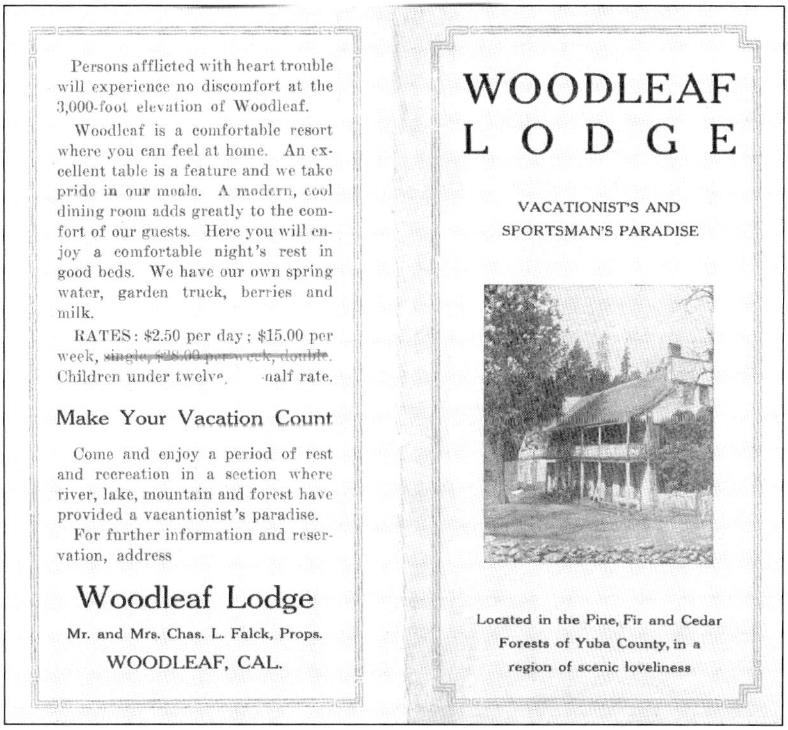

Persons afflicted with heart trouble will experience no discomfort at the 3,000-foot elevation of Woodleaf.

Woodleaf is a comfortable resort where you can feel at home. An excellent table is a feature and we take pride in our meals. A modern, cool dining room adds greatly to the comfort of our guests. Here you will enjoy a comfortable night's rest in good beds. We have our own spring water, garden truck, berries and milk.

RATES: $2.50 per day; $15.00 per week, ~~single, $28.00 per week, double~~. Children under twelve, half rate.

Make Your Vacation Count

Come and enjoy a period of rest and recreation in a section where river, lake, mountain and forest have provided a vacantionist's paradise.

For further information and reservation, address

Woodleaf Lodge

Mr. and Mrs. Chas. L. Falck, Props.

WOODLEAF, CAL.

WOODLEAF LODGE

VACATIONIST'S AND SPORTSMAN'S PARADISE

Located in the Pine, Fir and Cedar Forests of Yuba County, in a region of scenic loveliness

The Falcks promised fishing, swimming, and other pastimes in their brochure for Woodleaf Lodge. A stage line operated from Oroville to Woodleaf daily, except Sunday, and the round-trip fare from Sacramento was only $9.95.

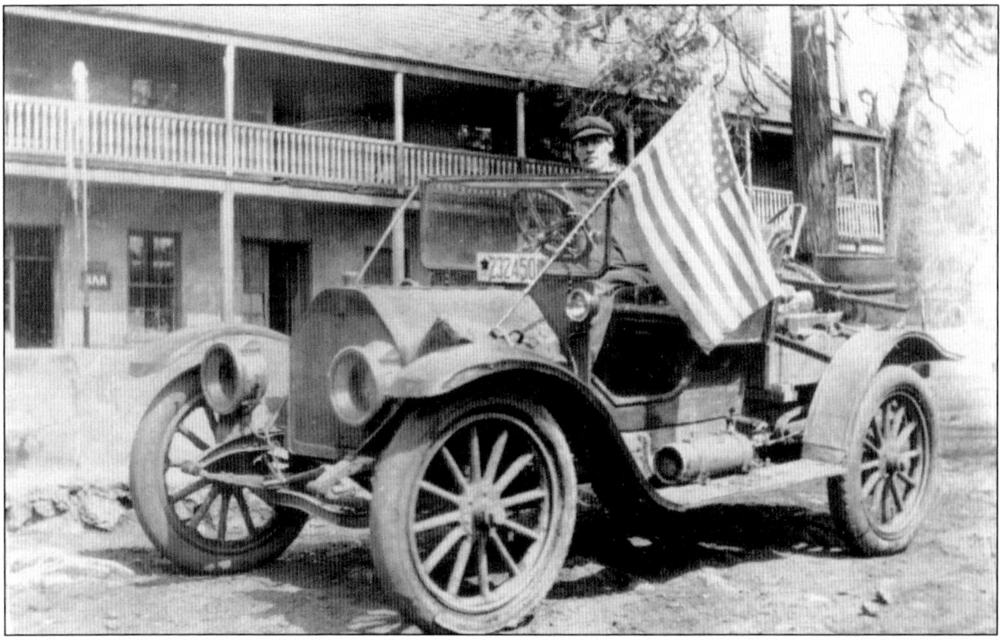

Bill Lang came by in his classy automobile, dressed in his military uniform and flying an American flag after World War I. At left is the water trough and fountain that ran year-round, gravity-fed from the spring on the hill north of the hotel.

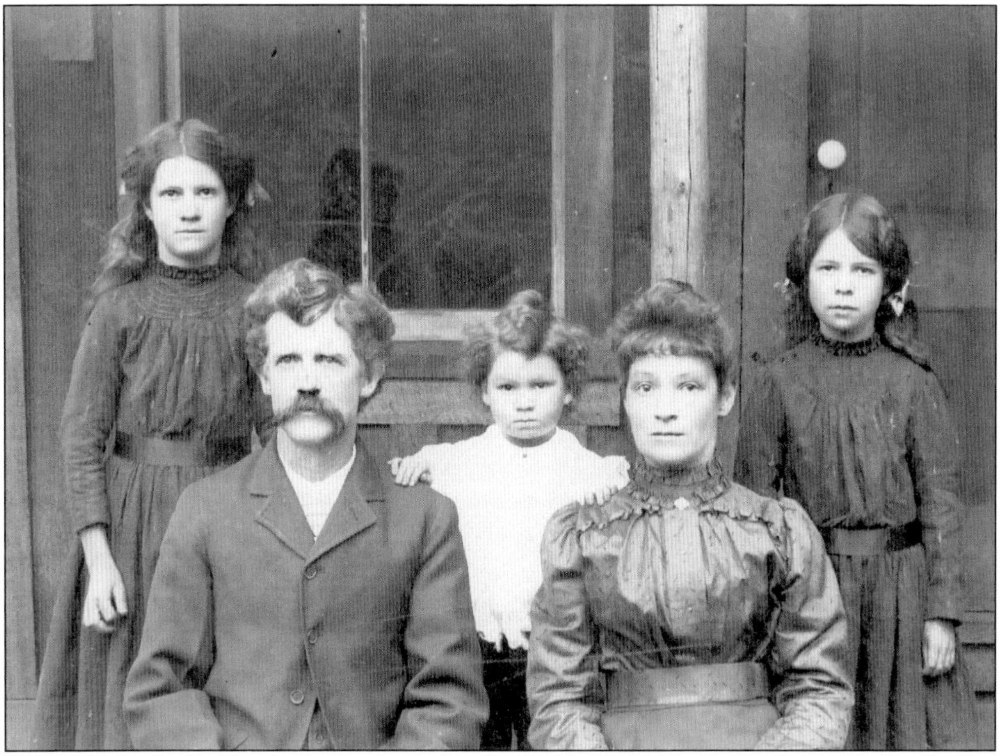

The Thurston family lived near Woodleaf where they had a large ranch and the Mount Hope Mine. Gertrude, Gordon, and Olive stand behind their parents, Thomas B. and Laura.

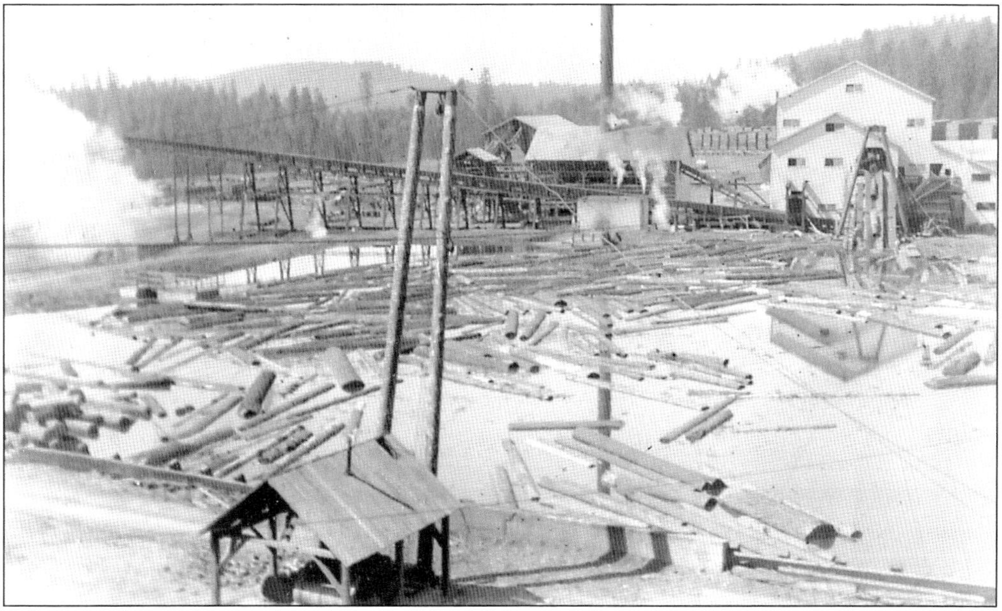

Sacramento Box and Lumber Company purchased most of the land at Woodleaf from the Falck family in 1943. They built a large mill powered with two steam engines, one from Fort Bragg, California, and another that once ran cable cars in San Francisco. A cookhouse, shops, and homes for the employees were also built during the 1940s. The mill was highly efficient, using sawdust and trimmings from sawn lumber to fire the boilers. The engines also provided electricity to the entire town when power lines failed during heavy snows.

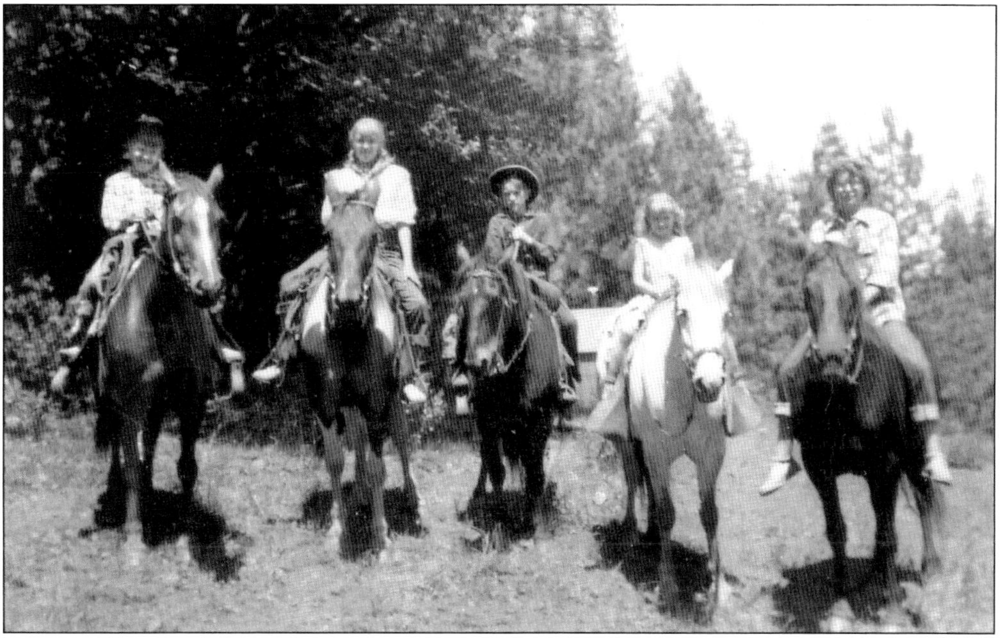

Life at Woodleaf from the mid-1940s until the mill closed offered great times, whether it was playing baseball with other town teams, skiing by moonlight, or horseback riding, as enjoyed by these young people. The meadow provided ideal pasture, and there were unlimited trails in the surrounding hills.

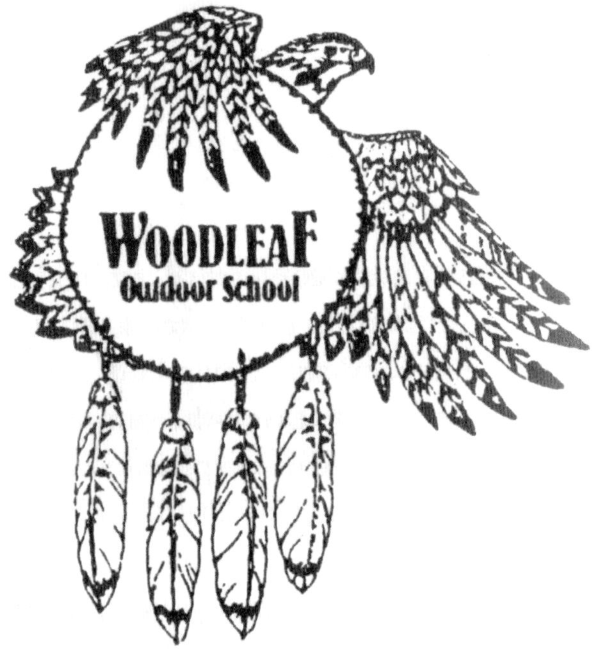


After the mill closed, Young Life, a Christian organization, purchased the property for their camping programs in 1966. In a separate endeavor, Woodleaf Outdoor School was developed by Sutter County in 1969 for elementary students and now hosts groups from many other counties. The camps feature sports, fishing, crafts, hiking, and wilderness survival during the fall and spring. Wildlife and weather are also part of the studies. "You're outside having fun, learning in a different way than if you were just sitting in the classroom with a book," explained a student. (Courtesy John Woodleaf Outdoor School.)

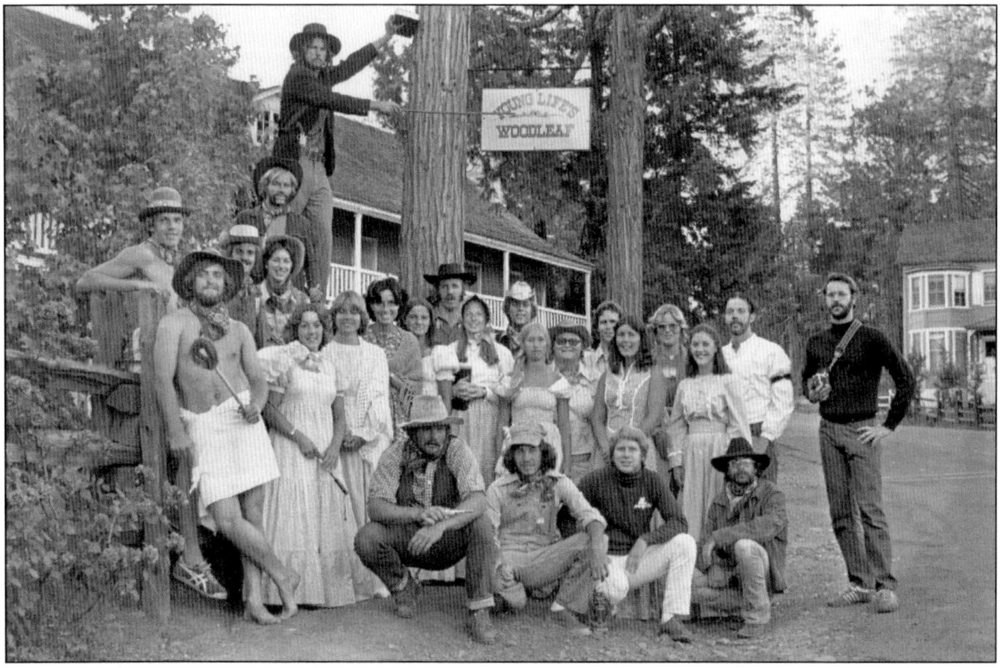


The staff during Young Life's summer program in 1976 portray characters from the past. The Christian organization reaches teenagers around the world through its resort facilities, and Woodleaf continues to grow to meet the changing needs. The town is the only one in the Yuba Feather Hills that is one parcel. Although several lots were separated at times, eventually the entire town of Woodleaf was brought together again under one owner.

# *Eight*

# Clipper Mills

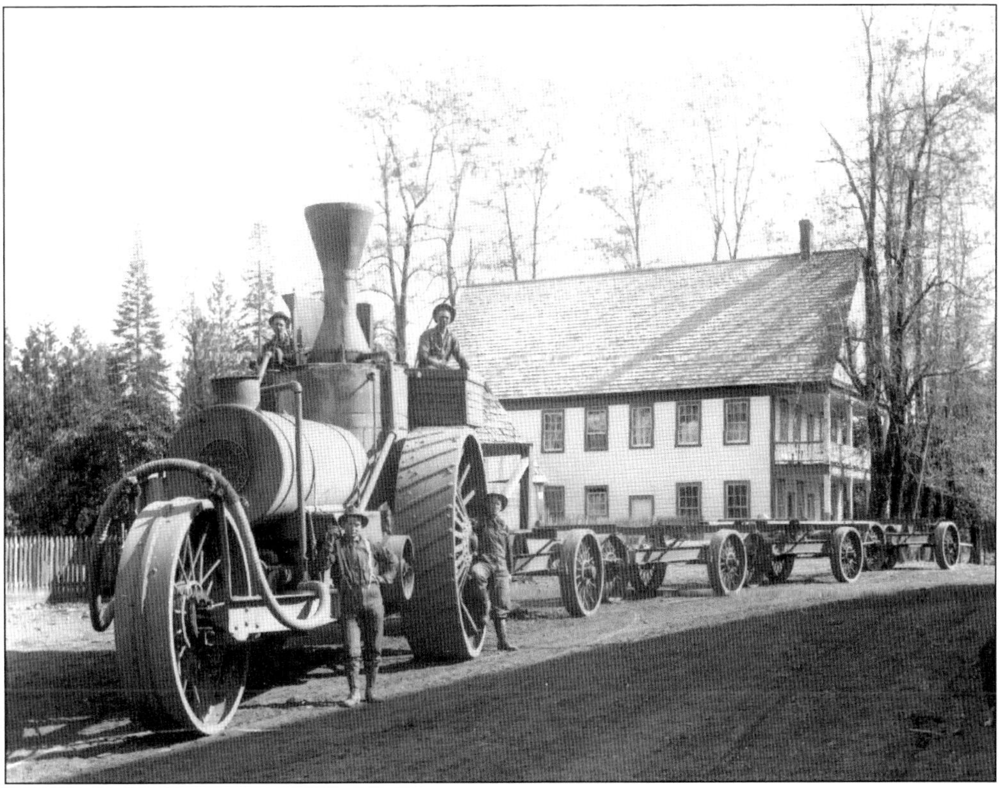

Clipper Mills, as its name suggests, began with lumber mills in the early 1850s, although there were also gold mines nearby. The water-powered mill on Grizzly Creek produced lumber for the Pine Grove House, at above right, built by Mr. Plant. The steam tractor passes the hotel on its way back to Barton House Mill for another load of lumber.

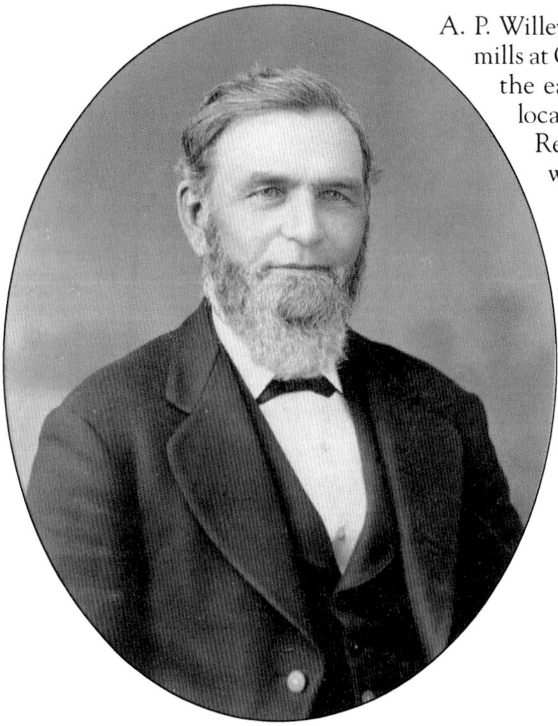

A. P. Willey, originally from Maine, was a partner in mills at Clipper Mills and Strawberry Valley during the early 1850s and 1860s. When he sold out locally, he moved his lumber operations to the Redwood Coast. By 1878, his headquarters were in San Francisco, where his elegant home graced the corner of Clay and Taylor Streets. (Courtesy Yuba County Library.)

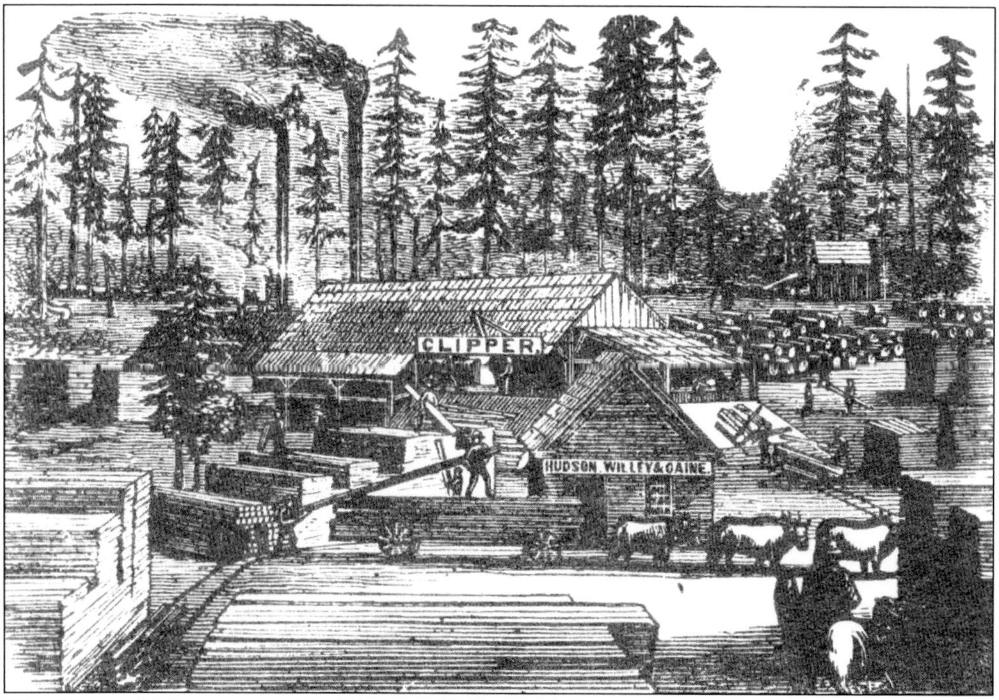


The Clipper Mill was owned by Hudson, Willey, and Caine in 1852. In the foreground, an ox-drawn wagon is being loaded with lumber. According to historian Florence Prater, the town was so named because some of the mill's machinery was sent from the east aboard a Clipper Ship. (1852 lithograph by unknown artist.)

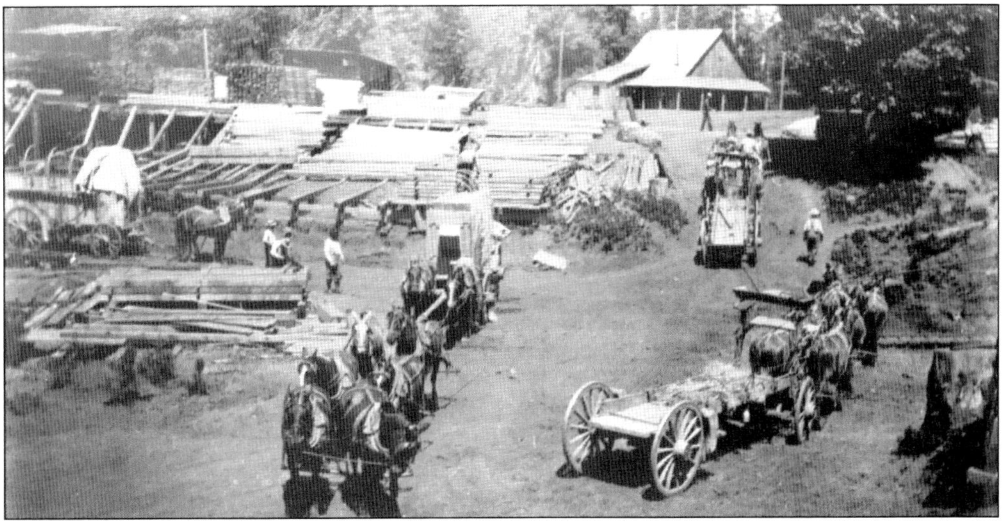

At the Clipper Mill lumber yard in 1865, a variety of wagons are loading and hauling lumber. The superintendent's house is in the right background.

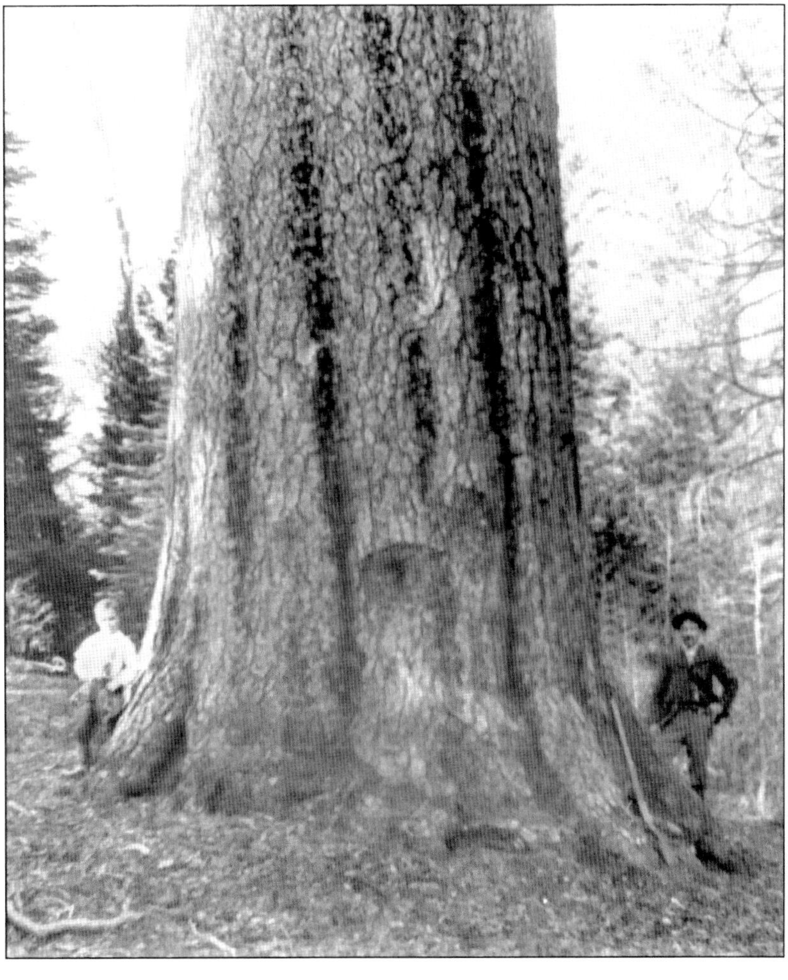

Trees grew to tremendous sizes in this region of the Sierra Nevada. This sugar pine measured nearly 15 feet in diameter at chest height. Bud Adams, at left, stands with his uncle Burt Adams in 1905. Sugar pine was valued not only for premium lumber, but for long-lasting roof shakes.

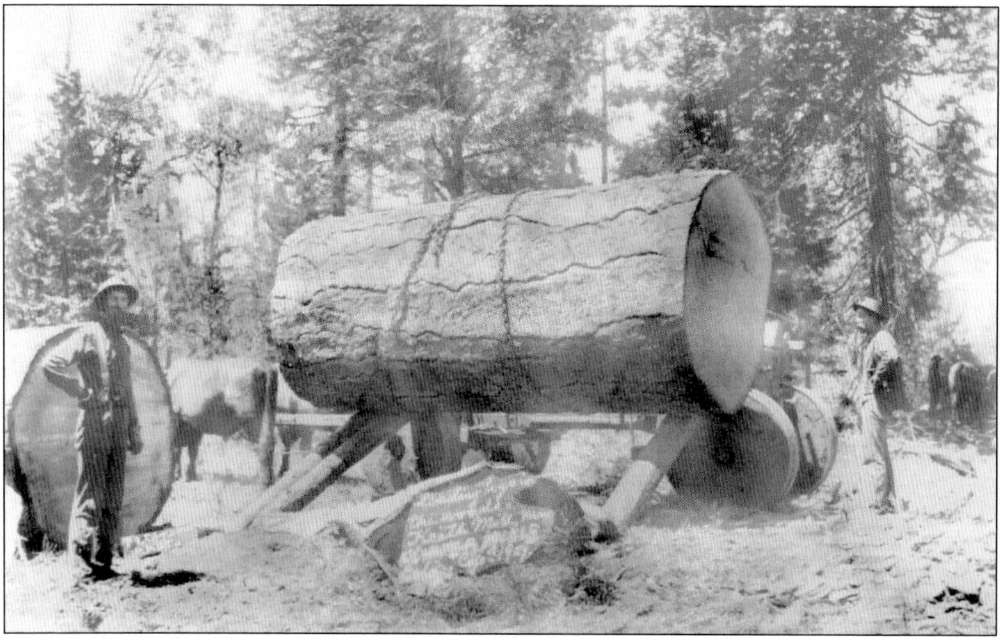

Teams of oxen provided the power to roll logs onto wagons and haul them to the mills. This ponderosa pine was harvested on Woodville Ridge and taken to the Keith Mill in July 1909.

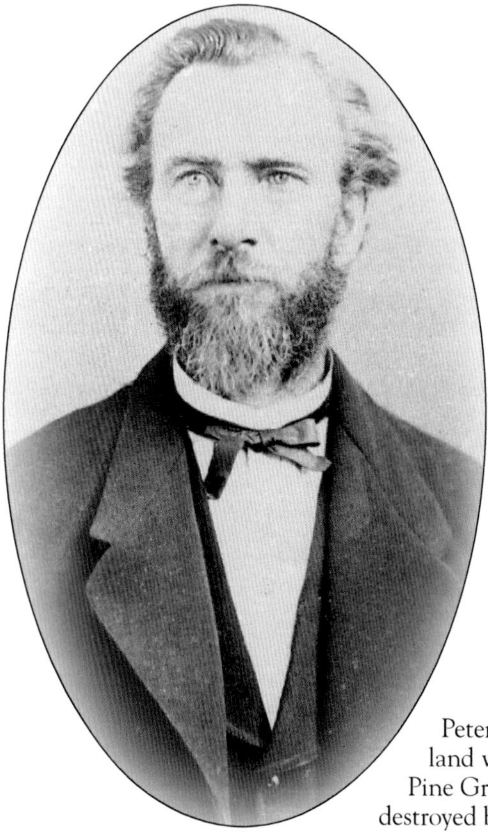

Peter Cornell, originally from New York, owned the land where Clipper Mills is now located. He built the Pine Grove House and operated it for years before it was destroyed by fire.

John Willey usually called the quadrilles for the balls at Pine Grove House, accompanied by the music of the violin and organ. Will Huk was a well-known fiddler who often played at the dances.

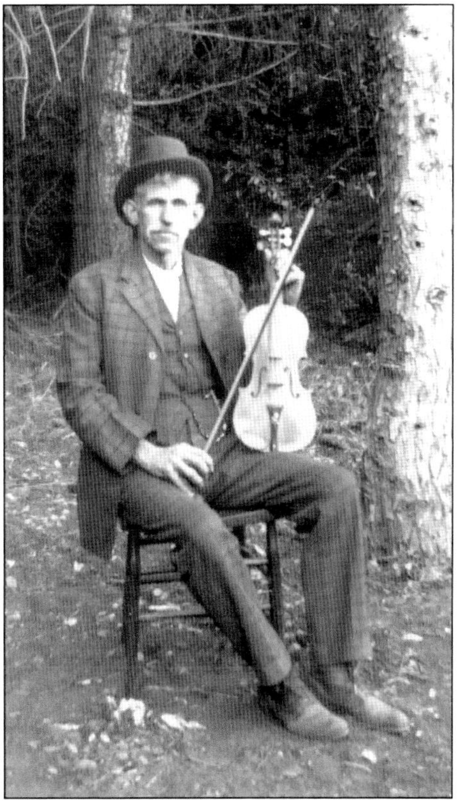

John F. Schultz rebuilt the Pine Grove House around 1874 and held dances in the upstairs ballroom. The hotel stood across the road from the present-day general store and post office. It burned to the ground in April 1917 and was not rebuilt. Only the black locust trees remain to mark the spot.

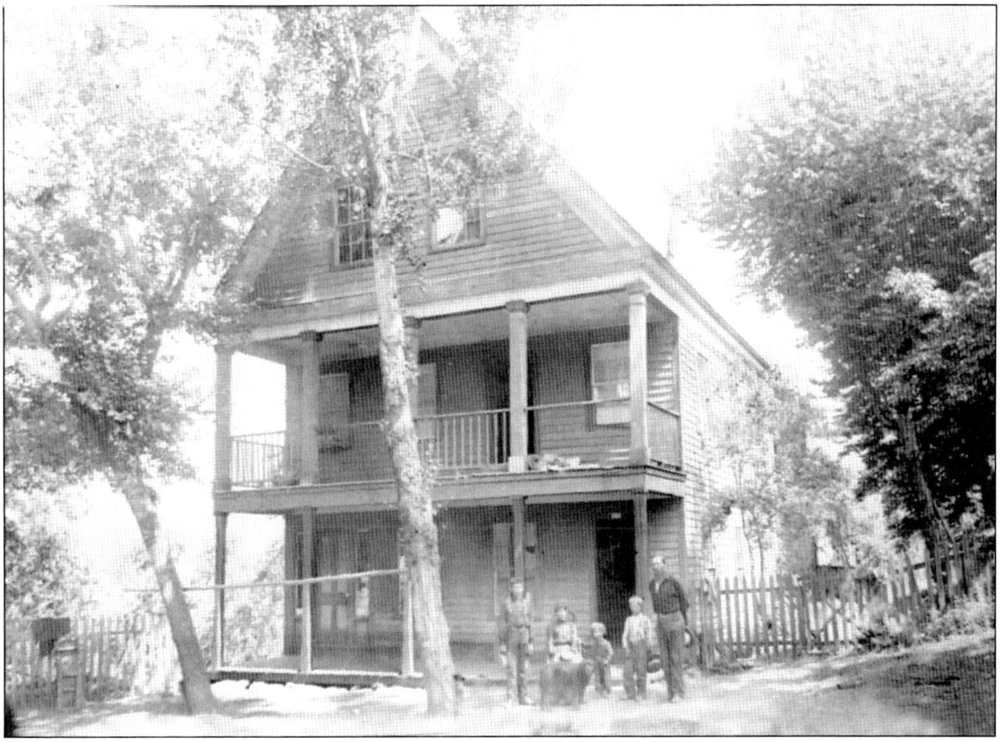

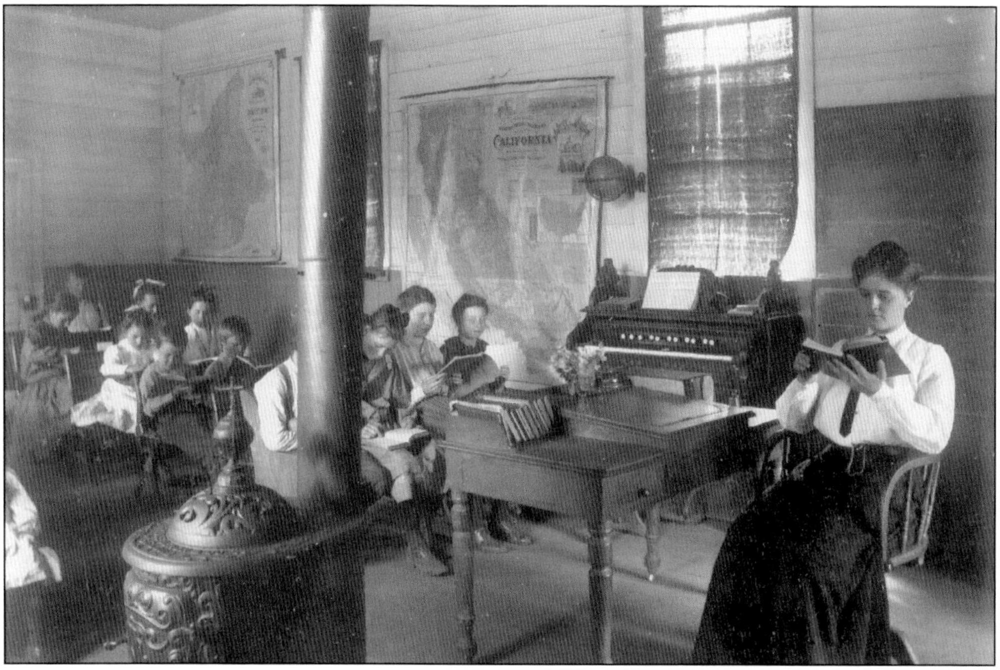


Students sat on benches at the Clipper Mills School, studying until the teacher, Miss Loveless, called for recitals at the front of the class. Around 1900, teachers were paid about $40 a month, and $20 went for room and board at the Pine Grove House. The first school was built near the present post office, and the second, which burned in the 1920s, was built near Oro Lewa Creek. The third was located nearby. The school joined Yuba Feather School District in 1960 and since then the old building has been a private home.

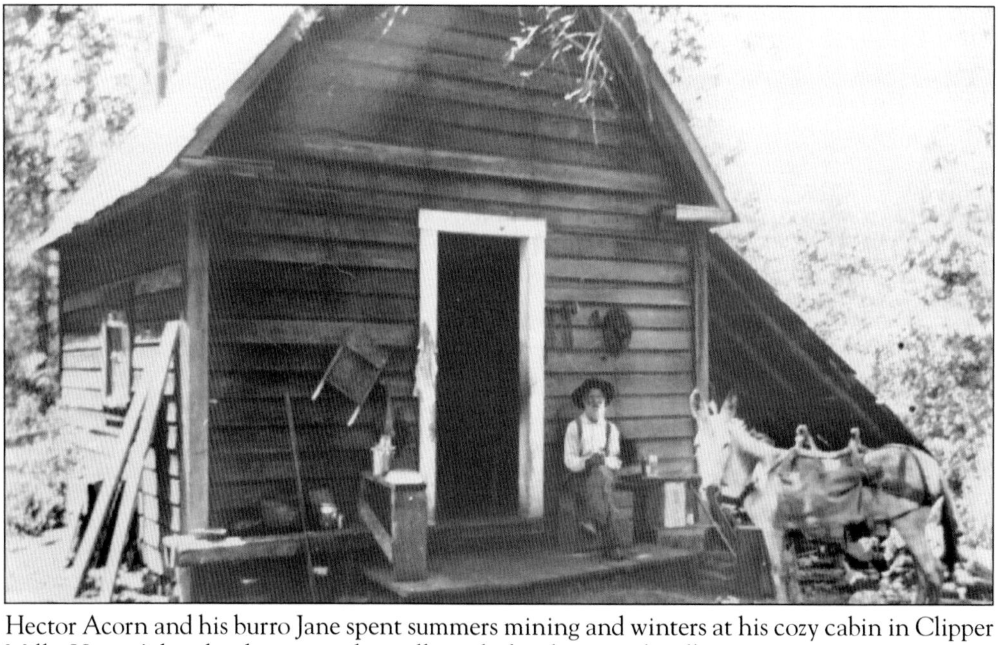

Hector Acorn and his burro Jane spent summers mining and winters at his cozy cabin in Clipper Mills. Hector's hatchet hangs on the wall, ready for chopping kindling.

Posing at right is Ming Chong Hay, a Chinese resident of Clipper Mills in the late 1870s and 1880s. This photograph was a *carte-de-visite*, or calling card, popular in the 19th century. They were given to a host or hostess when visiting their home.

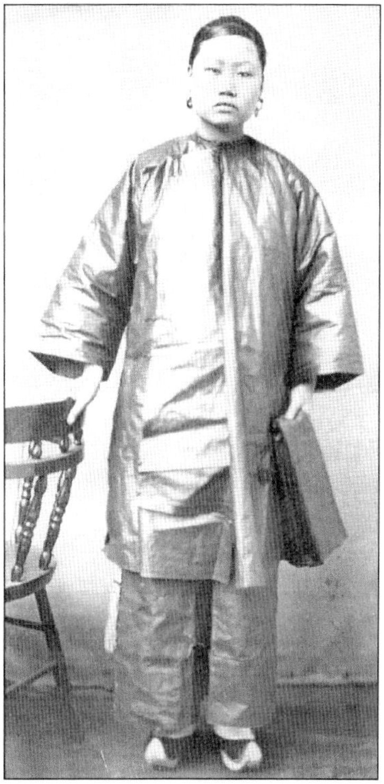

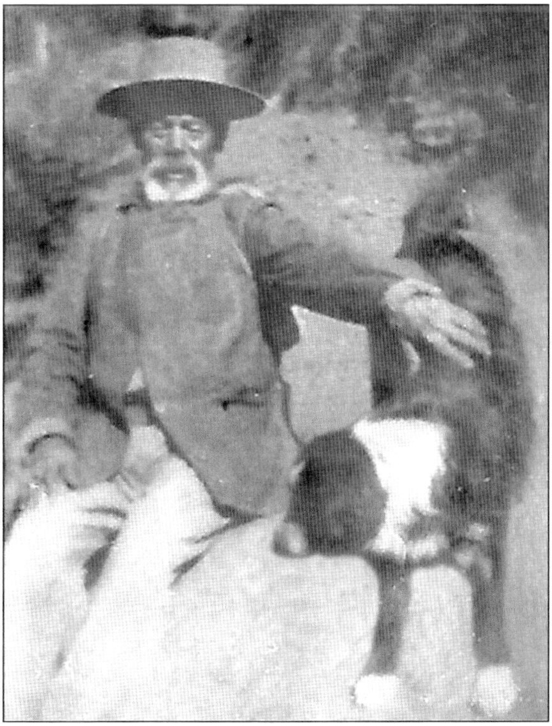

Sing Kee, at left in 1890, was a merchant in the Clipper Mills Chinatown, and a friend of the children. Lillie Bean remembered that he gave candy and Chinese nuts out on Chinese New Year.

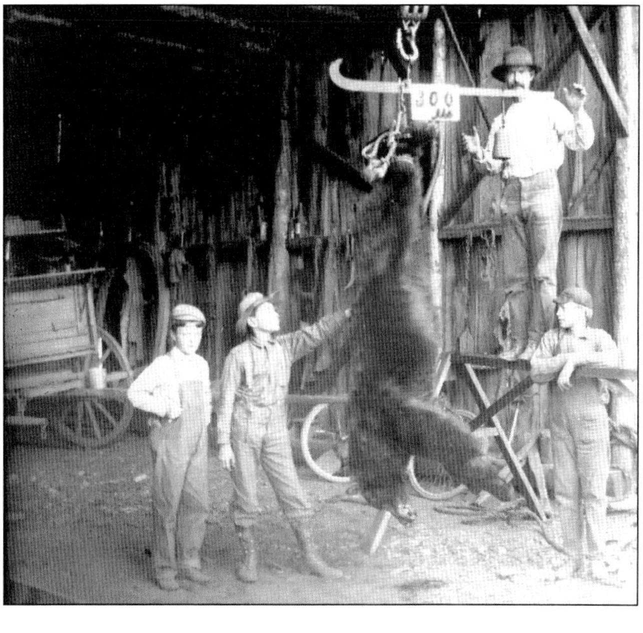


Mrs. Adams grew tired of the 300-pound bear ravaging her garden and orchard, so she shot and killed him. The men thought it as quite remarkable and they sent for Mr. Peterson, the photographer. Lou and Charles Wooley and Bud and Charles Adams posed near the beast, but Levina didn't get in this 1910 photograph.

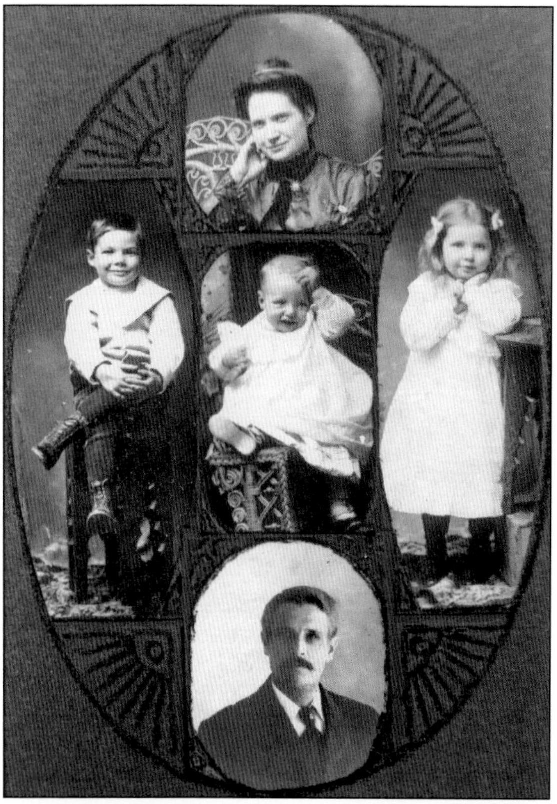

This collage includes photographer A. L. Peterson, his wife, and their children. He made hundreds of glass plates, recording the families and activities of the region.

The Peterson home, pictured in 1910, is still standing as a private residence. (Courtesy Ben Falck.)

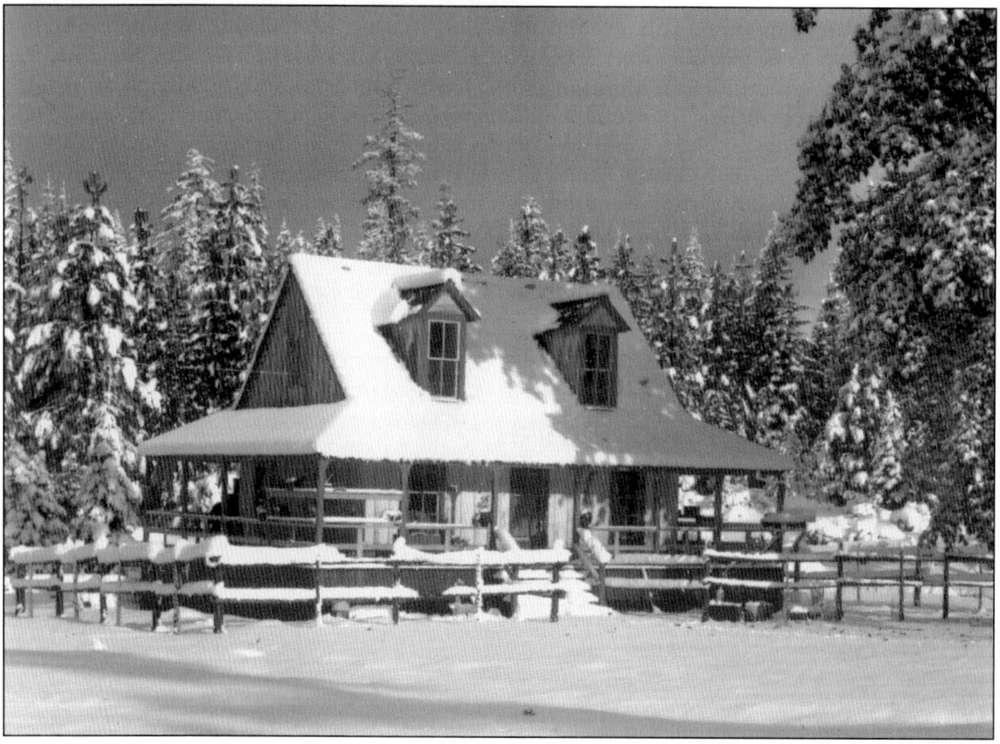

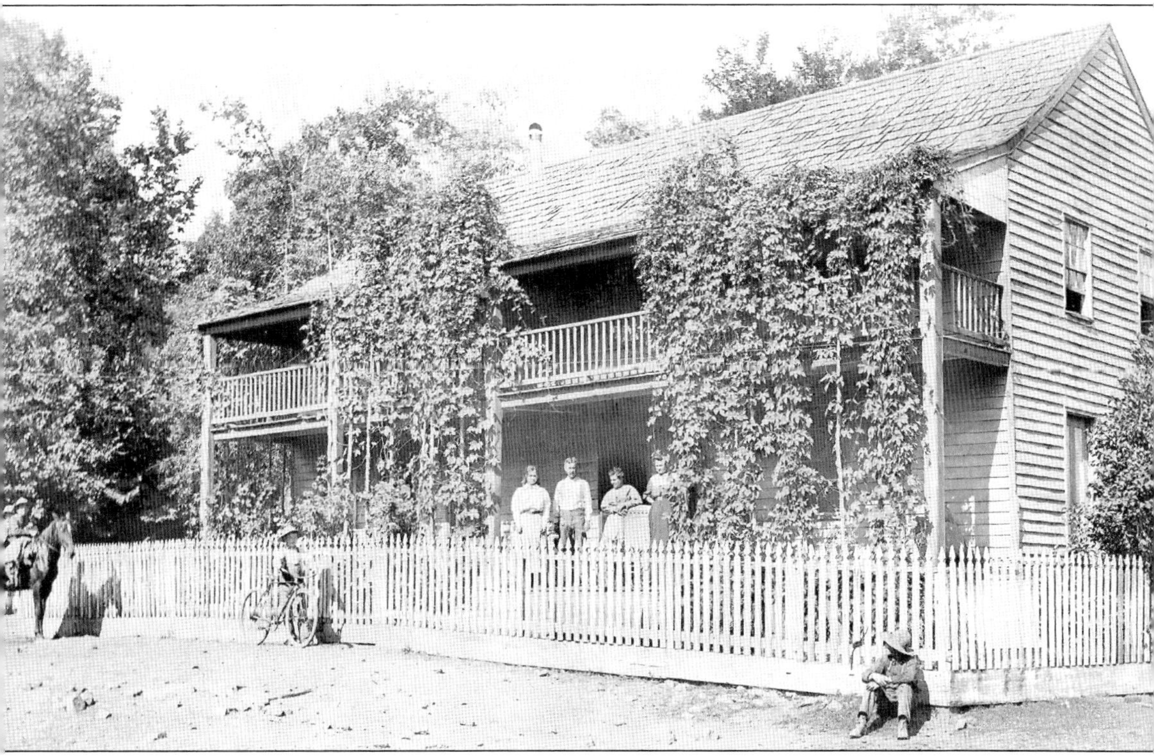

Eagle House Hotel was built by John D. Worden in 1852 at Oro Lewa and was operated for many years by the Adams family, who first settled here in 1848. Pictured here are Byron Stewart and Charles Gardener on the horse at left; Bud Adams on the bike; Emma, Charles, and Levina Adams, and Alice Peterson on the porch; and Earl Keith at right in front of the fence. Worden constructed his hotel entirely by hand without using any milled materials. The frame was of hand-hewn timbers, fastened with mortise-and-tenon joints. The floors were made of "puncheon" logs, hewn flat with an adze on one side and placed with the rounded side down. The roof and inside and outside walls were made of hand-split shakes. The inside walls were covered with canvas and eventually papered. Water was brought from the Oro Lewa Spring 900 feet away by log pipes. These were made by 3-inch holes the length of 10-foot logs that were then fastened together and sealed at the joints with caulking. When sparks from the chimney set the 92-year-old hotel on fire on June 9, 1944, it reduced to ashes the oldest landmark on the La Porte Road.

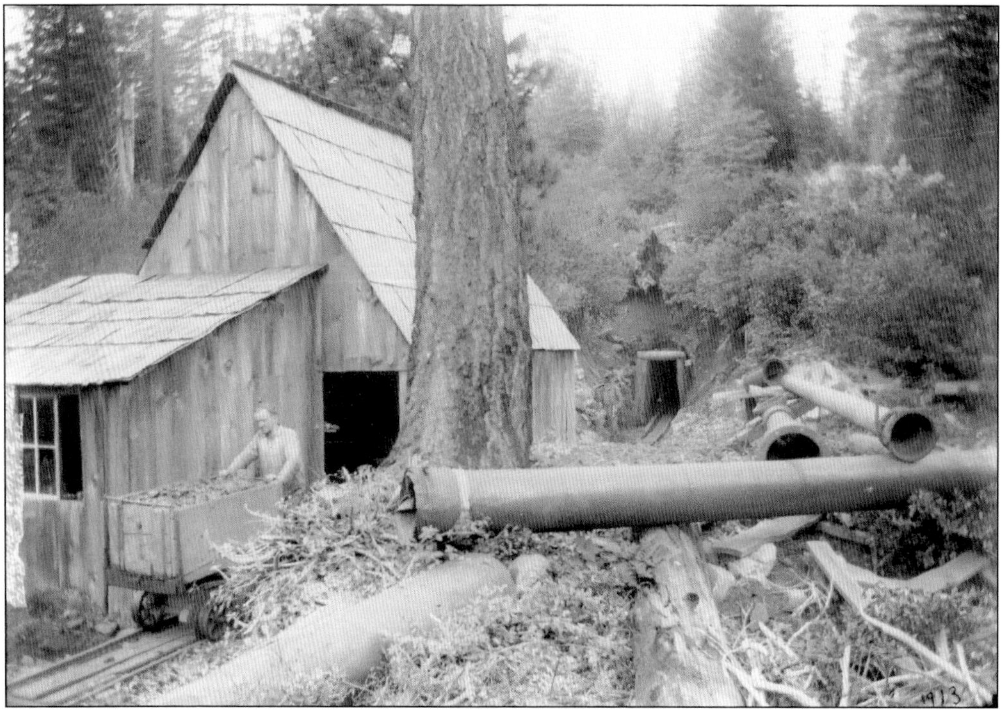

The Kingbird Quartz Mine was owned and operated by Rufus Bean, who is pushing an ore car out of the tunnel. Also operating at the time were the Klondike, McFarlin Hill, Burgotresser, Kickapoo, and Eagle Gulch Mines.

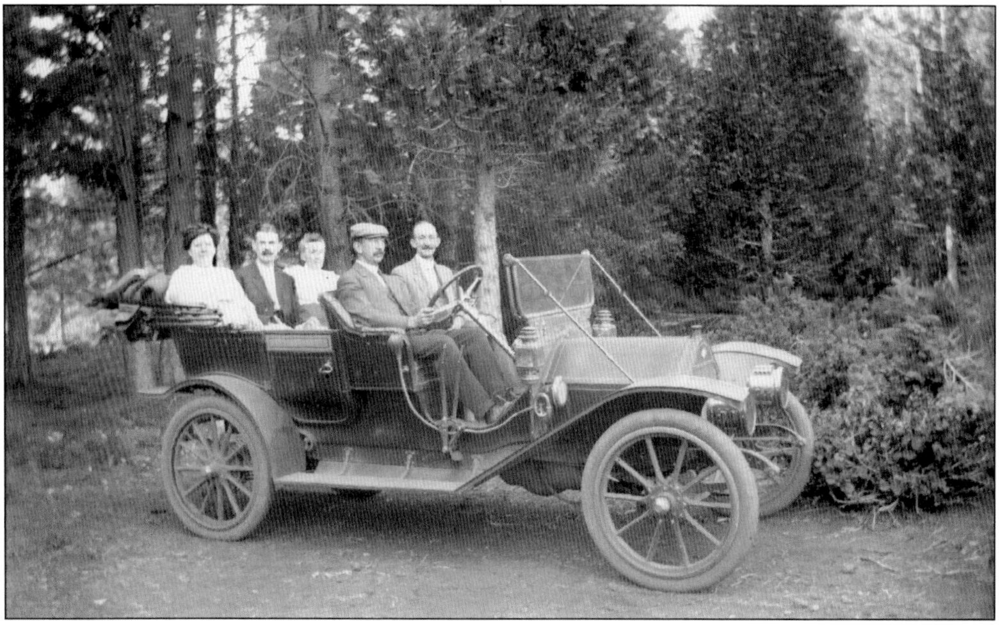

The Binet family was the first in the region to own an automobile and their jaunts through local towns were carefully noted. From his post as toll keeper at Woodleaf on June 19, 1907, Mr. Twogood noted, "The man with the auto passed by today." The Binets owned a lumber mill near their home on Grizzly Creek.

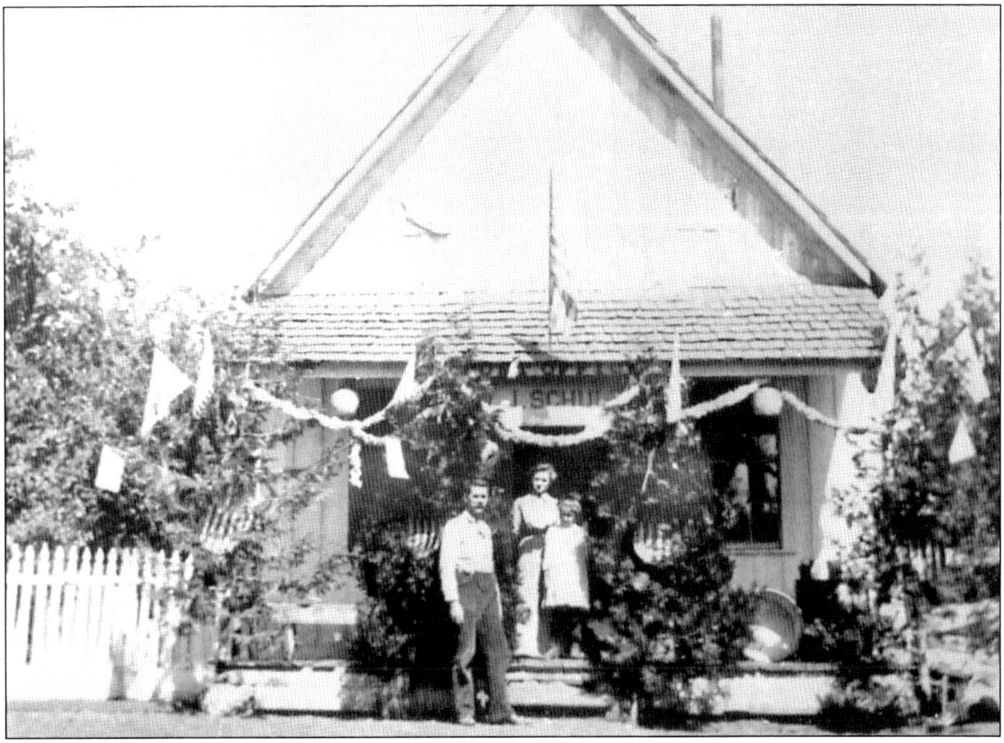

The post office opened in Clipper Mills on August 13, 1861, and Enoch Pratt built the first store across the road from the Pine Grove House. Will Schultz was the postmaster in 1900 and also owned the store. He and his family decorated the building with flags and bunting to celebrate the Fourth of July.

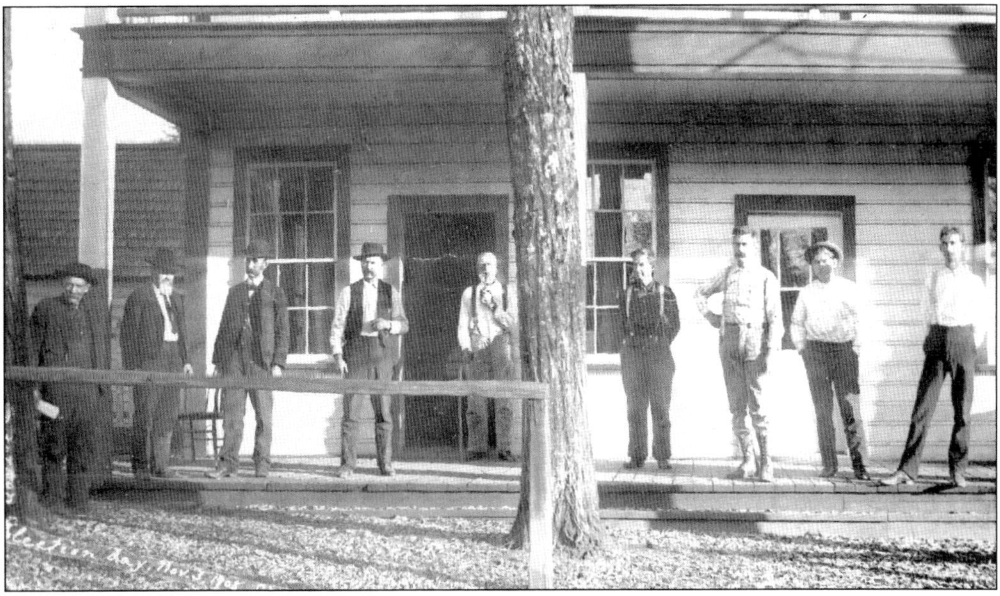

On election day, November 3, 1908, the men lined the porch of the Pine Grove Hotel, the polling place. Pictured here, from left to right, are Albion Bean, Rufus Bean Sr., Ed Binet, Charles Adams, Eddie Schultz, Lincoln Adams, Will Schultz, Walt Walker, and George Sharrer.

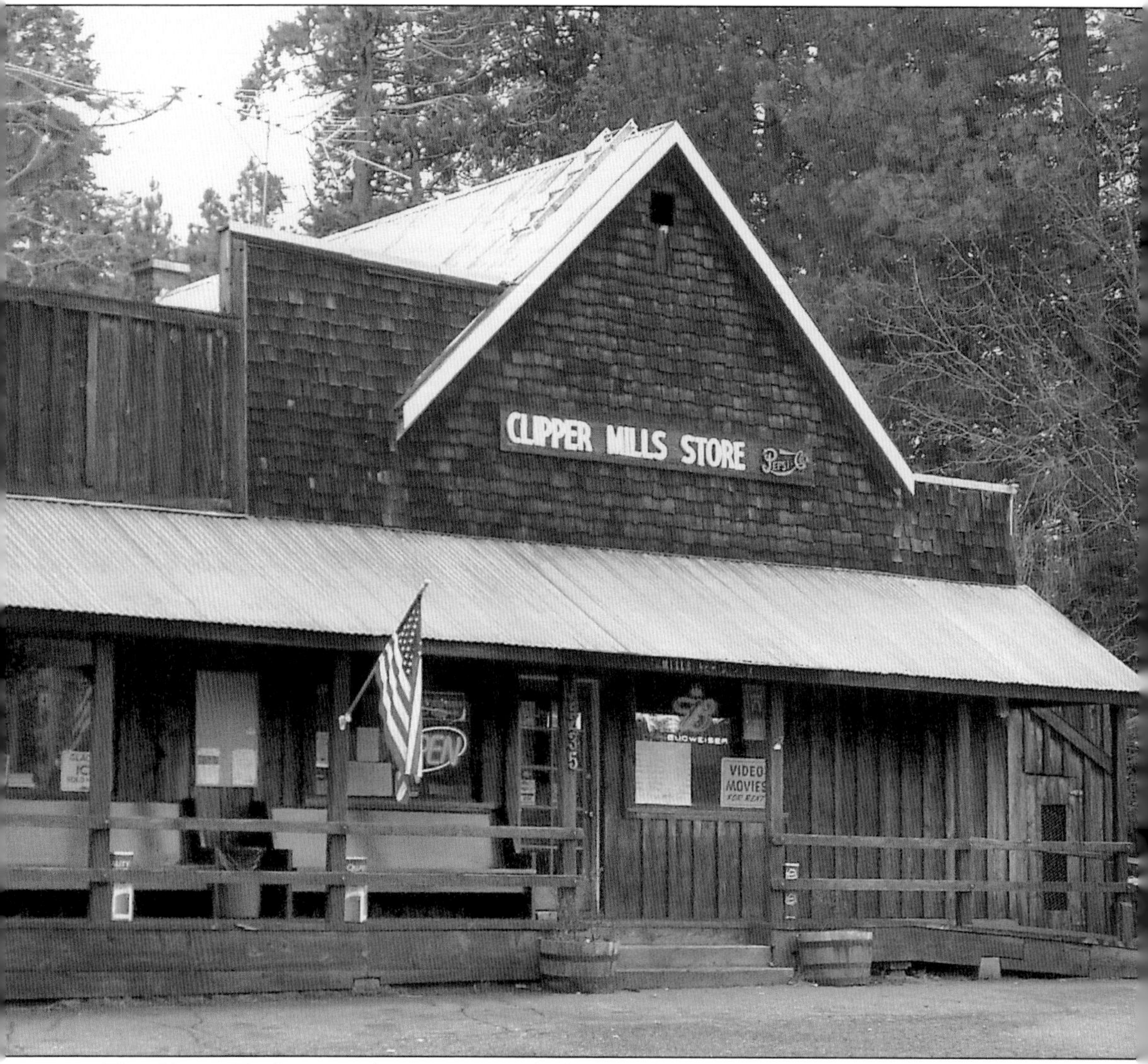


The Clipper Trader general store is in nearly the same location as the first one built in the 1850s. Clipper Mills today is home to residents who represent many walks of life. They proudly support their own fire department, and the town is the base for the *Rabbit Creek Journal*, a privately owned, weekly newspaper that has covered news of the Yuba Feather Hills since 1978. (Courtesy Aleta Joseph and Leonard Travis.)

# *Nine*

# STRAWBERRY VALLEY

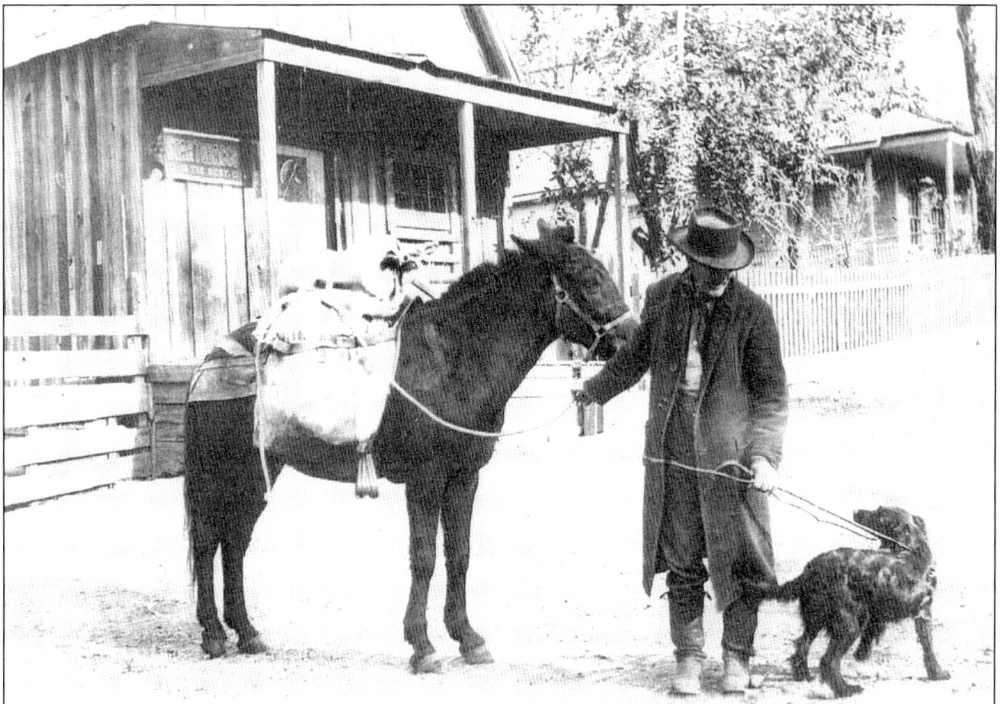

When gold seekers stopped for refreshment at a whiskey saloon under a brush shed, they also found the remains of a man with a rope around his neck. His identity and the reason for his execution was a mystery, but this wasn't enough to discourage a party of miners and entrepreneurs in 1850. Captain William and Wesley Mock, David Garvin, Boon and William Christopher, Joseph Vaughn, T. G. H. Jones, and John R. Perkins saw golden opportunities and built the Mountain Cottage Hotel. They used their old log cabin as an ice house and sold the ice in Marysville. The abundance of strawberry vines led Mock to choose the town's name. The general store, above, was built in 1853. A miner with his pack animal and dog leave James H. Drake's store with a load of provisions around 1870. (Courtesy Carl Mautz.)

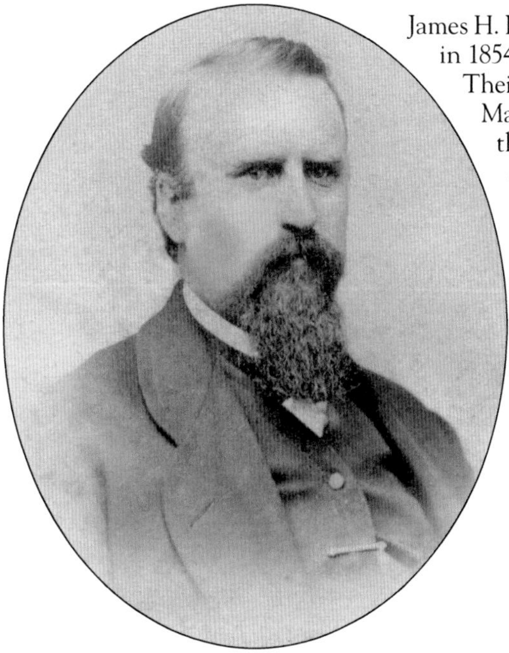

James H. Drake, a native of New York, came to California in 1854 and married Henrietta Buckius the same year. Their children, Harvey Scott, Edward DeForest, and Mary, grew up in Strawberry Valley. Drake bought the Corey store in 1857 and operated it until his sons took over. Wells Fargo established their express office in 1861, and Drake was the agent from 1880 to 1896. He also served as justice of peace and had interests in the Pinkard Creek Mine. Other mines in the region included Eagleville.

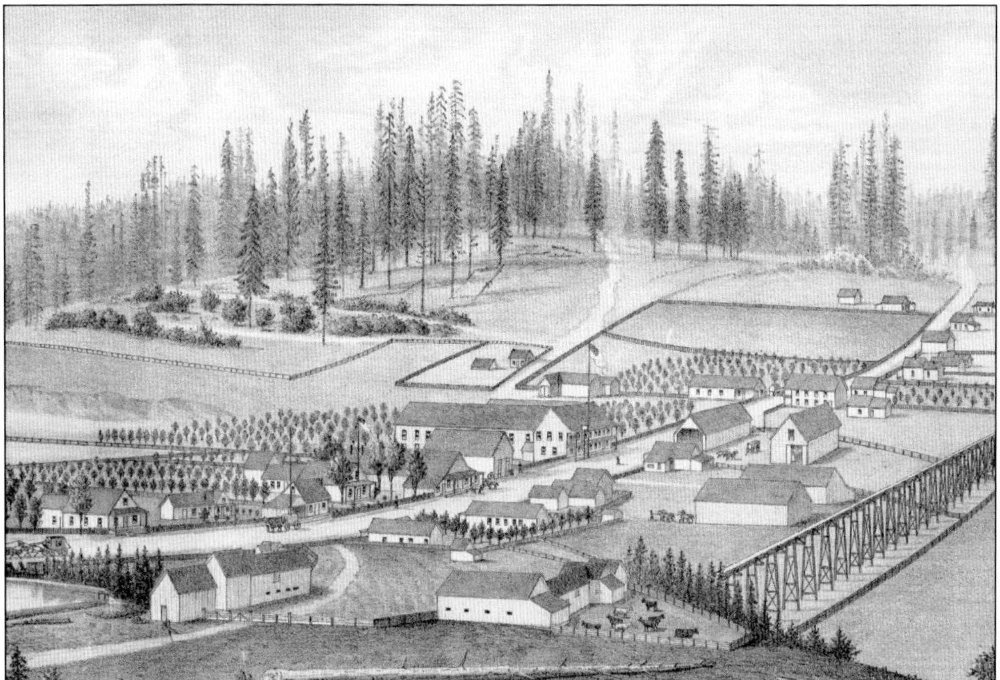

By 1879, the town was crowded with shops and businesses, including two hotels, a post office, Wells Fargo, a blacksmith, a butcher, a saloon, and a carpenter shop. Callaghan and Company built a hall for meetings of the Sons of Temperance and the Dashaway Club. The busy townsfolk also had a Sunday school, an Alpine Lodge International Order of Good Templars, an Excelsior Literary and Library Association, and a semi-monthly paper, the *Clarion*. (Illustration from *History of Yuba County*, Wells and Chamberlain, 1879.)

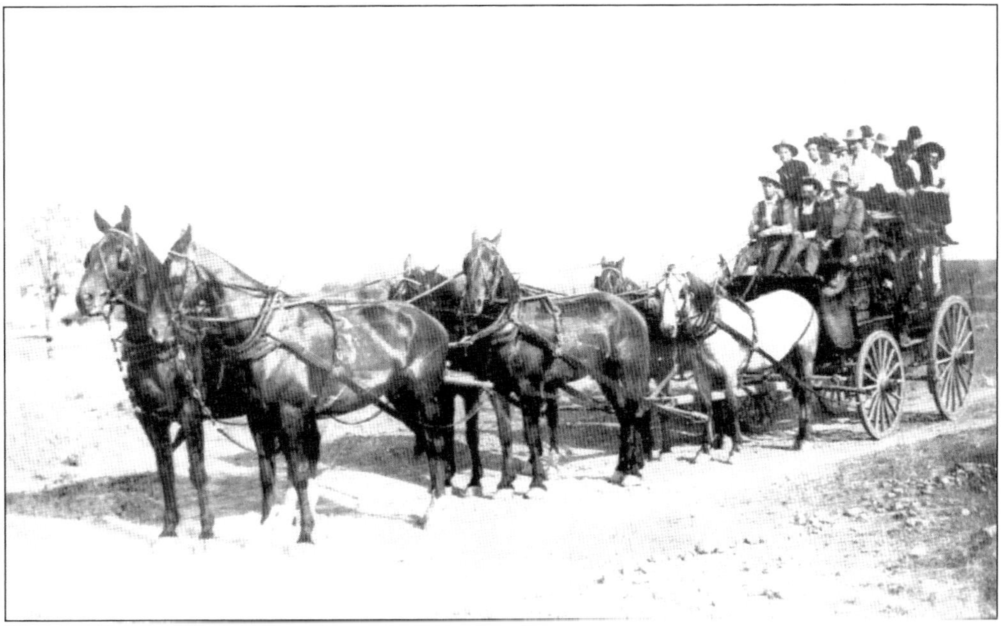

Oscar Pauly's stage was loaded with passengers inside and on top when it made a stop at Strawberry Valley on its way to La Porte. Pauly, a native of Germany, came to California overland in the 1850s and became an express agent on the route between Marysville and the mines in the high country.

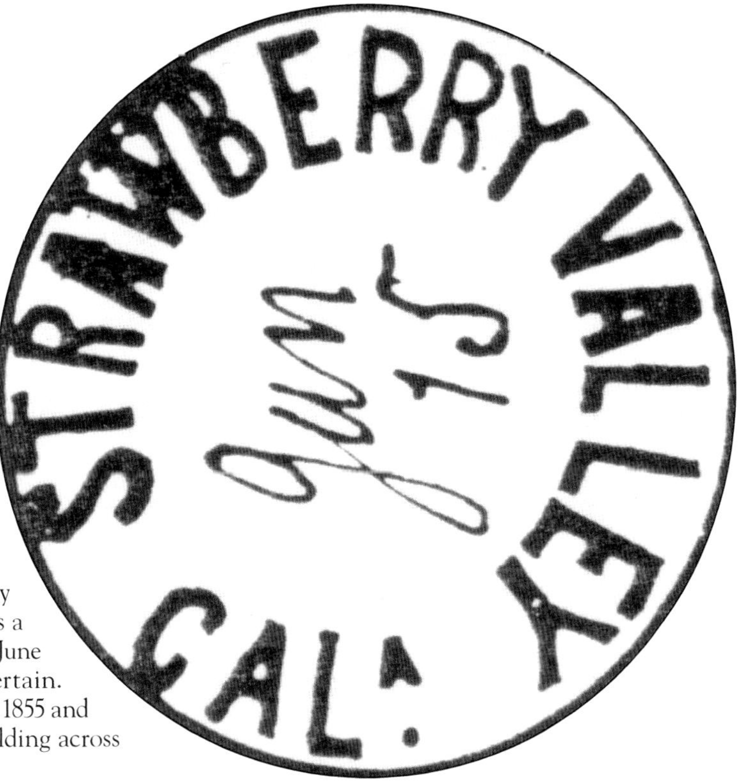


An early Strawberry Valley postal cancellation bears a hand-written notation of June 15, but the year is uncertain. The post office opened in 1855 and now operates from a building across from the general store.

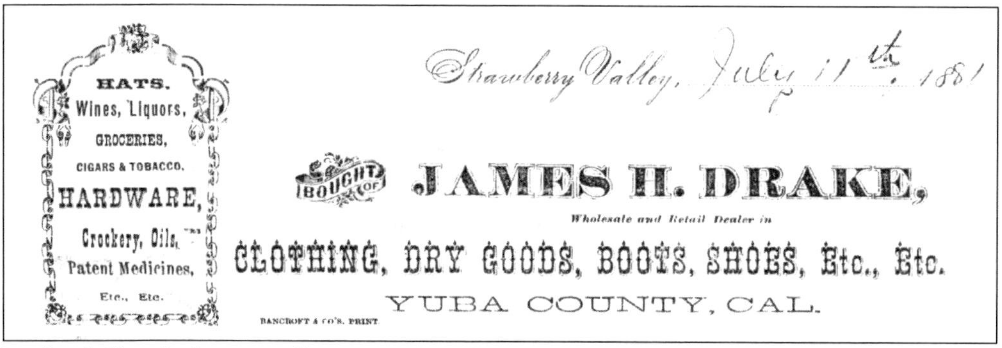
HATS.
Wines, Liquors,
GROCERIES,
CIGARS & TOBACCO,
HARDWARE,
Crockery, Oils,
Patent Medicines,
Etc., Etc.

Strawberry Valley, July 11th, 1881

BOUGHT OF JAMES H. DRAKE,
Wholesale and Retail Dealer in
CLOTHING, DRY GOODS, BOOTS, SHOES, Etc., Etc.
YUBA COUNTY, CAL.
BANCROFT & CO'S. PRINT

Drake's billhead advertises all manner of goods, including hats, liquors, groceries, cigars, tobacco, hardware, crockery, patent medicines, clothing, and shoes. He also provided services as a banker, making loans, trading gold dust for gold coin, and depositing money for clients.

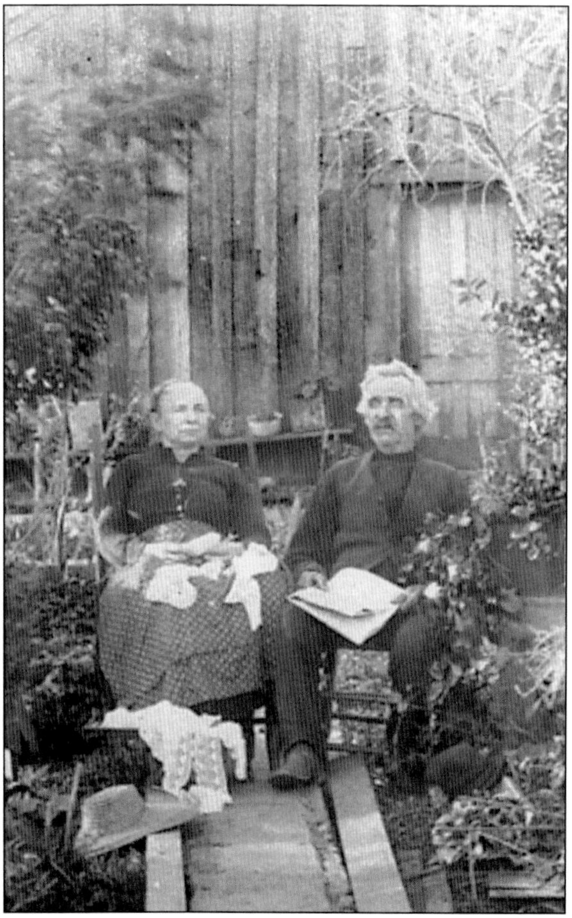

James T. and Elizabeth Birmingham enjoy lunch in their garden around 1890. James owned the toll road from Woodleaf to Strawberry Valley and was also the toll keeper. He sold the road to Yuba County for $600 in 1906. The toll rates were 25¢ for a man on a horse, 75¢ for a two-horse buggy and driver, 75¢ for a two-horse stagecoach, 3¢ for each sheep, 2¢ for each head of cattle, and it was free of charge for a miner and pack animal.

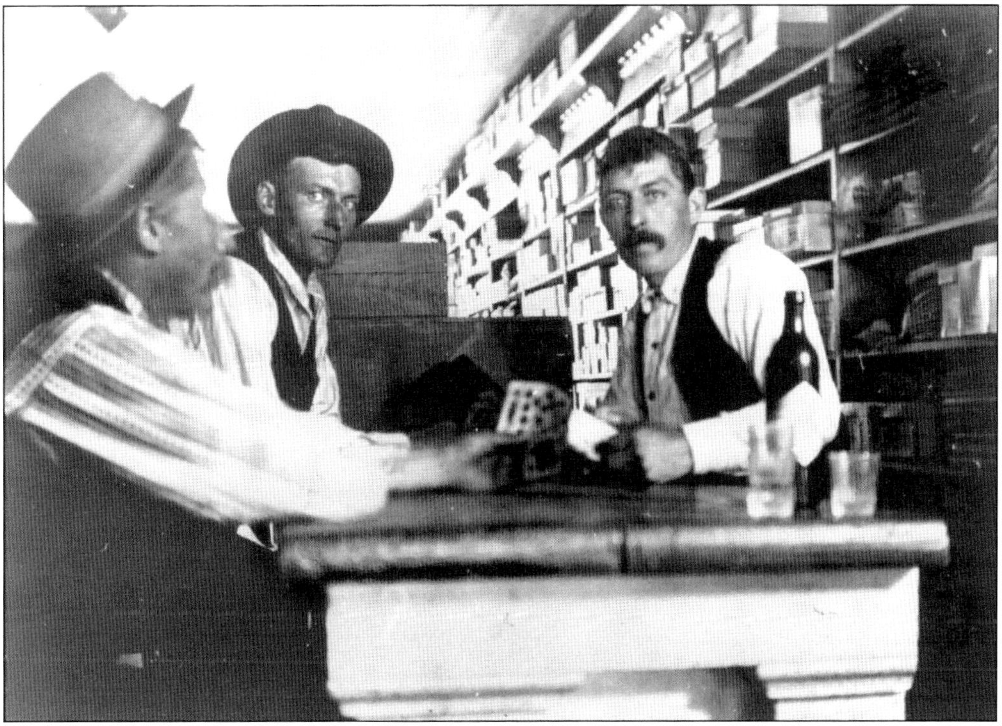

James H. Drake's sons Harvey S. and Edwin D. F. ran the store after their father died, and patrons not only shopped for essentials, but enjoyed occasional poker games with Ed, at above right. (Courtesy Jann Garvis.)

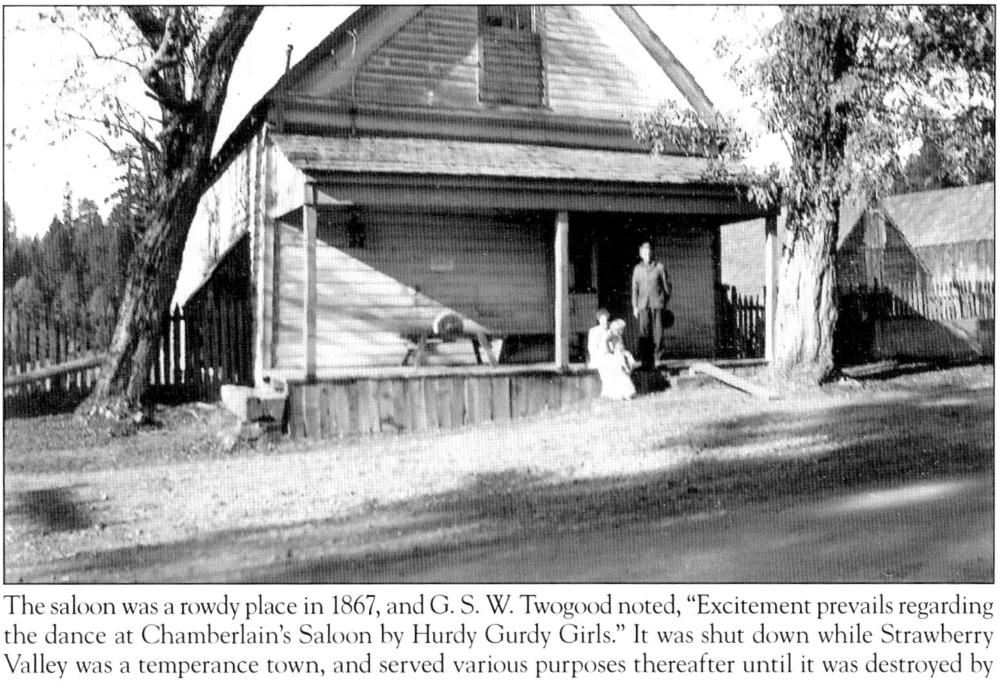

The saloon was a rowdy place in 1867, and G. S. W. Twogood noted, "Excitement prevails regarding the dance at Chamberlain's Saloon by Hurdy Gurdy Girls." It was shut down while Strawberry Valley was a temperance town, and served various purposes thereafter until it was destroyed by fire in 1965.

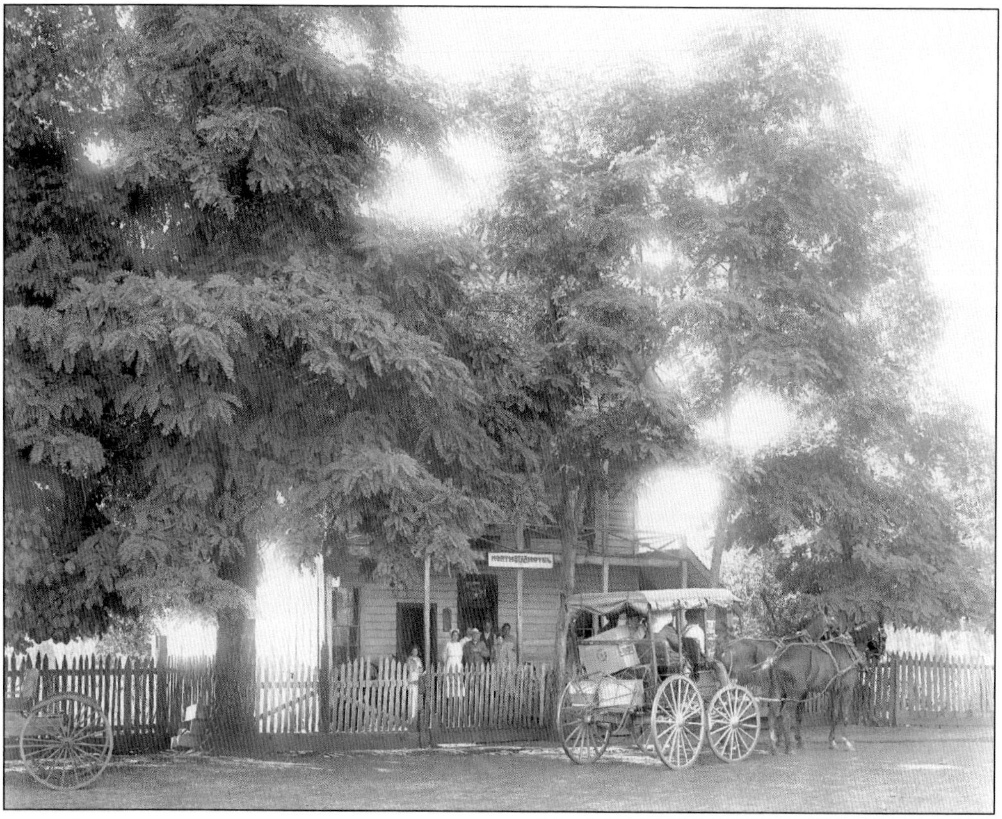

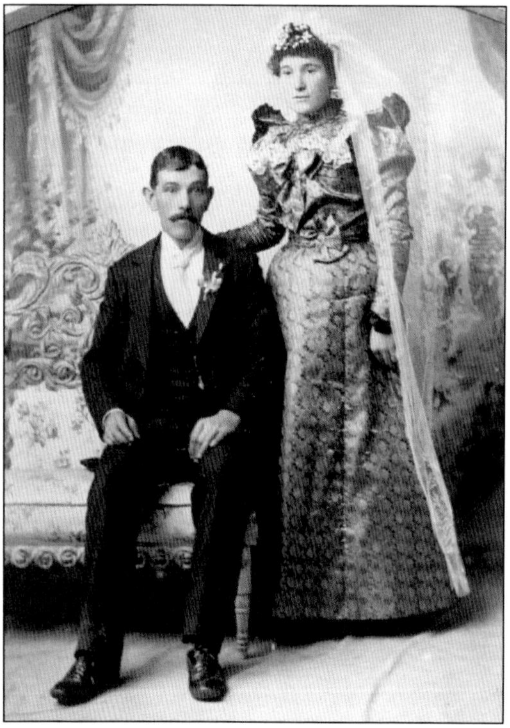

The Marysville–La Porte Stage had a regular stop at the North Star Hotel c. 1880 for passengers, their luggage, and the mail. The hotel was located a few miles up the road from Strawberry Valley. Frederick and Sophia (Burdewick) Onken came from Germany in 1852 and bought the hotel and 360 acres in 1875. Today, only the water trough and a few black locust trees mark the location.

William and Addie (Tompkins) Onken, at left, pose for a photograph on their wedding day. They ran the North Star Hotel after his parents died and, with their three daughters, marketed the apples, pears, and other fruit from their orchard. William was a trustee and clerk on the Strawberry Valley school district for years.

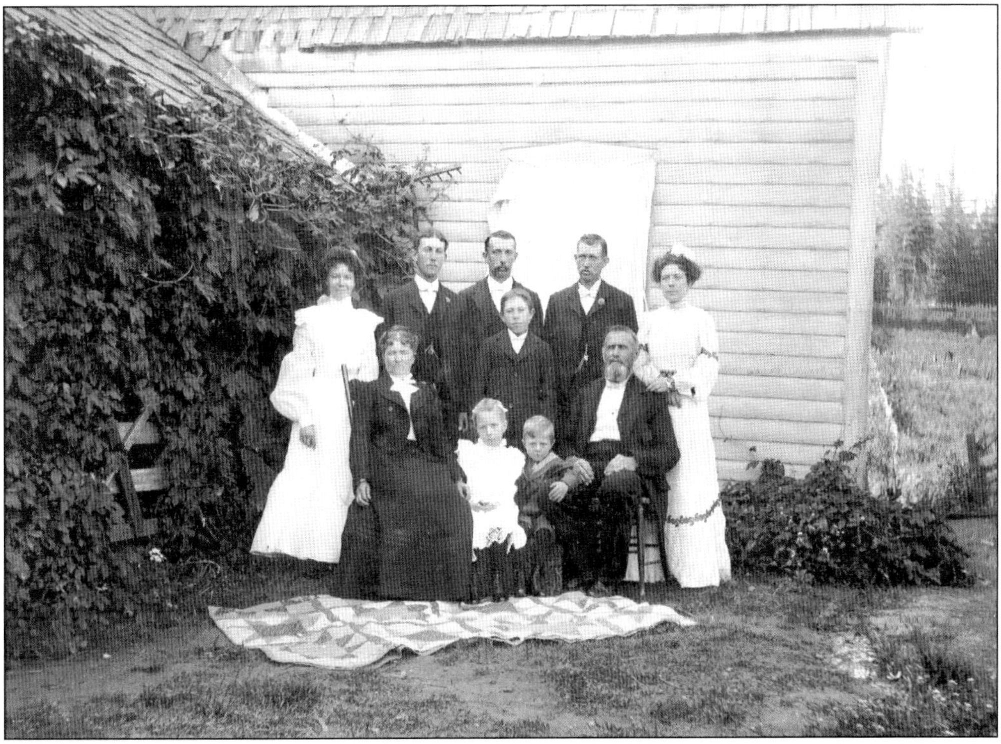

Joel Bean of Maine came to California in 1856 and held mining interests in Sierra and Plumas Counties. He was a member of the state militia at La Porte before buying the Scales Hotel. The family included, from left to right, Lincoln's children (first row) Nettie and Frank; (second row) Mary, Vernon, and Joel; and (third row) Amanda, Morgan, Lincoln, John, and Laura. Joel later bought the Columbus House in Strawberry Valley and moved there.

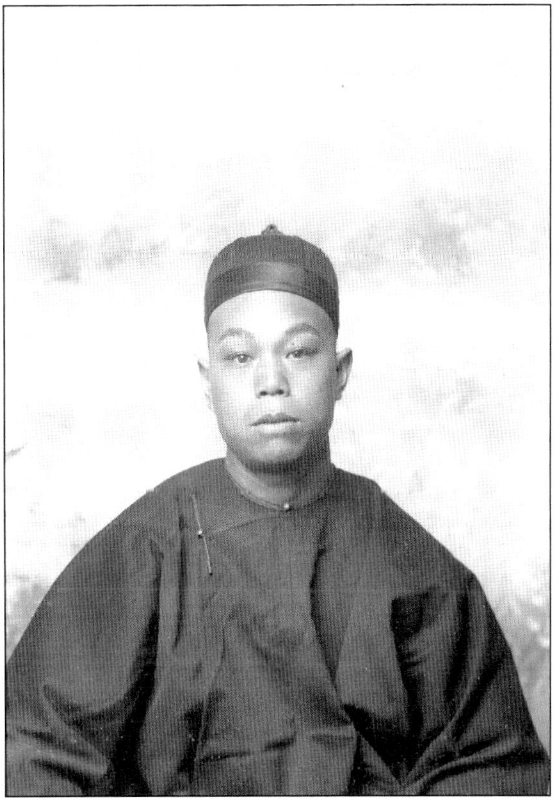

The Beans employed Ah Coon, the Chinese cook, whose talents were fondly recalled by Beryl Fry in a few words, "Oh, those great big sugar cookies!"

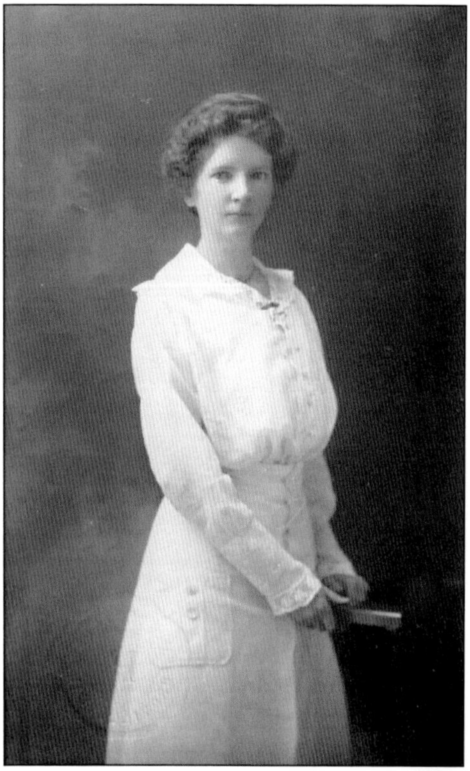

Nellie (Orr) Starr Bean taught in Humboldt County before marrying John A. Bean. She taught at the Strawberry Valley School from 1918 to 1930. Her starting wage was $75 per month, and by 1930 the salary had increased to $1,200 annually. Because of deep snow in winter, school classes began in April or May and ran until October. Nellie was fond of her students and bought Christmas presents for them every year, even after they graduated from school.

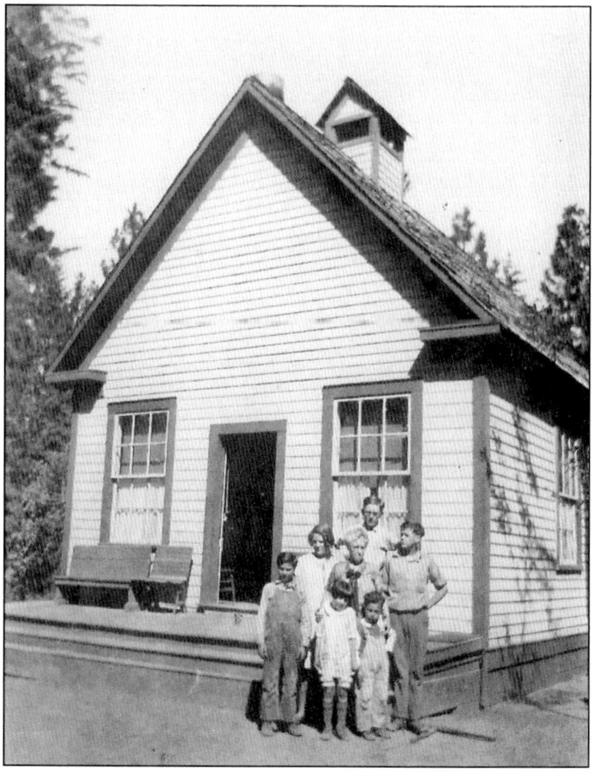

In 1910, the Strawberry Valley School had six pupils. Pictured here, from left to right, are (first row) Jimmy Williams, Bernice Bean, and Lloyd Silva; (second row) Loretta Gee, teacher Nellie Bean, and Stanley Travis, and (third row) Henry Gee. The school unified with Yuba Feather School in Challenge in 1949 and later became part of the Marysville Joint Unified District. The school bell was preserved and is mounted in the bell tower at Yuba Feather School in Challenge.

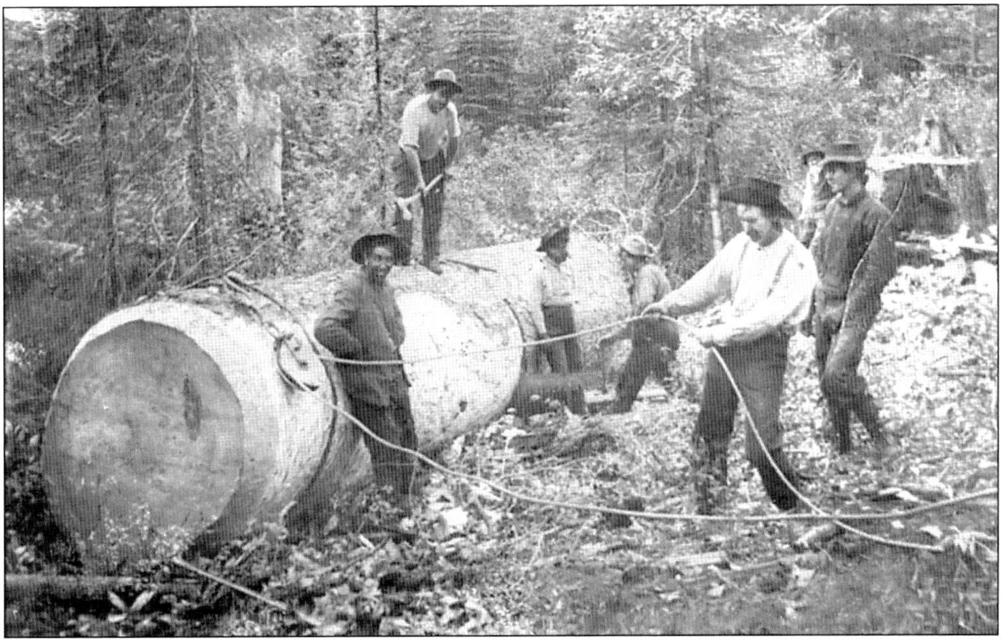

Bucking a log on Barton Hill near Strawberry Valley, the loggers use 10-foot saws called misery whips to cut the felled timber into manageable sections around 1905. The men in the foreground fasten cables around the log that are used to haul it to the mill.

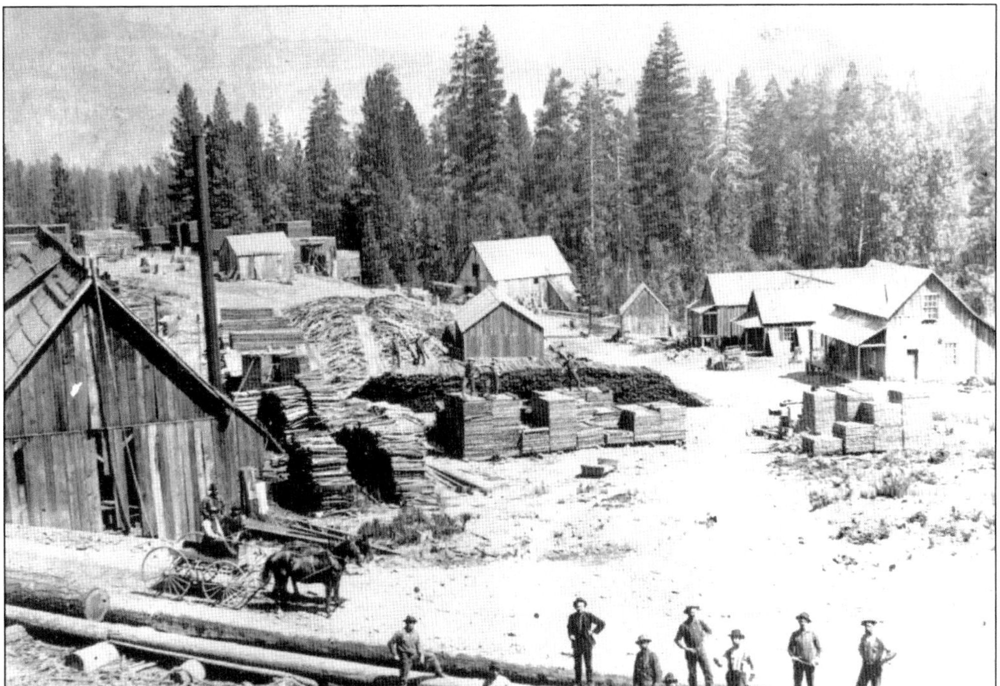

Lumberjacks paused in their work long enough for someone to photograph the mill at Strawberry Valley, c. 1885. Workers in the foreground stand in the chute where logs were dragged into the mill.

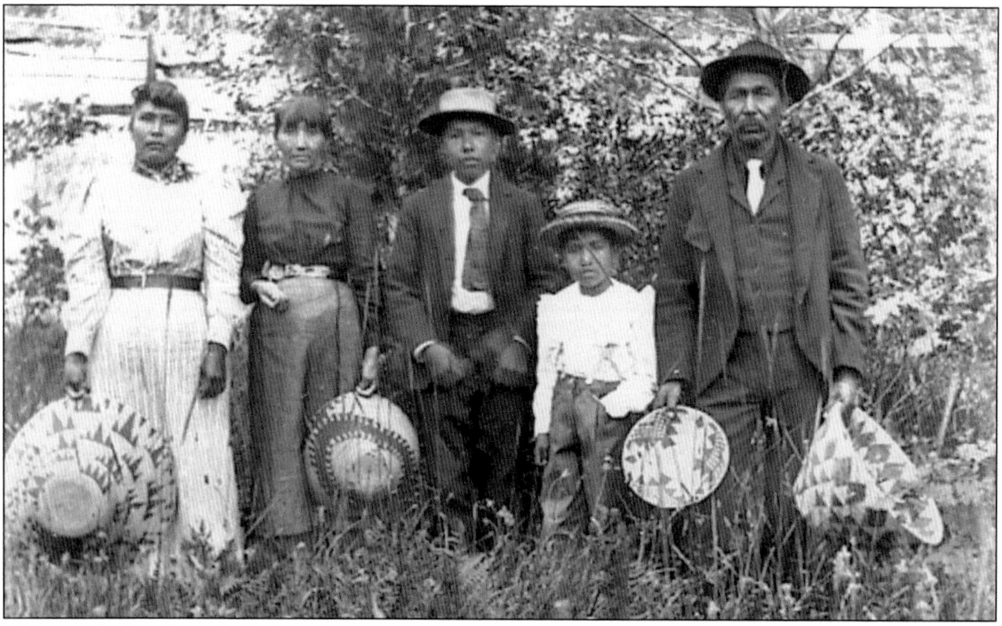

The Maidu family included Sophie Kennedy, her mother, Nellie Kennedy Johnson, Alex Picayune, Elizabeth Johnson, and Sam Johnson, Nellie's husband. Nellie and her family moved from her birthplace at Woodleaf after their tribe was granted a half-acre parcel in Strawberry Valley in 1916, the smallest reservation in the country. They hold some of the prized baskets made by the women. Nellie lived to age 110 and could recall the tribe's first contact with fur trappers around 1833.

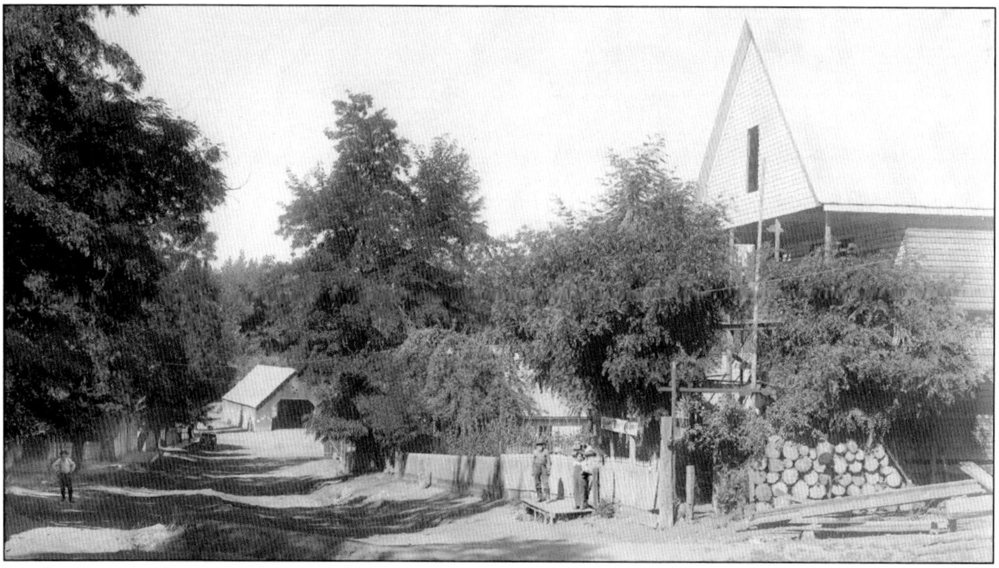

Looking west, the Strawberry Valley Hotel at right offers cigars, tobacco, and candies, and had an enormous vegetable garden in the front yard. Edwin Magruder bought the property in the 1930s and used the salvaged material from two hotels to build his home, which still stands today. Further down the road, the freight barn is visible. Huge doors on both ends enabled the freight wagons to drive through and unload, where goods were stored for the long winters. (Courtesy Yuba County Library.)

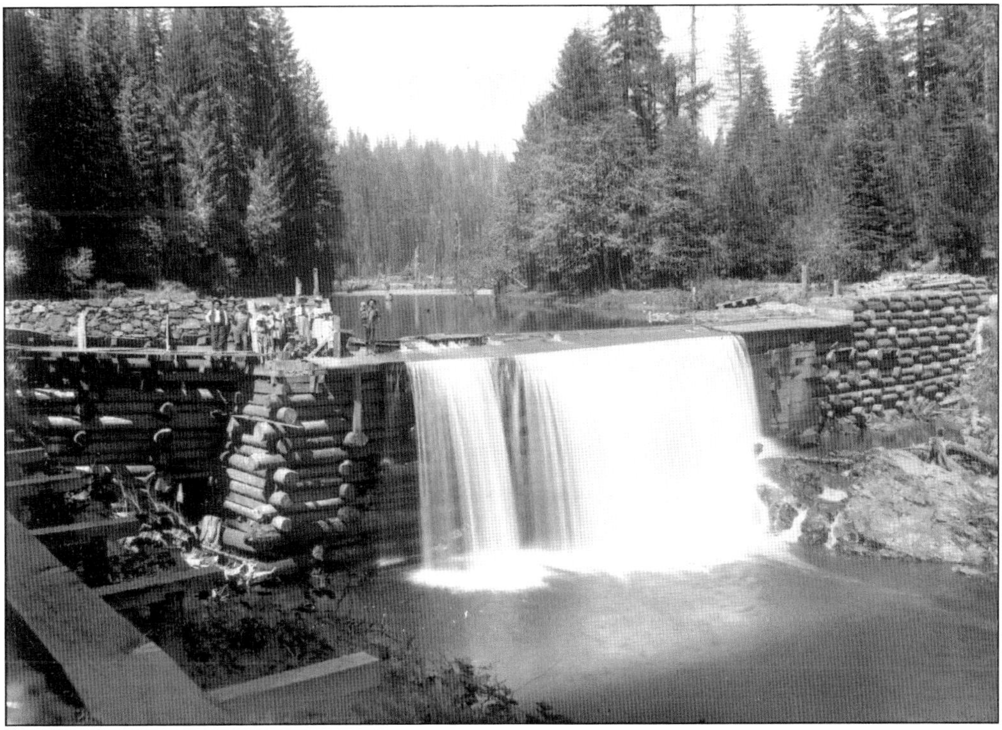

The log dam on Lost Creek was built by the South Feather Water Company to provide water for gold-mining operations and agriculture. This structure was later replaced with a larger, higher concrete dam.

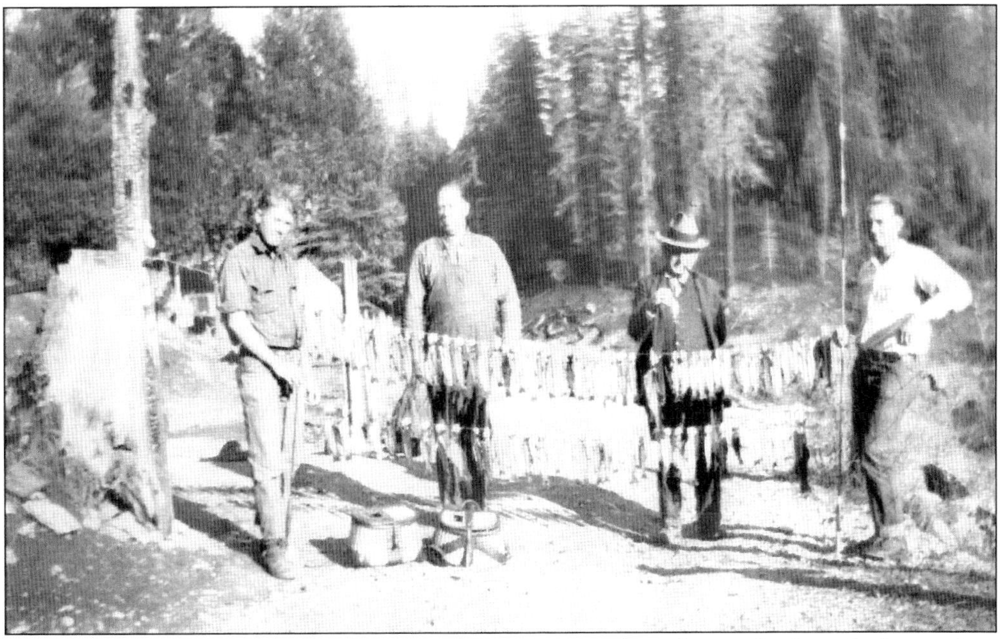

The pristine waters of Lost Creek attracted sportsmen such as these, who brought home their catch of trout for the town's fish-fry. Paul Stanfield, Vernon Bean, Mr. Hogan, and Frank Bean display the trout after a fly-fishing trip to Lost Creek Dam in 1920.

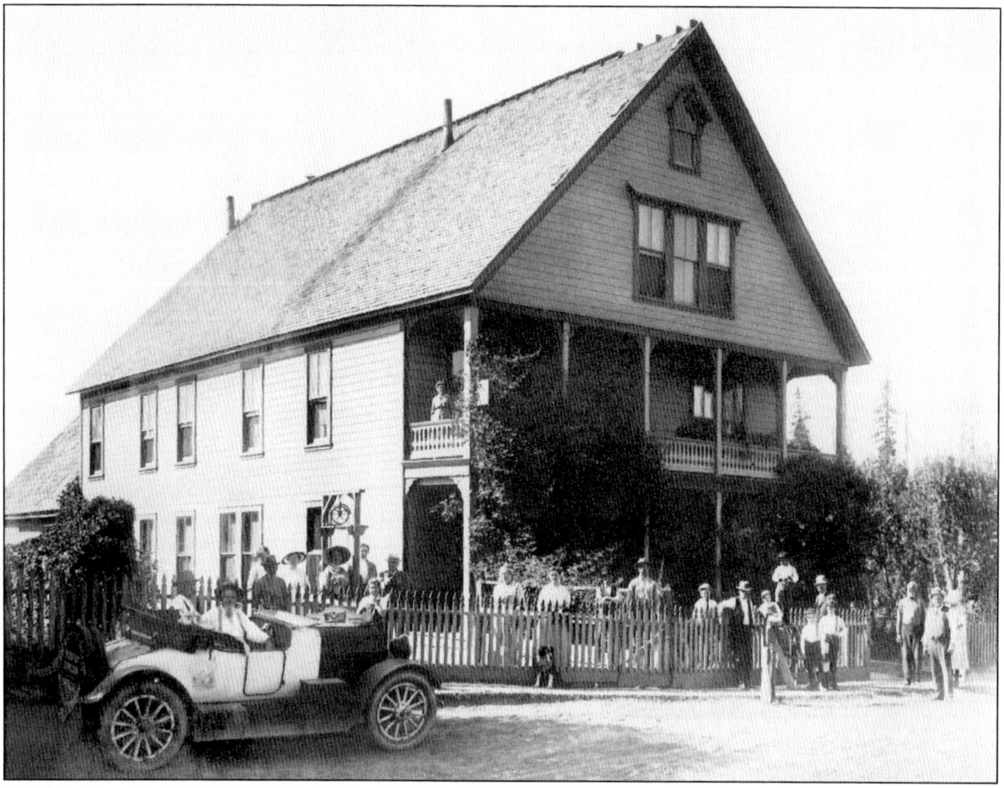

"Columbus House burned yesterday morn," wrote Charles Adams on May 1, 1900. The hotel was quickly rebuilt and furnished in the newest Victorian furniture. The celebration above took place in 1915. Present owner Brad Sharpe is restoring the hotel. (Courtesy Yuba County Library.)

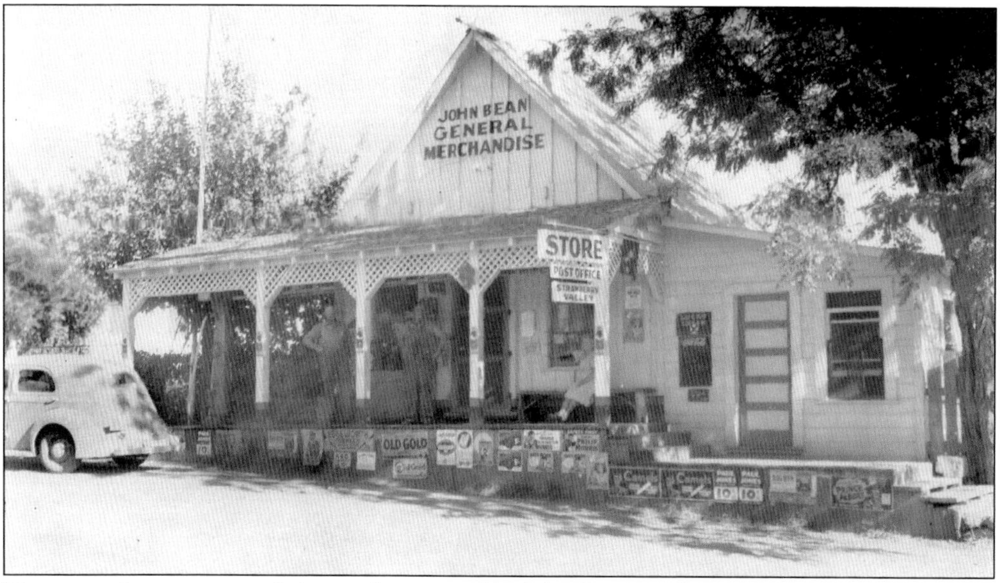


The general store, pictured above when owned by John Bean in the 1930s, also housed the post office. Posters advertising 12 different brands of cigarettes and tobacco decorate the side of the porch deck.

The present owner of the general store, Ben Borsoff, who stands on the porch, has preserved John Bean's office. John was also known as one of the best dope makers for the snowshoe races. He kept his secret recipes in the safe in his office and only brought them out when his door was locked and the window shades drawn. The dope, made of many kinds of waxes and oils, was manufactured by hand for all types of snow and weather conditions.

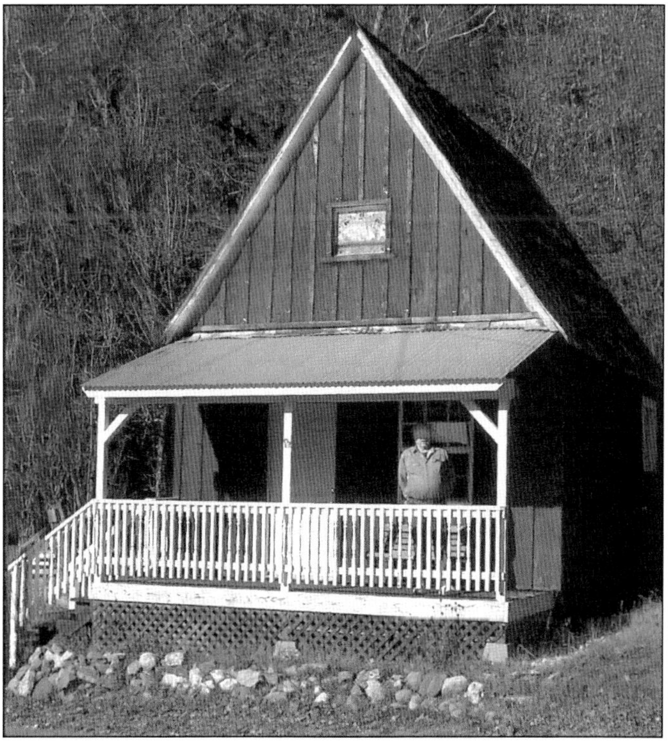

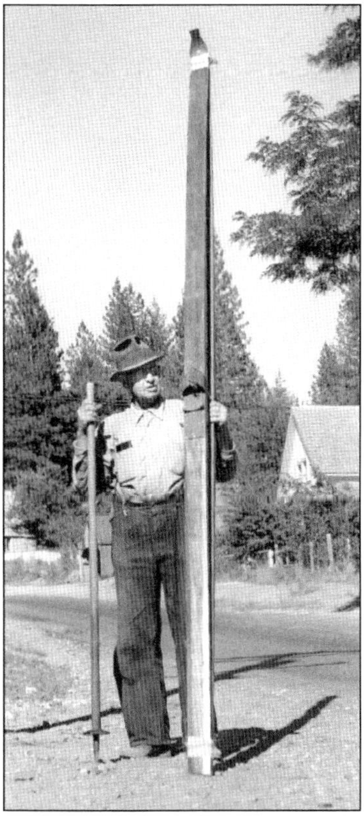

John Bean was a noted snowshoe maker, pictured here holding a pair of 12-foot-long racing "shoes" and a single pole. The shoes, which were introduced to Americans by Norwegians, were later called skis. John also served as justice of the peace, postmaster, and was affectionately known as the mayor of Strawberry Valley. Once, when a local man set a trap for bears, John feared for the safety of small children and dogs because it was too close to town. He slipped out at night, sprang the trap, and left a teddy bear in it.

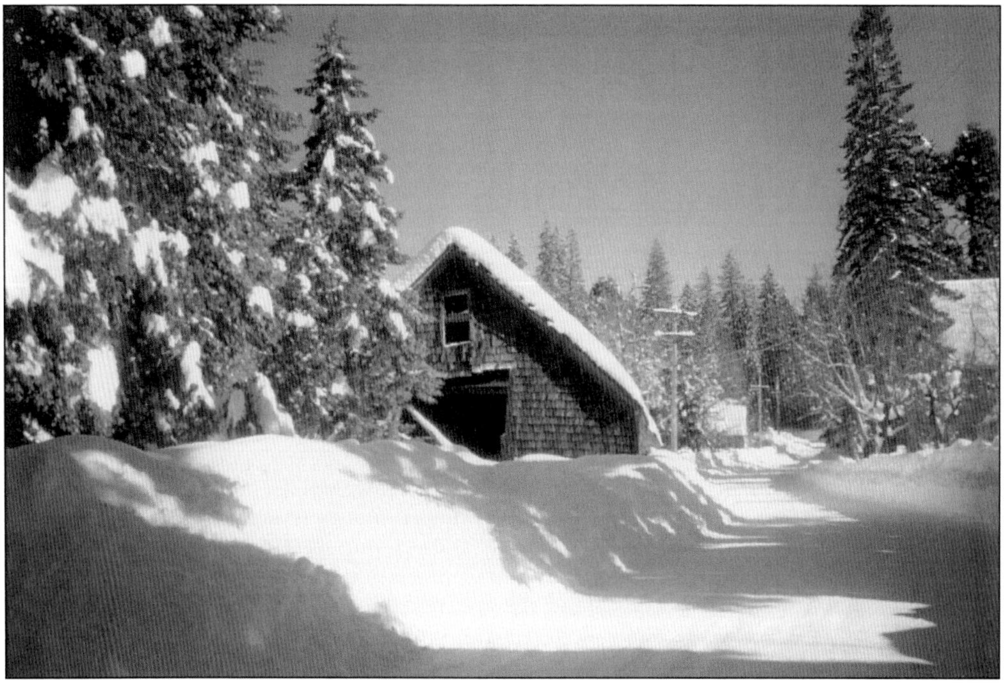

The freight barn, one of the last in the hills, was photographed in 1984 just before it collapsed from heavy snows. The freight teamsters drove the wagons through the large doors, visible on this side, unloaded them, and then proceeded up the road to the next stop. (Courtesy Brad Sharpe.)

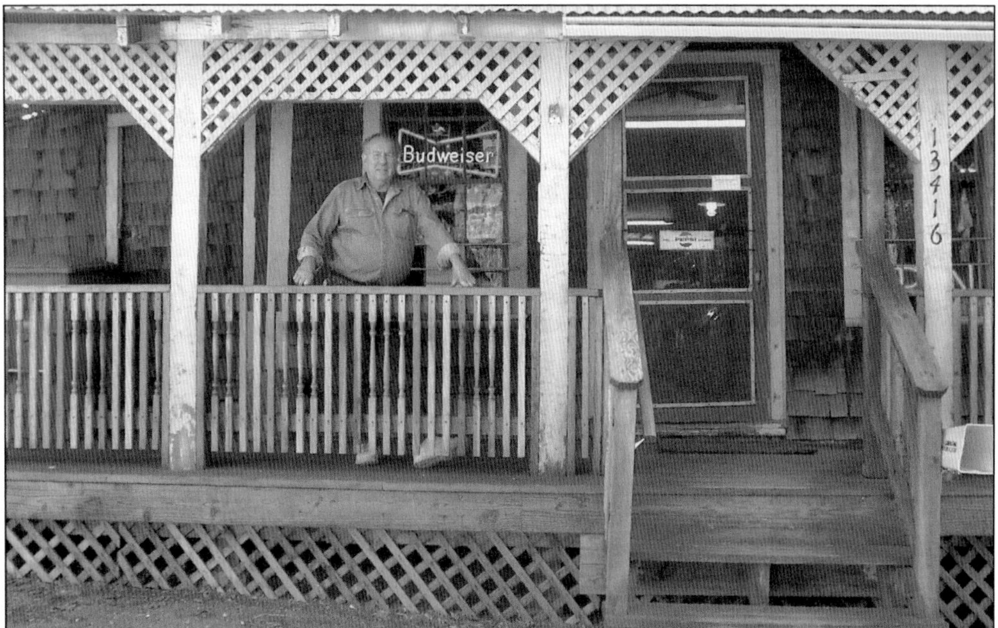


Strawberry Valley is still a small, close-knit community where people gather on the front porch of the general store and chat with neighbors at the post office. Those who appreciate the climate and beauty of the hills include newcomers and descendants of pioneers who have returned to their hometown to retire.

# *Ten*

# La Porte

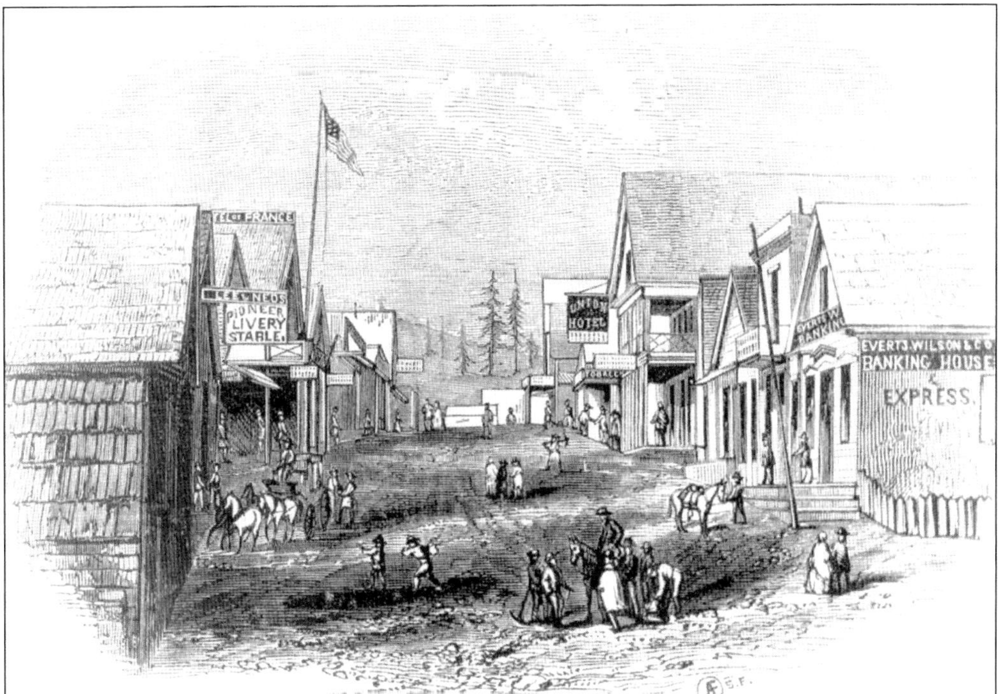


This town started with the name of Rabbit Creek in 1850, but when the post office was granted in 1855 the cancellation stamp read Rabbit Town. Neither name suited the residents and they changed it to La Porte after the Indiana hometown of one of their leading citizens, Frank D. Everts. By that time, there were 14 saloons, 3 hotels, 2 theaters, and a tenpin bowling alley. Among other businesses, the 1858 lithograph above shows Everts-Wilson Banking House and Express (right), the Union Hotel further up the street, the Pioneer Livery, and the Hotel de France (left). The town has been at the same spot since its origin, but the county lines wandered back and forth. Thus, La Porte was first in Yuba County in 1850, then in Sierra County in 1852, and finally Plumas County in 1864, where it has since stayed. Soon after its beginning, La Porte became the vital center for the Northern Mines. (Lithograph from *Hutchings' California Magazine*, 1858.)

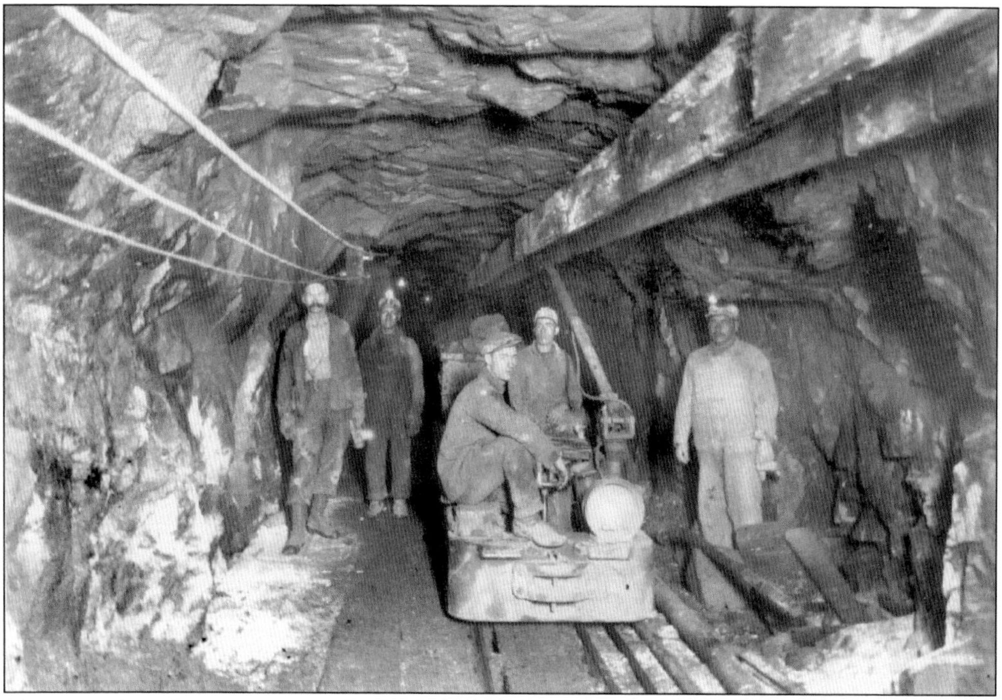

Miners used an electric ore car in the tunnel of the North American Mine near Whiskey Diggings. It was consolidated with four other mines, and was one of the richest in the region.

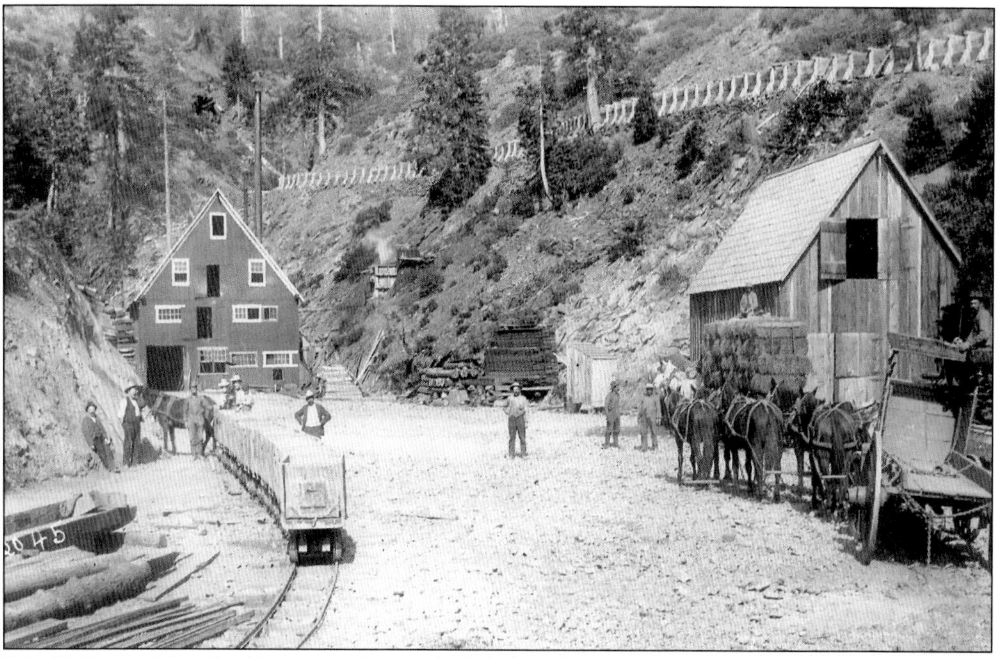

The Bellevue Mine buildings in 1901 included the adit structure and mule barn on this level, and six others down the hill. The wooden flume can be seen on the hillside above the buildings. Later, buildings were added for the boiler, blacksmith shop, and miners' changing room. (Courtesy Jann Garvis.)

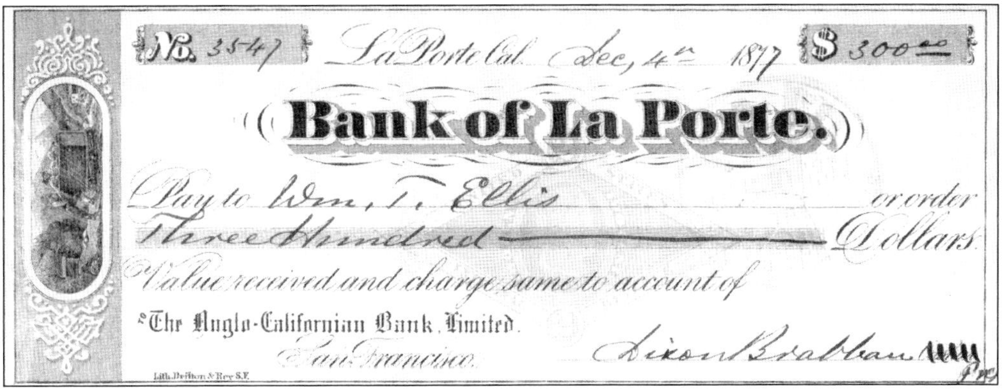

No. 3547 La Porte Cal. Dec. 4th 1877 $300.00

Bank of La Porte.

Pay to Wm. T. Ellis or order

Three Hundred Dollars

Value received and charge same to account of

The Anglo-Californian Bank, Limited.

San Francisco.

Dixon Brabban

Lith. Britton & Rey S.F.

The above $300 check was made out to W. T. Ellis of Marysville on December 4, 1877, and signed by Dixon Brabban, bank president at the time. Ellis was a leader in efforts to build levees to guard Marysville against floods of the Feather and Yuba Rivers.

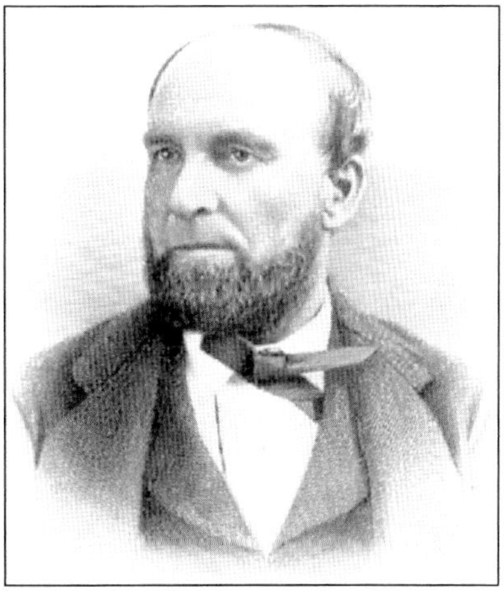

John Conly, at right, originally from New York, arrived in San Francisco in 1849 and spent a few years as a bank clerk in Marysville before opening the Bank of La Porte in 1855. The business was also known as the John Conly Bank and was located in a fireproof building on Main Street. Historian Jann Garvis documented a staggering 225 businesses operating in La Porte between 1860 and 1869 and a population of 1,134. La Porte was clearly the commercial center of the 25 towns and 880 gold mines in the surrounding high country. (Courtesy Jann Garvis.)

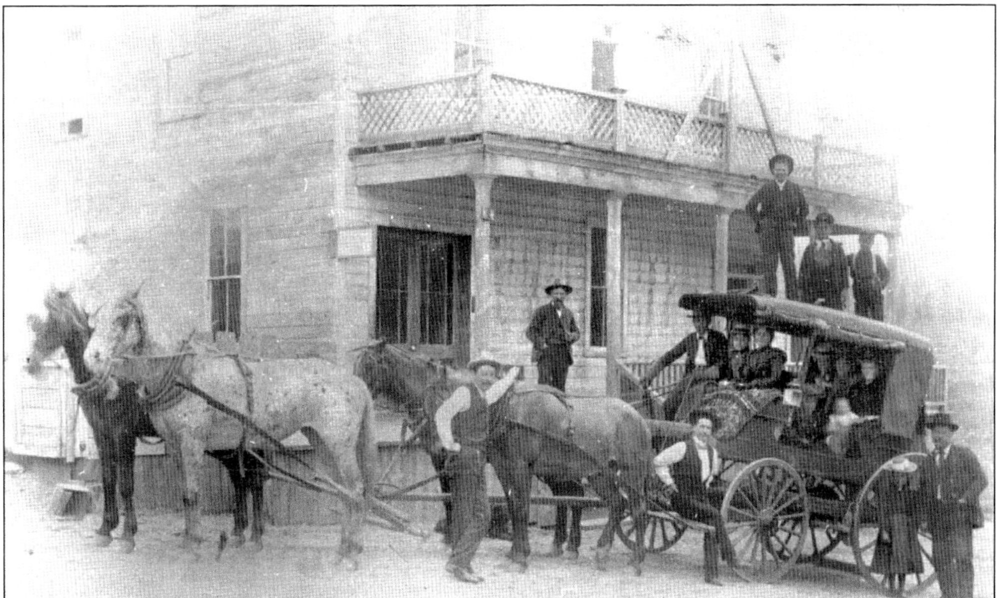

The private carriage of the Bustillos family, pulled by a team of four horses, is stopped in front of the Union Hotel in 1902. This hotel is one of only three that survive today in the Yuba Feather Hills.

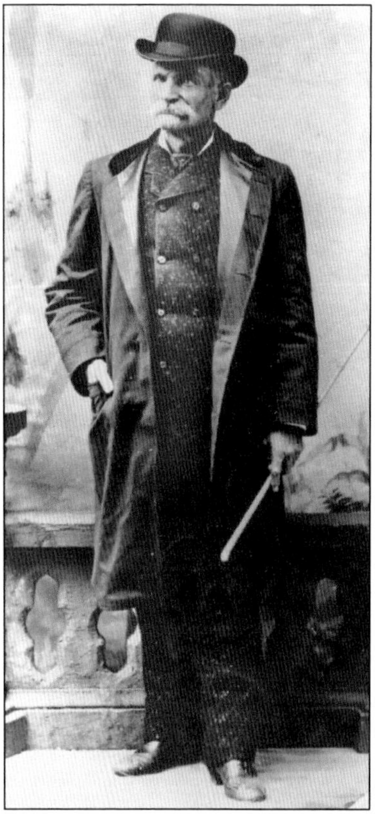

Charles Earl Bolles, known better as Black Bart, the scoundrel who terrorized the stage lines and Wells Fargo Express Company, appears to be a well-dressed gentleman, posing with his derby, walking stick, and tailor-made Harris tweed suit. But the photograph was made after he was arrested for armed robbery. He robbed the La Porte Stage on July 30, 1878, and July 13, 1882, and was linked to 26 other stage robberies where he escaped with the Wells Fargo treasure boxes. He sounded remorseful in letters he wrote to his wife and brother from San Quentin where he was imprisoned for four years, but he disappeared after his release, leaving a mystery unsolved to this day.

At the bar in Miguel's Saloon is bartender Tom Larimore and owner Manuel Miguel, at right. Miguel's Saloon burned in the La Porte fires of 1900, 1905, and 1919, but was not rebuilt after the last fire.

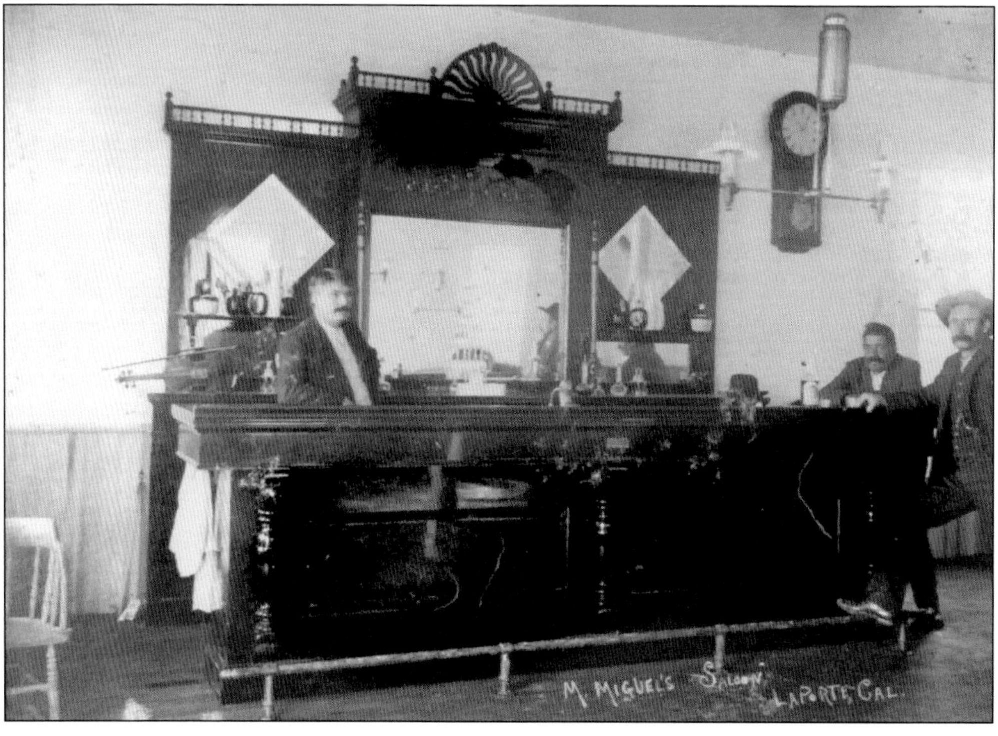

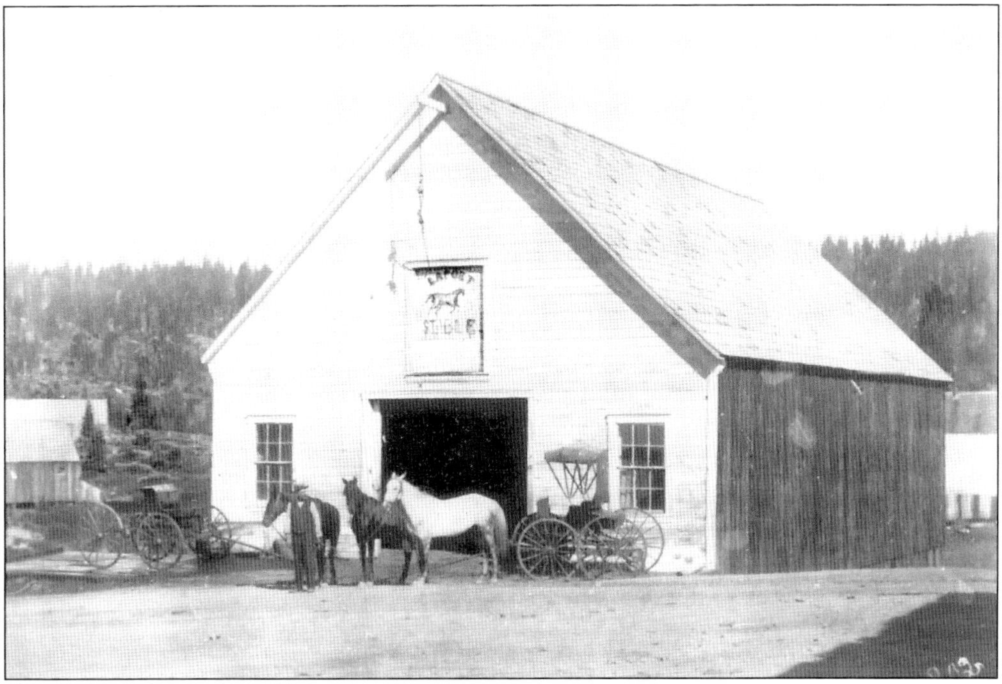

The La Porte Livery was located near the present Reilly's Saloon at the east end of town. It was destroyed by fire in 1919.

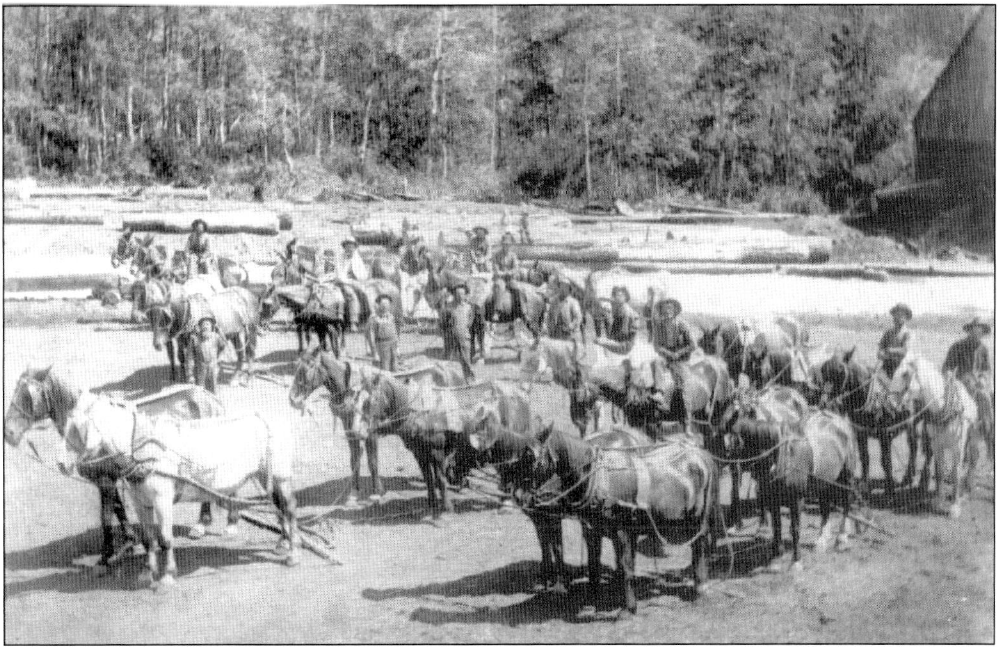

Jesus Bustillos ran a large freighting company, and some of his teams are harnessed and ready for the road. According to eyewitnesses, there was so much travel on the roads that one team was barely out of sight when one could hear the harness bells on the next team.

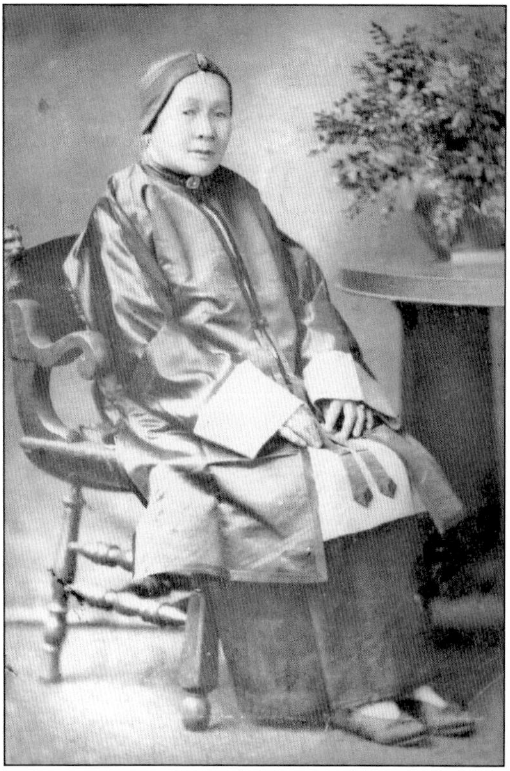

Chan Shee was the wife of Yee Ah Tye and the mother of seven children, all born at La Porte. Ah Tye was a wealthy merchant and mine owner who broke with all tradition, taking a wife without bound feet, educating all of his children (including five daughters), and telling his family to "bury my bones in America." He died in 1896, and his strange deathbed request was detailed in the June 14 issue of the *San Francisco Call*. Ah Tye was buried in the Chinese cemetery at Lone Mountain in San Francisco, the land he had given to the city for this use. The entire cemetery was moved to Colma in 1900 and is now Lincoln Municipal Golf Course. An inscription on the ruins of the Chinese temple translates, "Temporary resting place for Kong Chow sojourners," which is a reminder of the transition of returning bones to China, according to historian Lani Ah Tye Farkas.

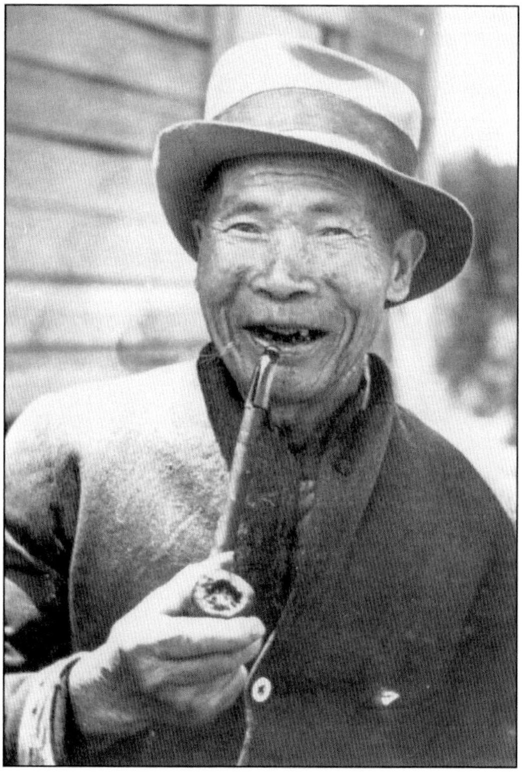

Ah Pok was born in China in 1852 and was a miner in La Porte for 55 years. He lived in the Hop Sing building owned by Ah Tye and was highly respected by the local people. He was the last Chinese resident in La Porte when he died in 1939.

Childhood friends Cleveland O'Rourke, Bill Pike, and Dilly Ah Tye bridged the gaps between cultures. O'Rourke's parents were from Ireland and Ah Tye's parents were from China. They were photographed in La Porte in 1894. After Dilly's father died in 1896, his family moved to San Francisco. Dilly married Rose Wong in a traditional Chinese ceremony on May 21, 1908. Many of the Ah Tye descendants still live in the Bay Area.

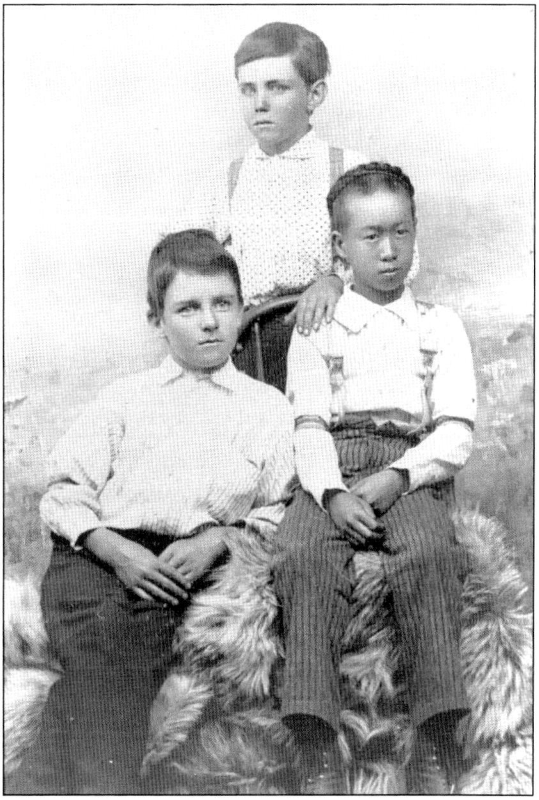

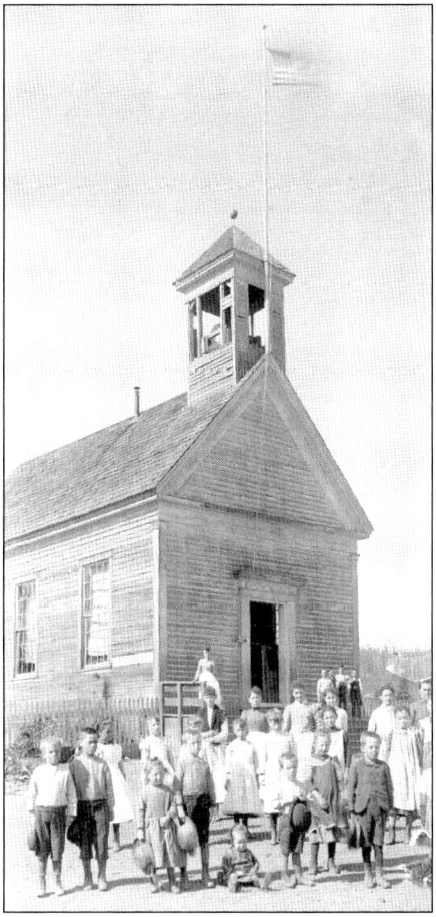

The Methodist Episcopal Church was built in 1858 and was valued at $2,000. Two years later, Reverend Dickinson raised $240 for a bell. "There are at present no suitable bells on sale in San Francisco, but when they arrive, one will be purchased," stated the *Mountain Messenger* on November 24, 1860. In 1880, the building was no longer needed as a church and was deeded to the La Porte School District. The pulpit was used as a teacher's desk, and the original pews were converted to student desks. This building was torn down in 1936 and a new one constructed, but by 1941 there weren't enough pupils to continue classes and the school closed.

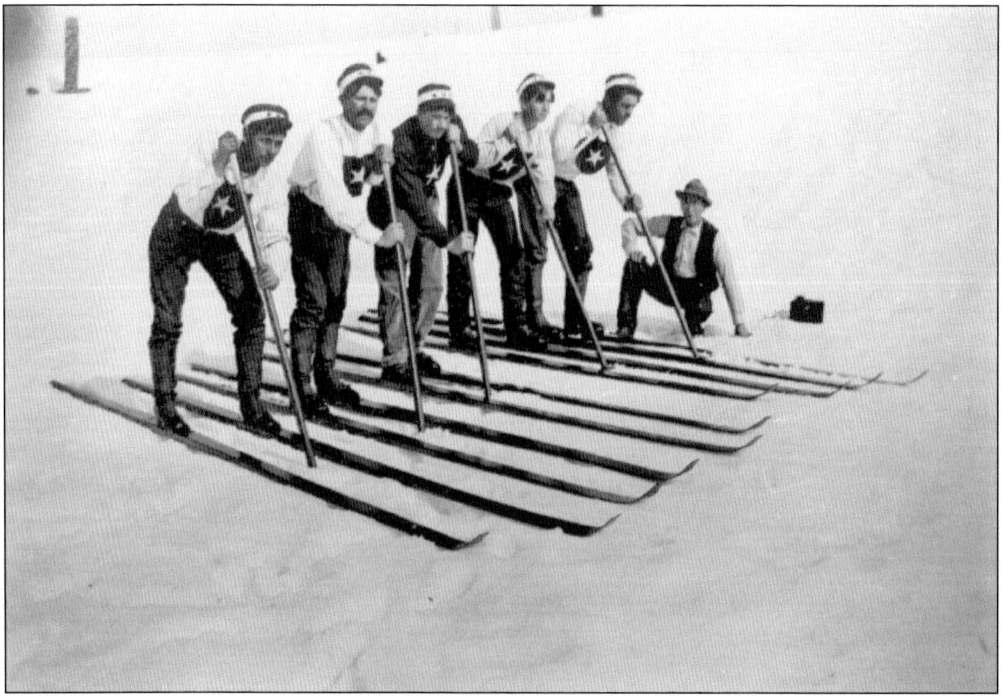

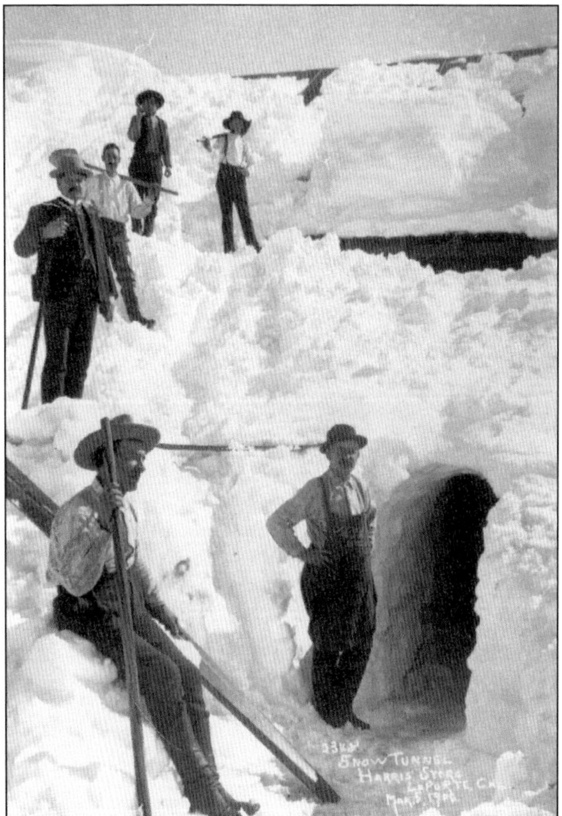


The La Porte team at the snowshoe races in 1910 included, from left to right, Mike Bustillos, Al Primeau, Clyde O'Rourke, Harold Pike, Will Primeau, and dope man Charles Ed Pike with his dope bag. The dope man played such an important role in the races that winners usually shared their prizes with him. The racers sometimes reached 80 miles per hour and the men had to nail their boots to the snowshoes to keep them on.

Aaron Harris's tin shop was accessible only by a tunnel in 1906. La Porte, at 5,000 feet, sometimes was nearly buried in snows more than 30 feet deep. Harris was in business from 1868 to around 1920. He made custom tin work, including bathtubs, tea kettles, and his own patented hydraulic pipe nozzles. He also made the buckle and stars that adorned the Snowshoe Champion belt.

This advertising poster announced four days of snowshoe races in 1868. The well-known John A. "Snowshoe" Thompson challenged the team but was defeated, clearly heralding the vital part played by dope. The dope man was one of the most important members of the team, providing dope, or wax mixture, for every type of snow, including wet, dry, powder, corn, ice, morning, midday, and for clear or cloudy weather. The recipes were closely guarded secrets, and the mixtures were brewed in pans on a wood stove and molded in blocks, labeled with the recipe number.

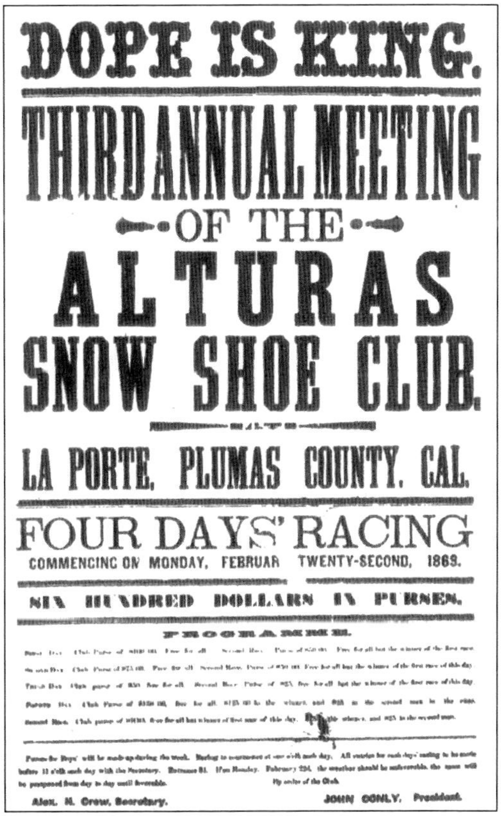


Four horses wearing snowshoes drew the La Porte Stage sleigh. A horse accustomed to wearing snowshoes could travel four to five miles an hour. The shoes were made of iron or a thin steel plate, about 9 by 11 inches, fastened on the hoofs with clamps. The horses were shod with long-heel caulks, which went through the snowshoes and prevented them from slipping when going up and down icy slopes.

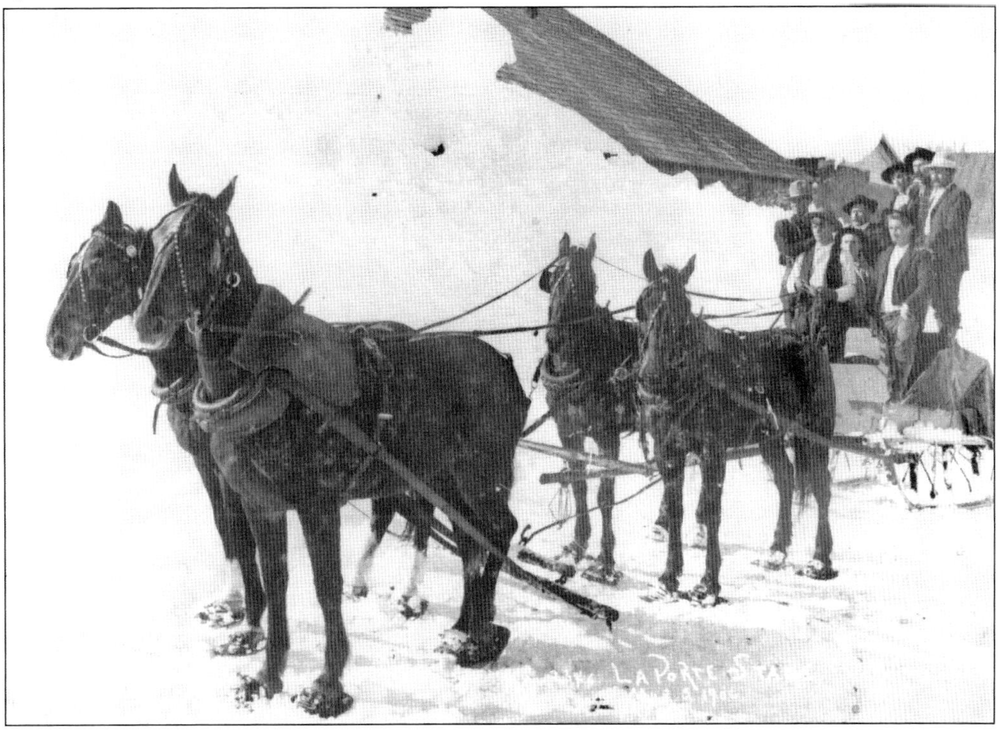

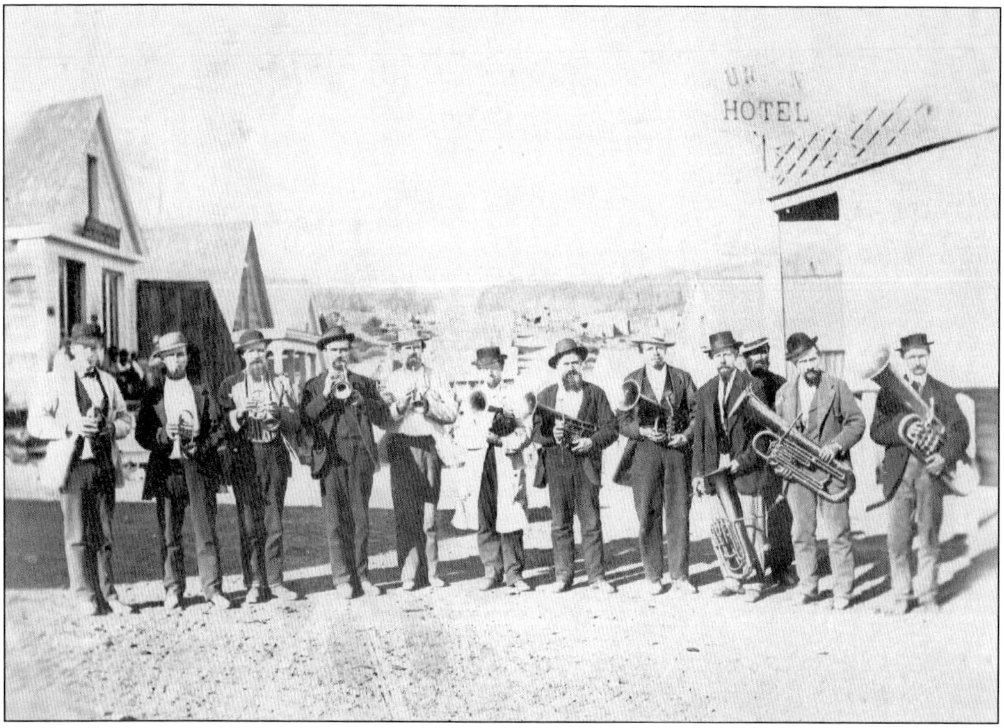


The La Porte Brass Band played for many special occasions throughout the hills. They gathered on Main Street for a photograph against a backdrop of the town's businesses 1870.

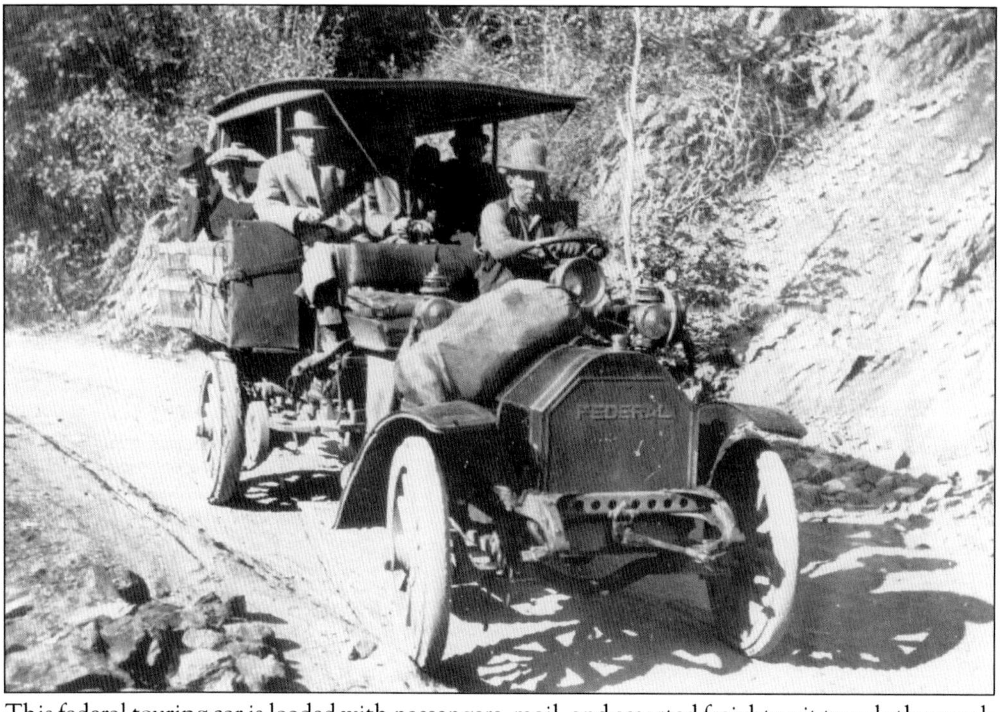


This federal touring car is loaded with passengers, mail, and assorted freight as it travels the rough roads to the mining camps in the summer of 1914.

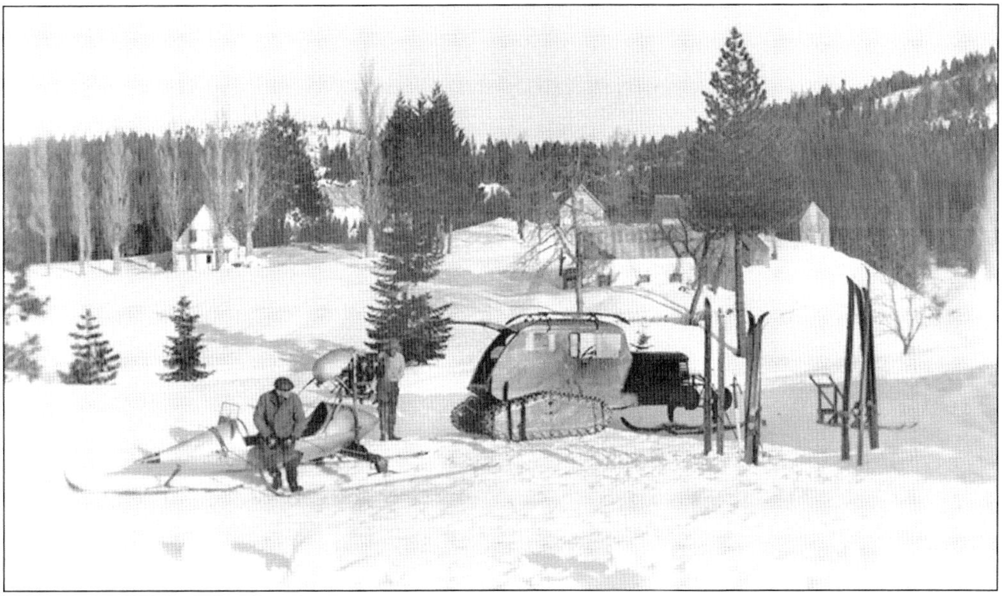

Delivering the mail from Strawberry Valley to La Porte in the winter has always been a great challenge, and in the past it has been accomplished on snowshoes, by horse-drawn sleighs, and by dog sleds. Dave Hall's unusual vehicle, the Snow Bird, was made of an airplane body and propeller, while Gould's snow cat, with its enclosed cab, was more comfortable for passengers.

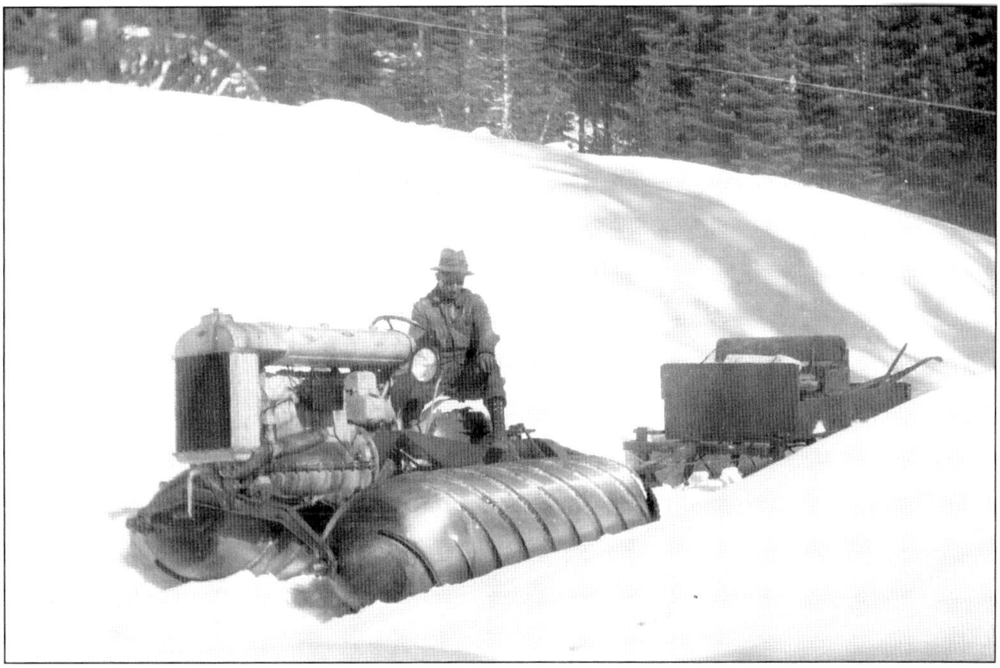

Another of Hall's ingenious inventions was this tractor engine mounted on pontoons that pulled a sled for freight and passengers.

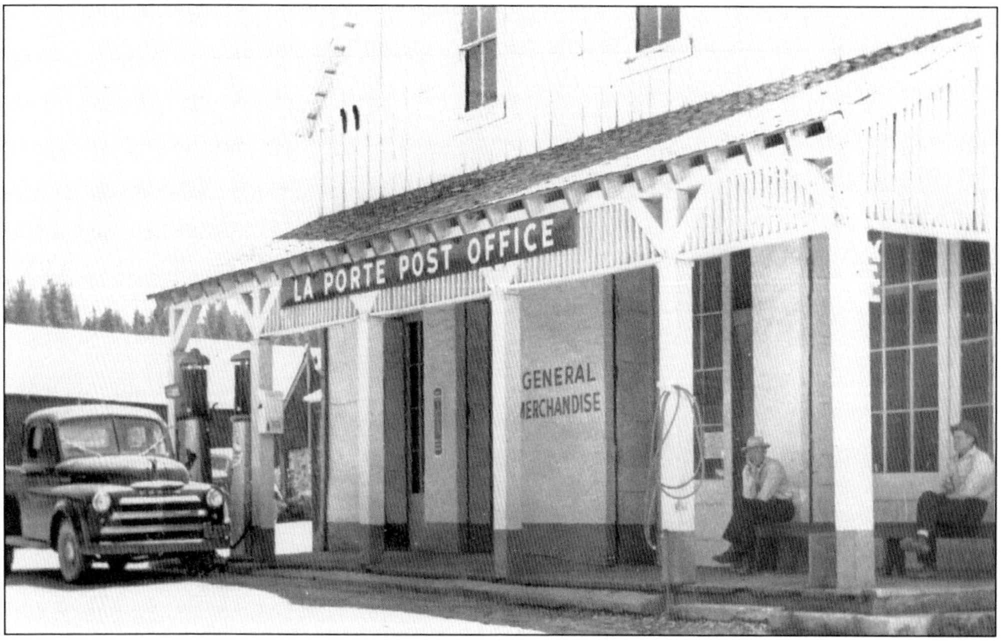


The general store, pictured here in 1950, was owned and operated by Helen and Truman Gould from 1950 to 1967, when it was destroyed by fire. The Goulds also lost their irreplaceable collection of firearms and historical artifacts.

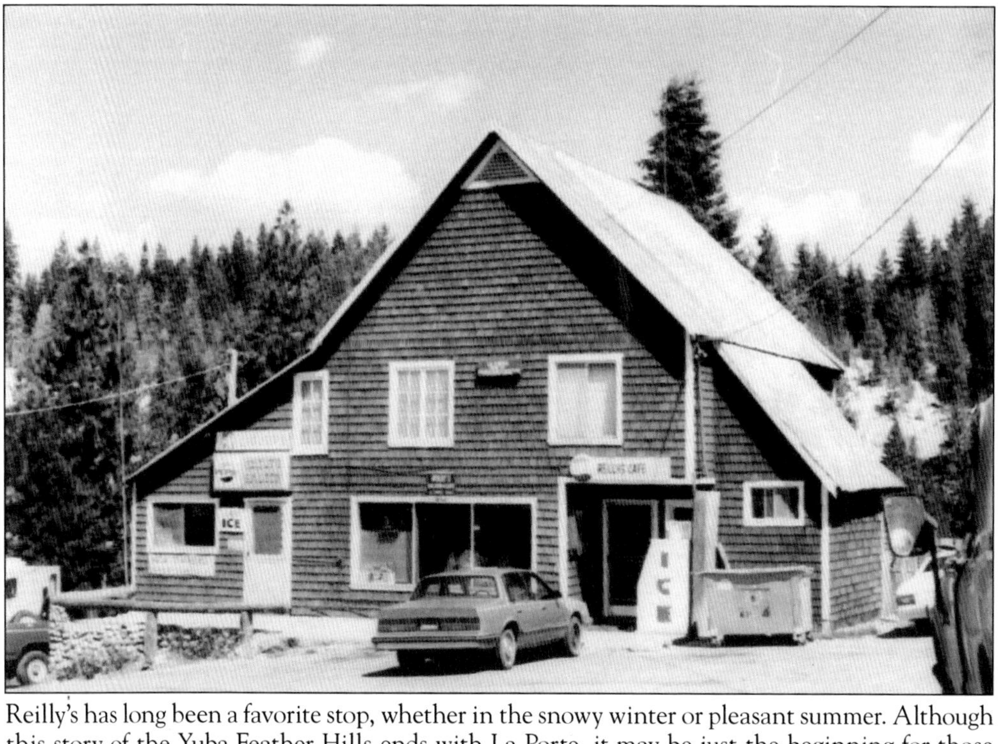


Reilly's has long been a favorite stop, whether in the snowy winter or pleasant summer. Although this story of the Yuba Feather Hills ends with La Porte, it may be just the beginning for those who seek adventures and stories of the lumberjacks and fabled gold mines.